THE FRONTIER EFFECT

A Volume in the Series
Cornell Series on Land: New Perspectives on Territory, Development, and Environment
Edited by Wendy Wolford, Nancy Lee Peluso, and Michael Goldman

A list of titles in this series is available at cornellpress.cornell.edu

THE FRONTIER EFFECT

State Formation and Violence
in Colombia

Teo Ballvé

CORNELL UNIVERSITY PRESS   ITHACA AND LONDON

First published 2020 by Cornell University Press

Library of Congress Cataloging-in-Publication Data

Names: Ballvé, Teo, author.
Title: The frontier effect : state formation and violence in Colombia / Teo Ballvé.
Description: Ithaca, New York : Cornell University Press, 2020. | Series: Cornell series on land: new perspectives in territory, development, and environment | Includes bibliographical references and index.
Identifiers: LCCN 2019020926 (print) | LCCN 2019981419 (ebook) | ISBN 9781501747533 (cloth) | ISBN 9781501747540 (paperback) | ISBN 9781501747564 (pdf) | ISBN 9781501747557 (epub)
Subjects: LCSH: Political violence—Colombia—Urabá. | Paramilitary forces—Colombia—Urabá. | Colombia—Politics and government—1974–
Classification: LCC F2281.U7 B35 2020 (print) | LCC F2281.U7 (ebook) | DDC 986.106/34—dc23
LC record available at https://lccn.loc.gov/2019020926
LC ebook record available at https://lccn.loc.gov/2019981419

Contents

Acknowledgments

As a bundle of debts both personal and professional, this book is a perfect example of how any finished product inevitably conceals the vast web of social relationships that actually made it possible. For starters, I will be forever grateful for the privilege of having worked with such a brilliant and generous cast of mentors at the University of California, Berkeley that have guided this project since its infancy. Michael Watts is simply a phenomenon and will always remain an inspiration. Gillian Hart had a profound impact on my understanding of praxis and scholarship. Donald Moore stimulated and refined my thinking through hours upon hours of conversation. Nancy Peluso—and who better?—introduced me to political ecology. At Berkeley I was also sustained by the friendship and comradery, intellectual and otherwise, of Erin Collins, John Elrick, Anthony Fontes, Zoe Friedman-Cohen, Gustavo Oliveira, Shaina Potts, and Alberto Velázquez. I am thankful to have found an equally supportive community of colleagues within the Peace & Conflict Studies Program and the Department of Geography at Colgate University.

My sincere thanks are owed to the Social Science Research Council (SSRC). The SSRC's International Dissertation Research Fellowship (IDRF) and the Drugs, Security, and Democracy Fellowship (DSD) provided me with the precious opportunity of full immersion into the research for this book from 2012 to 2013. Administered alongside the Universidad de Los Andes in cooperation with funds from the Open Society Foundations and Canada's International Development Research Centre, the DSD program is a paragon of what an intellectual community can and should be.

A 2010 summer fellowship from the Human Rights Center at UC Berkeley funded what turned out to be some of the most productive months of fieldwork. A mini-grant in 2013 from the Berkeley Center for Right-Wing Studies gave a boost to the final stages of fieldwork. The Harry Frank Guggenheim Foundation afforded another immersive luxury: a year of generous financial support to simply write. A grant cofunded by Fulbright Colombia and the Colombian Institute for Education and Technical Studies Abroad (ICETEX) along with a Picker Fellowship from Colgate University floated the final stages of writing.

During my research *Verdad Abierta,* the premier source of analysis, reporting, and documentation on Colombia's armed conflict, was a tremendous source of support. I owe special thanks to César Molinares, María Teresa Ronderos, and especially Juan Diego Restrepo. In Medellín and Urabá my fieldwork received a helping hand from César Acosta and his staff at the Unidad de Restitución de Tierras in Apartadó, Mario Agudelo, "Cocinero," Fiscalía de Justicia y Paz in Medellín (Despacho 48), Forjando Futuros, Carlos Paez of Tierra y Vida, and many others who asked to remain anonymous.

Throughout the writing process many fellow *colombianólogos* read portions of the text and provided crucial feedback that helped sharpen both my arguments and my prose: Julio Arias, Alex Fattal, Meghan Morris, Diana Ojeda, Eduardo Restrepo, Winifred Tate, Austin Zeiderman, and especially Kimberly Theidon. The text also benefited from the supportive critiques of two anonymous reviewers. Over the years the participants of many conferences and workshops—too many to name—gave valuable feedback. The editors of the Cornell Series on Land, Wendy Wolford, Nancy Peluso, and Michael Goldman, gave me their enthusiastic support and sharp criticism.

This book, particularly its historical chapters, builds on the dedicated work of several scholars of Urabá, and mere citation of their publications would not adequately reflect my debt to them: Clara Inés Aramburo, Fernando Botero, Clara Inés García, Carlos Ortíz Sarmiento, James Parsons, Claudia Steiner, Andrés Suárez, William Ramírez Tobón, Maria Teresa Uribe, Mary Roldán, and Juan Ricardo Aparicio. Alejandro Santos, the publisher of *Semana* magazine, generously supplied some of the photos that appear in the book. My heartfelt thanks to all of these allies and institutions.

Above all, I am most thankful for my family. Mom and Dad, you have been unconditional sources of love and support—always and in everything. Marcelo, Sole, and Cuti: despite our endlessly far-flung locations, you constantly prove there is at least one thing that renders geography meaningless: the bonds of siblinghood. Over the course of this project my life was enriched by two incredible miracles: Pablo and Cecilia—now, seven and four years old. Your impatience with *el libro gordo* (the fat book, as they called it) was a welcome and life-affirming distraction.

Finally, and most important, my deepest gratitude and appreciation go to Angela Carrizosa Aparicio. Your labor is contained in every single page of this book. The burdens you have shouldered since that cross-country road trip so many years ago have been far greater than we ever anticipated. Your strength, irrepressible optimism, and undefeatable joy have made this book possible. For that, and for so many other reasons, I love you.

Abbreviations

ACCU	Autodefensas Campesinas de Córdoba y Urabá (Campesino Self-Defense Forces of Córdoba and Urabá—also known as the Casa Castaño)
AFP	Alliance for Progress
AGC	Autodefensas Gaitanistas de Colombia (Gaitanista Self-Defense Forces of Colombia—also known as Los Urabeños)
AHA	Archivo Histórico de Antioquia (Antioquia Historical Archive)
Asocomún	Asociación Comunitaria de Urabá y Córdoba (Communal Association of Urabá and Córdoba)
AUC	Autodefensas Unidas de Colombia (United Self-Defense Forces of Colombia)
BEC	Bloque Elmer Cárdenas (Elmer Cárdenas Bloc)
CNMH	Centro Nacional de Memoria Histórica (National Center for Historical Memory)
Corpourabá	Corporación para el Desarrollo Sostenible de Urabá (Corporation for the Sustainable Development of Urabá)
ELN	Ejército de Liberación Nacional (National Liberation Army)
EPL	Ejército Popular de Liberación (Popular Liberation Army)
EPM	Empresas Públicas de Medellín (Public Utility Company of Medellín)
FARC	Fuerzas Armadas Revolucionarias de Colombia (Revolutionary Armed Forces of Colombia)
Funpazcor	Fundación para la Paz de Córdoba (Foundation for Peace in Córdoba)
PASO	Proyecto de Alternatividad Social (Project for a Social Alternative)
PCC	Partido Comunista Colombiano (Colombian Communist Party)
PDS	Promotor de Desarrollo Social (Promoter of Social Development)
PEUD	Plan Estratégico Urabá–Darién (Urabá–Darién Strategic Plan)
MADU	Municipios Asociados de Urabá (Urabá Association of Municipalities)
UP	Unión Patriótica (Patriotic Union)
USAID	U.S. Agency for International Development
UNDP	United Nations Development Program
UNODC	United Nations Office on Drugs and Crime

FIGURE 1. Map of Colombia showing Bogotá, Medellín, and Urabá.

(Credit: Author)

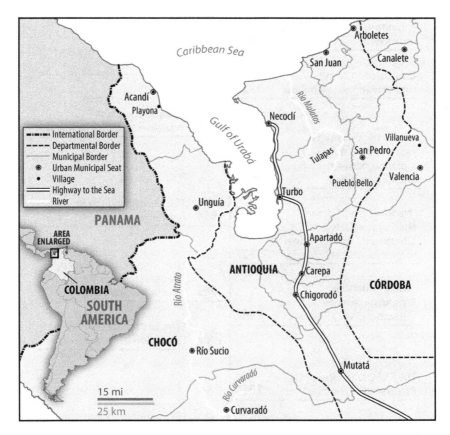

FIGURE 2. Map of Urabá showing its municipalities, main highway, major rivers, and some of the villages mentioned in the book. As administrative-territorial divisions, Colombia's county-like municipalities usually encompass not only their namesake urbanized municipal seat but also the towns and rural areas in their jurisdictions. Urabá's most populous municipality, Apartadó, for example, is almost entirely an agrarian space dotted with small towns and villages, even though its municipal seat is a bustling city of 150,000 residents.

(Credit: Author)

Panama wins independence from Colombia.	**1903**		
		1905	Urabá again becomes part of Antioquia.
Construction of the Highway to the Sea begins.	**1926**		
		1928	Striking United Fruit Company workers massacred near Santa Marta.
Jorge Eliécer Gaitán's assassination sparks La Violencia between Liberals and Conservatives.	**1948**		
		1954	The Highway to the Sea is finished.
"National Front" power-sharing deal between Liberals and Conservatives formally ends La Violencia.	**1957**		
		1963	The United Fruit Company chooses Urabá as the site of its new banana enclave.
Fuerzas Armadas Revolucionarias de Colombia (FARC) founded.	**1964**		
		1967	Ejército Popular de Liberación (EPL) founded.
The FARC forms the Unión Patriótica (UP) party.	**1985**		
Autodefensas Campesinas de Córdoba y Urabá (ACCU) founded.			EPL demobilizes and forms political party.
Cooperatives of Private Security and Surveillance (Convivir) introduced by national decree.	**1994**	**1991**	Colombia ratifies a new Constitution.
El Alemán's group of para-military gunmen names itself the Bloque Elmer Cárdenas (BEC).		**1995**	Alvaro Uribe elected governor of Antioquia.
The Autodefensas Unidas de Colombia (AUC) paramilitary umbrella group founded.	**1997**		

FIGURE 3A. Timeline I

(Credit: Author)

The U.S. military aid package Plan Colombia begins implementation.	**2000**	
		The paramilitary-backed "Urabá Grande" electoral coalition is launched.
	2001	
Alvaro Uribe elected president of Colombia.	**2002**	
		Paramilitaries sign deal with the Uribe administration and begin their demobilization.
El Alemán introduces his bloc's Project for a Social Alternative (PASO) demobilization program.	**2003**	
Paramilitary leaders begin confessional transitional justice trials in exchange for reduced sentences.	**2005**	
		The Bloque Elmer Cárdenas is the last paramilitary group to demobilize.
	2006	
The Urbaeños declare their existence, calling themselves the Autodefensas Gaitanistas de Colombia.	**2008**	
		Juan Manuel Santos elected president of Colombia.
	2010	
Law on victims' reparations and land restitution begins implementation.		
Peace talks with the FARC begin in secret.		
Sergio Fajardo, ex-mayor of Medellín (2004-7), elected governor of Antioquia.	**2012**	
		El Alemán released from jail after fulfilling the terms of transitional justice process that began in 2005.
	2015	
Final peace accord with the FARC ratified.	**2016**	

FIGURE 3B. Timeline II

(Credit: Author)

THE FRONTIER EFFECT

INTRODUCTION

The plaza in front of the main courthouse in Medellín is usually a drab, bureau-cratic setting. But on the morning of June 5, 2007, the trial of Freddy Rendón was about to begin and the plaza was buzzing. Rendón, better known as El Alemán (The German), had led one of Colombia's largest and bloodiest paramilitary groups. For more than a decade he had terrorized the people of Urabá, a war-torn region in the far northwest corner of the country. Once labeled by the media "the *Führer* of Urabá," El Alemán was finally due for a reckoning with justice.

A crowd of about three hundred people streamed into the plaza in front of the courthouse. They arrived with dancers in colorful costumes and a live band blasting popular Colombian folk music. Showers of confetti and reams of red and white carnations completed the impromptu carnival. Amid the festivities, revelers waved professionally printed banners expressing support for the mass murderer: "We want peace, bring Freddy back to Urabá," read one sign. "The people of Urabá are free thanks to you," claimed another. All of this for a man about to stand trial for mass atrocities and war crimes.

Before turning himself in to the authorities as part of an amnesty deal El Alemán had been a rising star in the loose federation of private armies that com-prised Colombia's right-wing paramilitary movement. He had signed up as a twenty-two-year-old recruit in the mid-1990s. In those years paramilitary groups had started cropping up all over the country. They grew out of a complex alliance of agrarian elites, drug traffickers, and moonlighting members of the Colombian military who had joined together to fight against the country's leftist guerrilla groups.

From the beginning, besides counterinsurgency the paramilitary war machine was fueled by plunder and illicit enrichment, especially via its most lucrative venture: drug trafficking. All told, paramilitary groups like the one led by El Alemán ended up killing almost one hundred thousand defenseless civilians in the name of fighting *la subversión*.[1] But El Alemán's supporters chanting in the plaza described him in heroic terms. They said he had liberated Urabá from the grip of the leftist insurgencies, and they celebrated his so-called social work in the region.

El Alemán was escorted into the sixth-floor courtroom by prison officers. He wore a navy corduroy blazer, jeans, and a pink dress shirt unbuttoned down to the middle of his chest. Some say his nickname came from the strict discipline he

FIGURE 4.   Prison officers escort the paramilitary chief Freddy Rendón, "El Alemán," to his opening day in court in Medellín on June 5, 2007.

(Credit: AP Photo/Luis Benavides)

demanded of his troops, but it might as well have come from the contrast of his white complexion against the various black and brown hues of his soldiers—and of the people of Urabá more broadly. At least six feet tall, he had dark, shoulder-length hair that was slicked back into a tight ponytail. A few moments before the hearing began he leaned out the window and saluted his mass of supporters below. The crowd went wild.

At this point a group of protesting human rights activists who had been huddled in a corner of the plaza gave up their solemn attempt at reading the names of those killed or disappeared by El Alemán and his troops. Nationwide, paramilitaries had systematically slaughtered Colombia's human rights movement. Understandably intimidated, the protestors ceded the plaza to the festivities, a move that symbolically reenacted another mainstay of paramilitary violence: forced displacement. Between 1985 and 2014 Colombia's armed conflict displaced some 6.5 million people from their homes: paramilitaries were responsible for the lion's share of that dispossession.[2]

When a reporter asked the protesting human rights activists about the show of support for El Alemán, one of them responded, "We know this isn't a spontaneous demonstration by the people of [Urabá]. It's a product of the control these paramilitary chiefs still have in the region."[3] But El Alemán's spokesman denied that the crowd was a farce. "They aren't circus clowns or mourners-for-hire [pla-ñideras]," he said. "They are men and women who genuinely love Rendón. They respect him, and they see him as a leader."[4] The truth is that both sides—the paramilitary supporters and the human rights activists—were engaged in a performance. Both groups were attempting to cast the past in a particular light, a way of setting the stage for the politics of the present. "The past is never dead," wrote William Faulkner. "It's not even past."[5] And in this case it was playing out right in front of me.

At the time, I was working as a journalist covering El Alemán's trial for an investigative piece on paramilitary land grabs in Urabá. Watching the scene, I dismissed the throng of support for El Alemán as a public relations stunt, a whitewashing of paramilitaries' gruesome history. Since they were so widely feared and hated, I naïvely disregarded the possibility that paramilitaries might have actually managed to cultivate a meaningful base of genuine grassroots support—or, as the combatants call it, una base social. For any irregular armed group, winning at least some degree of support or collaboration from civilian communities is a practical necessity. And it turns out that El Alemán was something of an expert in this regard.

His opening statement began with some family history.[6] The Rendóns had suffered the same history of violence and displacement endured by most Colombians of humble rural origins. During the country's previous civil war in the late

1940s—known to this day as La Violencia—guerrillas had forced El Alemán's father to flee his family farm. La Violencia was a decade of ruthless partisan warfare between Colombia's equally oligarchic Liberal and Conservative parties. The farm the Rendóns left behind was in Amalfi, a town in the department (or province) of Antioquia and a hot spot of the conflict.[7]

A government security report from Amalfi in 1953 observed, "Everyone has abandoned their farms, and all agricultural activities have ceased because of *bandolerismo*."[8] *Bandoleros* (bandits) was Conservatives' preferred pejorative for the Liberal Party's guerrillas. The most radical faction of the guerrillas eventually morphed into one of the world's longest-lived rebel organizations, the communist-inspired Fuerzas Armadas Revolucionarias de Colombia (FARC). La Violencia evolved in slow motion into today's still-simmering armed conflict, which by most accounts began in 1964, the year the FARC formally declared its existence.[9] In the decades that followed, guerrilla organizations multiplied across the country, and the Rendón family was uprooted two more times, on both occasions by the FARC.

El Alemán pinned the blame for his family's tragedies squarely on the state, citing its inability to protect their "life, honor, and property." Throughout his trial he repeated the same phrase several times: "The state shone by its absence" (*el estado brillaba por su ausencia*). Rehearsing a well-worn narrative, he accused the state of having abandoned places like Amalfi and Urabá to the mercy of the communist insurgencies. Like most paramilitaries, he justified their reason for being entirely on this claimed absence of the state. "Our interest as a politico-military organization in arms," he told the court, "was not only to win the war against Colombian society's number one enemy, the guerrillas, it was also for the state to gain a presence in those areas."[10]

As a journalist I had dismissed paramilitaries' self-proclaimed role as state builders as yet another political façade, a way of concealing their self-serving economic interests beneath a veneer of laudable political purpose. But during the two years of research I conducted for this book I began to see things differently.[11] Paramilitary statecraft was indeed smoke and mirrors, but, like the crowd cheering for El Alemán outside the courthouse, it was also much more than that. The tremendous power attained by these ultraviolent militias across the country was in no small part due to the way in which they positioned themselves and were hailed as state makers in places where the state's institutional presence and authority had supposedly lapsed or never existed.

For anyone unfamiliar with Colombia's conflict it might be hard to imagine the prevalence of this narrative of statelessness. But almost any explanation of the armed conflict will inevitably mention *la ausencia del estado* (the absence of the state) as the main cause of the country's violent history. The same Hobbesian thesis about the absence of the state devolving into the fabled "war of wall against all" also finds its way into countless government and even scholarly studies of the roots of the armed conflict.[12]

In Urabá, regardless of whom I spoke with—from ex-guerrillas to former paramilitaries, displaced peasants to agribusiness executives, and even local mayors and military officers—it was the only thing everyone seemed to agree on: Urabá's violent history and its unruly contemporary condition can be largely explained by the absence of the state. It came up so often that I soon realized this discourse about statelessness is not only recurrent and pervasive but also powerful and productive. It makes things happen.

This book is about the ways in which imaginaries of statelessness have structured the political life of a rural hinterland in Colombia. It asks, How are the limits of state power imagined and acted upon in a place where the state supposedly doesn't exist?[13] It is about state formation, not as an abstract concept but as something in which people actively and sometimes self-consciously engage.[14] By exploring the kinds of political formations that emerge at the assumed limits (or frontiers) of the state, the book is a story about how statelessness became and remains a powerful ideological and material force in Colombia.

In telling this story, I take an analytical approach that at first blush may seem contradictory. On one hand I maintain a critical stance toward these claims of statelessness so as to avoid glossing over the actual persistence of governmental structures and practices. But I also take commonsense notions about the absence of the state seriously, recognizing their powerful ability to shape the imaginaries, practices, institutions, and relationships of political life in Urabá. My goal, in other words, is to understand the purported absence of the state historically and ethnographically, not to debunk it as some bizarre case of false consciousness.

Ultimately, rather than classifying Urabá as a case of state absence or failure I argue that Colombia's violent conflicts have produced surprisingly coherent and resilient regimes of accumulation and rule—yet this is not to say they are benevolent. I show how Urabá's economies of violence are not necessarily anathema to capitalist development and projects of liberal rule. In the case of paramilitaries, for example, I highlight the ways in which plunder, the laundering of drug money, and political violence worked alongside development projects aimed at institution building, good governance, and political participation. Even government-led initiatives aimed at shoring up the rule of law became functional to paramilitary strategies.

Conceptual Bearings

Through its fine-grained historical and ethnographic analysis of Urabá's violent regimes of accumulation and rule, this book challenges dominant thinking on the political economy of development and conflict. It questions the prevailing view of "civil war as development in reverse," a phrase coined by the economist Paul Collier and his colleagues at the World Bank.[15] While Collier and others recognize the obvious fact that armed conflicts bring down basic human development indicators, they ignore the surprising compatibilities between war and development projects. They also perpetuate superficial notions of statelessness by taking Max Weber's heuristic conception of the state—that which successfully claims a monopoly over the use of legitimate force—as if it were an achievable empirical reality.

By revealing the inextricable links between politics and economics in the configuration of violence, my arguments also counter crude versions of the New Wars framework and simplistic dichotomies of greed versus grievance.[16] In the case of Colombia these analyses, besides leaving state absence unquestioned, overemphasize the economics of the drug trade to the point that guerrillas and paramilitaries end up standing in for greedy, depoliticized warlords while cocaine becomes an avatar of the resource curse.[17]

Scholars in Colombia have produced a much richer body of literature on the political economy of civil war. Rather than analyzing Colombia as a deviation from a normative model of political development, their work rightly positions the conflict as an integral part of state formation in the country.[18] In making these arguments, some of these scholars directly dispute or at least qualify the claim of state absence.[19] Fernán González and his colleagues, for instance, document the spatial distribution and history of political violence in Colombia with an emphasis on the "differential presence of the state across space and time."[20] Although I join these scholars in critiquing both popular and scholarly presumptions of statelessness, my contribution, without predetermining what counts as statehood or state building, is a deeper look into the question of state absence itself and the political configurations produced in its name.

My findings raise fundamental questions about the commonplace notion that state building, usually associated with tropes about institution building and good governance, is a lasting antidote to lawlessness and violence in conflict-affected areas. Put simply, an overarching argument of this book is that state building does not necessarily result in peace building. This perspective questions the way international aid agencies have pushed state making to the top of their agendas in response to geopolitical handwringing around so-called fragile states and ungoverned spaces. Some security-minded policymakers have argued even that state building should become a "new development paradigm."[21]

Experts from institutions like the United Nations and the U.S. Agency for International Development (USAID) now see security and development as so inseparable that scholars critical of this conflation call it the security–development nexus.

The World Bank, in the vanguard of this trend, has sponsored major studies on the links between conflict, security, and development, advocating for more "bottom-up" and "resilient" forms of state building.[22] But Urabá demonstrates how the grassroots solutions being endorsed by the bank are not necessarily incompatible with and can in some cases even facilitate illicit economies and violent political projects. Part of the problem with the literature on the political economy of both development and conflict is its lack of concern with how space and, by extension, territory are enmeshed in the rough and tumble world of human power relations. Civil wars produce extremely fraught, contested, and violent territorialities because the question of who calls the shots in a given space is precisely what's at stake. In analyzing these inseparable ties between space and power, I draw on the work of the Marxist philosopher Henri Lefebvre, whose ideas about "the social production of space" constitute the main theoretical foundation of the arguments in this book.[23]

Lefebvre's key insight was that space plays a formative role in shaping society while society, at the same time, plays a formative role in shaping space. He claimed that all spaces are socially constructed, which is not to say they exist only in our mind; it means that spaces are as much the product of our collective imagination and everyday experiences as the result of our physical constructions and material interventions. His crucial contribution to my arguments is that space is both a medium and an outcome of social relationships and conflicts rather than some inert plane on which these unfold.

The reason a more social understanding of space is so important for studying civil wars and their complex political economies is that struggles over territory, as several scholars have noted in passing, are a defining feature of irregular warfare. But this scholarship has never subjected territory itself to any further conceptual scrutiny. A territory is a spatialized political technology, a form of social control over a defined fragment of space.[24] Scholars like Stathis Kalyvas, among others, have noted that the territorial imperative of armed groups is what gives civil wars their tremendous capacity for fragmenting space.[25] The logic of civil wars, according to Kalyvas, is that violence against civilians is most intense in areas where the territories of competing combatant groups overlap and bleed into each other.

But a deeper analytical concern with territory itself—and a social understanding of space more broadly—raises key questions: How are these territories produced in the first place? How are they made, unmade, and remade through the course of violent conflict? Close attention to the social dimensions of space reveals a crucial insight: territories are never held by force alone; they are always a delicate balance of coercion and consent. They must be maintained, in other words, through the workings of what another Marxist thinker, Antonio Gramsci, called hegemony.[26]

As conceived by Gramsci, hegemony describes a fluid process of struggle through which specific configurations of rule are established and naturalized, making alternative arrangements seem practically unviable or even unthinkable. But more than a way of thinking about consent, I use "hegemony" as a way of understanding struggle.[27] The literary critic Raymond Williams put it this way: "A lived hegemony . . . does not just passively exist as a form of dominance. It has continually to be renewed, recreated, defended, and modified. It is also continually resisted, limited, altered, challenged by pressures not at all of its own."[28]

For my purposes what this means is that an armed group's territorial hegemony is never simply imposed but is always to some degree a negotiated process. Understood in this way, hegemony is always and already shaped by the resistance and struggles it has in practice emerged to control; this is what makes it such a dynamic, elastic form of domination. In a civil war, as rival combatant groups build up their localized territorial hegemony, these spaces begin to accumulate, overlap, and, fatefully, collide. The inevitable backlash from centralized authorities against such territorial fragmentation is what explains Kalyvas's provocative claim that "civil war is, at its core, a process of integration and state-building."[29]

By putting hegemony and spatiality at the center of its analysis, this book contributes to critical research on the anthropology of the state. It has become scholarly commonplace to point out that the state is not a unitary sovereign entity with functional desires. If not a complete fiction, the state, most scholars would agree, lacks the coherency and unity of purpose we so often attribute to it.[30] What this literature has not yet fully accounted for, however, is the way in which the state, even via the negativity of its absence, gains practical shape and meaning in everyday life through the production of space.[31]

Urabá, in this respect, is contradictory: on the one hand, the absence of the state implies a fetishized, even personified, monolith that willfully neglects the region. It is a complaint that indicates a profound sense of political alienation from the collective construction of rule. Locals indeed decry their abandonment by the state, expressing what Diana Bocarejo, my Colombian colleague, describes as an intense "longing for the state."[32] At the same time, however, people in Urabá are not as blinded by state mystification and fetishism as the broader literature on the anthropology of the state would suggest. My point is that scholars are not the only ones who are aware of the state's contradictory qualities as an incoherent, heterogeneous, political assemblage.

I approach the state as a dynamic ensemble of relations that is both an effect and an instrument of competing political strategies and relations of power. The advantage of this approach is that it remains open to people's subjective political imaginaries by not predetermining what counts as statehood or state building while at the same time revealing the mutually constitutive relationship between those imaginaries and concrete configurations of rule. Rather than seeing the state as a preformed autonomous entity, I examine how its symbolic and material formation is an always-emergent effect of social practices, relationships, discourses, and lived experiences. While recognizing the state as an abstraction, this conceptualization foregrounds how it nonetheless structures and organizes social life in very real, concrete ways.[33]

In embracing the slippery contradictions surrounding the state rather than trying to resolve them, I follow the analytical approach of the feminist scholar Begoña Aretxaga, who writes, "I attempt to leave the state as both an open notion and an entity, the presence and content of which is not taken for granted but is the very object of inquiry. By thinking about the state in this way, I want to emphasize the power it still conveys; its social and political presence can hardly be ignored."[34] Urabá is a paradoxical confirmation of her final point: even amid the purported absence of the state, "its social and political presence can hardly be ignored." By means of the long, ghostly shadow cast by its absence, the state, as the dominant referent of modern politics, still structures the relationships, discourses, practices, and institutional formations of rule in frontier zones. In Urabá, for instance, groups from across the political spectrum, armed and otherwise, all end up trying to give concrete coherence to the inherently unwieldy abstraction of the state in a space where it supposedly doesn't exist. The way this absence exerts a generative political influence is what I refer to as the frontier effect.[35]

The frontier effect describes how the imaginary of statelessness in these spaces compels all kinds of actors to get into the business of state formation; it thrusts groups into the role of would-be state builders. Under the sway of the frontier effect, they become engaged in what the geographer Bob Jessop calls "state projects." Urabá bears out his suggestion that "whether, how, and to what extent one can talk in definite terms about the state actually depends on the contingent and provisional outcome of struggles to realize more or less specific 'state projects.' For, whatever constitutions might declare about the unity and sovereignty of the modern state as a juridical subject, there are often several rival 'states' competing for a temporary and local hegemony within a given national territory."[36] As spaces of presumed statelessness, frontiers are especially prone to the proliferation of state projects; in fact, such projects are an integral part of the way in which rival groups vie for territorial hegemony in these spaces.

A major reason frontier actors are so bent on advancing their respective state projects is that they are instruments for determining access to and control over land. Conflicts over land and thus over property are a constitutive element of the frontier effect, not only because those fighting over land so often see the existence of such struggles as proof of the state's absence but also because those involved inevitably invoke the state's presence through appeals to the law, rights, authority, and enforcement.[37] The frontier effect turns land into a particularly productive springboard for state formation. Indeed, rather than an index of state absence or failure, violent struggles over land are an essential part of everyday state making in these spaces; they are what make frontiers into such crucibles of competing political authorities and the rival state-building projects they bring in tow. As the fundamental basis for the accumulation of both wealth and power in frontier zones, land constitutes the violent meeting place between cold economic interests and heated political battles.

And yet in most stories of frontier zones, whether the narrative is critical or triumphalist, land is ultimately the primary vehicle for the definitive consolidation of state control. In these accounts unruly struggles over land eventually give way, via the survey, the grid, and private property, to the high-modernist powers of legibility, simplification, and abstract space. These forces bulldoze all opposition and lay waste to whatever existed before. The standard ending of most frontier stories is a transformed social and ecological landscape that enables the smooth operation of state power and the circulation of capital. But Urabá is proof that enduring conflicts over land can be just as conducive to projects of accumulation and rule.[38]

Mapping Urabá and the Organization of the Book

Urabá is not an official administrative–territorial division of any kind. As is typical of most informal subnational regions—say, Appalachia or the Outback—Urabá is a profoundly subjective, contested, and fluid historical construction. Its boundaries and even its name are matters of debate. At its most expansive Urabá encompasses the entire area surrounding its namesake gulf in the far northwest of Colombia, including the northern tips of the departments of Antioquia and Chocó along with the western reaches of Córdoba (see fig. 2). For consistency and simplicity I use "Urabá" in this expansive sense as shorthand for the entire area surrounding the gulf. But to many locals and most Colombians Urabá is most closely associated with the swath of land along the eastern side of the gulf that belongs to the department of Antioquia. The reason for this—that is, how and why Antioquia claimed the coastal region as its own—is where I begin this story.

The first two chapters of the book are about the production of Urabá as a frontier zone. Chapter 1 shows how the main force behind the making of this frontier was the city of Medellín's neocolonial designs on the region. During the first half of the twentieth century Medellín's urban elites, mostly white and famously conservative, set out to subjugate Urabá and its overwhelmingly Afro-Colombian population. For locals, the violent relations between land, labor, and capital at the heart of this internal colonialism came to define the frontier as a lived experience. Chapter 2 continues in the 1970s and 1980s, when the Cold War drew Urabá's economies of violence into the vortex of insurgency and counterinsurgency, reinforcing the region's reputation as a stateless frontier. Amid the region's profound crisis of authority, the insurgencies believed they had finally achieved what they called a revolutionary situation, but the brewing paramilitary movement would soon deliver them a crushing defeat.

The middle three chapters of the book present an in-depth account of paramilitary state building via the case of the militia led by El Alemán. Chapter 3 examines the practices by which paramilitaries sought to methodically build a state presence in the region. Chapter 4 highlights the cultural politics of paramilitaries' revanchist state project by detailing their attempt to build an electoral political movement. Making clear that paramilitary state building was by no means a selfless public service, chapter 5 dissects how grassroots development initiatives enabled the creation of a vast criminal economy.

Finally, the last two chapters consider the way in which expectations surrounding Colombia's postconflict transition have become the latest impetus for state building in Urabá. Through a fine-grained account of the government's flagship land restitution program in the region, chapter 6 delves into the country's ongoing experiment with transitional justice, illustrating the messy renegotiations of rule the postconflict entails. Finally, chapter 7 concludes the book by returning to the fraught relationship between Medellín and Urabá, which in its latest iteration involved an elaborate regional planning effort aimed at creating, once and for all, a meaningful, lasting state presence in the region.

Ultimately, this book disputes one of modernity's founding myths: that the state saved humanity from a life that the political philosopher Thomas Hobbes famously described as "solitary, poor, nasty, brutish, and short."[39] Hobbes's dystopian "state of nature" still colors the main lens through which dominant geopolitical imaginaries in Colombia view the country's war-torn agrarian spaces. Prominent discourses portray these areas as spatial aberrations and historical anachronisms, places where the state of nature inexplicably lives on. Regions like Urabá appear in the media as the unintegrated Outsides of the Colombian state, spatial Others in desperate need of incorporation. They are seen as dystopian Edens: lawless and stateless spaces bursting with untapped natural riches and populated (if at all) by expendable populations.

Deep-seated colonial conceptions of race and nature underwrite the view of these spaces as lying beyond the pale of civilization and modern statehood. A respected local journalist, for example, described Colombia's civil war as "a constant battle against geography, resembling the conquest of the Wild West."

She concluded, "You can't build the State in a scorching climate, amid a swarm of mosquitos, and where taking a sack of corn to the market requires navigating entire rivers and scaling the Andes."[40] With clear echoes of Hobbes, she reduced decades of conflict—some would say centuries—to the problem of statelessness as an inevitable result of interrelated geographical, environmental, and racial determinisms.

Paramilitaries seemed especially haunted by the ghost of Hobbes. In his first appearance in court, the music of his supporters still blaring from the plaza below, El Alemán described violence as Urabá's primordial condition: "It's always been a spot of violence, even before the arrival of the Spanish conquistadors." He claimed that disregarding this history would make it seem as if the paramilitaries had fallen out of the sky "like armed paratroopers landing in the Garden of Eden." To him, Urabá, far from being an innocent paradise, bore a closer resemblance to a hellish state of nature.

As he selectively paraphrased the Colombian Constitution, he kept reminding the court of the threat guerrillas posed to "life, honor, and property."[41] Channeling Hobbes and later liberal philosophers, El Alemán added, "Our military doctrine was philosophically inspired by the natural right to self-defense." Instead of compounding the fabled war of all against all, paramilitary leaders set out to decide its conclusion. In the mold of Carl Schmitt's fascist political theory, these leaders justified their armed struggle as an extralegal necessity for preserving the state's legal order against the existential threat posed by the guerrillas.[42] But paramilitary commanders took things a step further and made state building a key part of their strategic vision—and no one did so more than El Alemán.

The first time I met El Alemán was in September 2012. As per the terms of his deal with Colombia's transitional justice program, he was at that time still serving out his eight-year jail sentence at a maximum security prison near Medellín (he was released in 2015). Apparently he had been keeping tabs on my research from afar through his people in Urabá. This was chillingly revealed to me the first time I contacted his former troops. "Oh, you're the one who's been going around talking to the victims," said the voice on the phone. "My *comandante* told me about you." After years of having my interview requests go unanswered, I still don't know for sure why El Alemán finally agreed to speak with me; he deflected the question when I asked. I suppose he liked what he had been hearing about my research. After all, I was taking seriously the paramilitaries' self-appointed role as state builders, something most people, including me at one time, dismissed out of hand as hollow political theater.

Our meeting took place in the warden's office at a large table next to an open window overlooking a small, enclosed cement prison yard in which inmates were milling around. The guards brought El Alemán into the office, and after a brief greeting he yelled out the window for someone to bring us some juice. Both the location of our meeting and the orders he barked out the window made clear his high standing and authority within the prison. Even the guards showed deference to the jailed commander.

As we waited for the juice I nervously tried to pretend that meeting an infamous paramilitary commander was no big deal. He asked me about my background. When I told him I was born in Argentina and grew up mostly in the United States he joked that my accent sounded "more *cachaco* than *argentino*." My six years of living in Bogotá, making me a *cachaco*, as people from the interior of the country are known, had erased most traces of my Argentine accent. But Colombians could still immediately detect, if not quite place, my foreignness. I gave El Alemán a canned description of my research, after which our conversation—more of a monologue, actually—went on for nearly four hours. At one point during the interview I interrupted him to note that he sometimes described Urabá as a place where the state shone for its absence, as he liked to say, but at other times said it had been *un estado guerrillero* before his arrival.

"Well, which was it?" I asked. "The absence of the state or a guerrilla state?"

"It's the same thing," he said instantly, launching into yet another lengthy monologue: "Look, the police may have had control of an area here or there without any problems, but the economic, social, political, and military power really belonged to the guerrillas. So, what did we do?" He paused for dramatic effect and cracked a smile before saying, "We took that power away and replaced it with our own, *bit by bit*."[43] It was at this "bit-by-bit" scale that paramilitary state building went to work.

On my way home from the prison that day I thought back to my first meeting with Gerardo Vega, a former operative of the Ejército Popular de Liberación (EPL), initially a Maoist rebel outfit.[44] In the 1960s and 1970s the EPL and the FARC competed for influence in Urabá among the human fallout generated by the arrival of the infamous United Fruit Company. The region's dispossessed peasantry and exploited workforce proved to be a receptive social base for the rebels. By the 1980s, as conflicts around land and labor heated up, the EPL decided it needed a trusted lawyer in the area, so they sent one of their own, Gerardo, who was young, idealistic, and just out of law school. Now graying and middle-aged, Gerardo is the director of a scrappy human rights NGO based in Medellín. The bulk of his organization's work is aimed at helping displaced peasants reclaim lands stolen by paramilitaries.

We met at the NGO's offices and during my usual pre-interview small talk, I mentioned something in passing about paramilitaries positioning themselves as state builders. "Paramilitaries?" he scoffed, obviously offended. "In Urabá *we* were the ones who built the state!" Offering examples of the EPL's work, he cited its support of popular struggles over land, labor, and public services in Urabá. He pointed out that political parties linked to the insurgencies had controlled most of Urabá's municipal administrations in the 1980s. Reciting this history and still openly annoyed by my characterization of his sworn enemies as state builders, Gerardo emphasized, "*We* were the ones who brought the labor code to Urabá. *We* made it respected, and it was thanks to *us* that there's now an Office of Labor Affairs and Social Security in the region."

Perhaps these were the kinds of things El Alemán had in mind when claiming that, in those days, Urabá had been a guerrilla state. The contrasting positions taken by the EPL's Gerardo Vega and El Alemán—the first emphasizing labor exploitation and the other threats to private property—reflect how Colombia's violent political struggles arise not from the absence of the state but from radical disagreements about the very meaning and purpose of political community. Their comments also indicate how violent relations between land, labor, and capital are at the crux of the region's perceived status as a stateless frontier.

Despite their centrality to the story, guerrillas and paramilitaries are by no means the only actors discussed in this book. The cast of characters includes military strategists, agrarian elites, dispossessed peasants, technocratic planners, and many more. The other protagonists of this story are the multiply scaled forces that have been just as consequential in shaping Urabá's history: from global security paradigms to national development regimes; from the cultural politics of Colombian regionalism to the intimate conflicts of community. All of these actors and forces have at one time or another played integral roles in shaping the region's unruly frontier state formations (in the plural)—the sometimes fleeting, sometimes durable political configurations produced at the imagined limits of the state. Indeed, the problem for Urabá has never been as much the absence of the state as the proliferation of state-building projects. And no single group assumed the mantle of state building with the same ferocity and dedication as the paramilitaries.

It was my interest in paramilitaries that led me, as a reporter, to attend the start of El Alemán's trial in 2007. I looked on in disbelief as his supporters basked in the sun beneath the towering structures of Medellín's judicial buildings. What could they possibly admire so much in the man whose trial was about to begin? The ensuing testimonies of top commanders like El Alemán began revealing the full extent of the paramilitary phenomenon and its tentacular reach into almost every imaginable institution of social life. What slowly came to light is that the paramilitary movement had succeeded in building a new cartography of state power in Colombia. Their state project had won the day, and Urabá was its proving ground.

As he started winding down his testimony, El Alemán claimed he had led his troops to an unequivocal victory in the war. "The one thing I know is that I left an Urabá free of guerrillas," he said. "Today, the region is in the hands of the state, and seeing it able to enjoy liberty and harmony is my greatest satisfaction." The reality is much more complicated than that. Newer drug-trafficking militias, one of them founded by El Alemán's brother, took control of the territories once held by previous generations of fighters. Urabá is still the pipeline for a sizable portion of the world's cocaine supply, and it remains a major hot spot of organized violence in what is misleadingly called postconflict Colombia.

After six hours of testimony and with his voice growing hoarse, El Alemán asked for a recess until the next day. By then, the boisterous crowd had long since dispersed from the plaza outside the court building. Littered confetti and trampled carnations were the only signs of the morning's festivities. The plaza had regained its banal bureaucratic stateliness: people rushing about, others waiting anxiously in line, almost everyone cradling papers and folders in their arms as they quietly went about their business with the state.

PRODUCING THE FRONTIER

Suddenly, as if a whirlwind had set down roots in the center of town, the banana company arrived, pursued by the leaf storm. A whirling leaf storm had been stirred up, formed out of the human and material dregs of other towns, the chaff of a civil war that seemed ever more remote and unlikely. The whirlwind was implacable. . . . In less than a year it sowed over the town the rubble of many catastrophes that had come before it, scattering its mixed cargo of rubbish in the streets.

—Gabriel García Márquez, *Leaf Storm* (1955)

In preparation for his trial El Alemán wrote a book-length manuscript on the history of Urabá. One of the first sections of the text bears the title "Urabá: A Land without a State."[1] It begins with a story about an engineering mission that set out for Urabá from Medellín in 1927. It took the group five weeks of travel by car, foot, horseback, and boat to reach the waters of the Gulf of Urabá. According to El Alemán, the mission had to bushwhack much of the way, so the "only guide for navigating through the treacherous jungles" was a lone telegraph line.

The leader of the mission was Gonzalo Mejía, a famous businessman from Medellín and a "visionary *antioqueño*," according to the jailed paramilitary chief (*antioqueño* is someone from the department of Antioquia). Mejía helped pioneer so many modern industries in Colombia, including automotive, aviation, and cinema ventures that the press had dubbed him "the dream maker."[2] But his most ambitious plan of all was the one that had led him to trudge through the swamps of Urabá: the construction of a road connecting Antioquia's capital of Medellín to the department's only outlet to the sea, the Gulf of Urabá.

Through an elaborate marketing and public relations campaign, Mejía had whipped up a frenzy of support for the project among his fellow antioqueños. Medellín's newspapers fanned the excitement, predicting the road would be Antioquia's "magnum opus." Mejía and his allies claimed the "Highway to the Sea," as they branded it, would be "una obra redentora" (a redemptive public work).[3] The Highway to the Sea inspired nothing less than a creole version of Manifest Destiny, but rather than Horace Greeley's "Go West, young man," the call was "¡Hacia Urabá! ¡Al Mar!" (To Urabá! To the Sea!)[4]

FIGURE 5. "To the Sea!" The February 1927 cover of *Progreso*, the in-house magazine of the Society for Public Works, a business lobby group founded by Medellín elites.

Antioquia's version of Manifest Destiny had just as racialized an underpinning as its U.S. counterpart and was based on the same master narrative of all frontiers: the duel between civilization and barbarism. "Yes, we're heading west to both civilize and civilize ourselves," wrote one newspaper columnist, "to repel barbarism and attract healthier elements of morality and work." He described Urabá as the unconcluded business of colonial conquest: "Let's finish what those audacious Spanish conquistadors were unable to do: subjugate and exploit that promised land."[5]

Despite the feverish enthusiasm behind it, the construction of the two-lane road, spanning a mere two hundred miles, dragged on for three decades. The Highway to the Sea opened in 1954, two years before Mejía's death. The project stalled repeatedly due to administrative disarray, the financial strains of the Great Depression, and the ruggedness of the terrain. In his manuscript El Alemán

points out that the rainy season still occasionally renders the highway impassable, a fact he laments as proof that "*even today*, the road is holding back Urabá's
genuine progress." In his eyes the civilizing mission begun by Mejía remains,
"even today," a work in progress.

The torturous construction of the Highway to the Sea exemplifies the paradoxical quality of frontiers as spaces produced by both the power *and* the limits
of reigning regimes of accumulation and rule. On one hand, frontiers are spaces
undergoing profound material transformation, epitomes of the "wreckage upon
wreckage" witnessed by Walter Benjamin's angel of history, its face turned toward
the past and a violent storm caught in its wings. "This storm irresistibly propels
him into the future to which his back is turned," wrote Benjamin, "while the pile
of debris before him grows skyward. This storm is what we call progress."[6] And
yet frontiers are also spaces in which these storms of "progress" have supposedly
not yet run their course. Frontiers, then, are made by forces that somehow manage to be both brutal and brittle.

They achieve this contradictory feat because frontiers are consummate examples of what Lefebvre meant by the social production of space: frontiers are ideological and discursive formations as much as material ones; they are, in every
sense, both real and imagined.[7] The symbolic realm of, say, myths and maps are
just as integral to their production as the physical materiality of, say, railroads
and landscape transformations. Frontiers are also inherently relational spaces:
every frontier is the frontier of somewhere for someone. In the case of Urabá, the
somewhere was Medellín and the someone was the city's light-skinned, ultra-
conservative elites.

The historical–geographical contours of Urabá's production as a frontier zone
was driven by a profoundly racist set of cultural politics emanating from the city.
Following a classic metropole–satellite relation, the frontier emerged via Medellín's attempt to bring the gulf region into the city's cultural, political, and economic orbit, and the construction of the Highway to the Sea was a central part
of this process.[8] The relationship turned into a form of uneven development: the
accumulation of wealth by a small elite in Medellín was systematically linked to
the accumulation of exploitation and poverty in Urabá.[9]

In the language of Latin American dependency theory, Medellín's relationship
with Urabá was a form of internal colonialism, a term with intentionally racialized overtones.[10] As a concept, internal colonialism highlights the way in which
the uneven development of Urabá as a frontier zone was as much a racial and cultural process as a structural effect of the geographies of capitalism. However, the
fact that this form of colonialism is primarily internal or subnational does not
mean it happens in a vacuum; internal colonialism is not divorced from forces
operating at other scales. Indeed, as I show, the making of Urabá into a frontier

was the product of global interconnections: from the tentacles of the United Fruit Company to the wide-ranging geopolitics of the Cold War.

Urabá's statelessness in these years was problematized and expressed from the point of view of Medellín through racialized idioms of civilization and barbarism and claims about the region's lack of progress and abandonment. As late as 1950 an army fact-finding mission reported, "The place is dreadfully abandoned; there's no Inspector, no Police, no official form of authority of any kind."[11] Driven by the imperative to resolve these problems, the frontier effect unleashed a succession of state projects in Urabá led by urban elites based in Medellín.

Frontiers as Racialized Spaces of Uneven Development

Frontiers have a long and infamous history in Latin America.[12] As the product of colonial discourses, frontiers in the region are as old as Christopher Columbus's first letters from the Caribbean and the early myths of El Dorado. Once Latin America gained independence from Spain, frontiers became an integral part of the ways in which early nation builders shored up fledgling forms of national identity. Perpetuated by everything from the geographical expeditions of Alexander von Humboldt and his successors to Domingo Sarmiento's influential classic *Civilization and Barbarism*, frontiers were what the new "imagined communities" of Latin America were to be formed against.[13] They became, in the words of the anthropologist Margarita Serje, "the opposite of the nation."[14]

Race and identity were central to why these spaces were cast out as areas beyond the pale of the nation. In post-Independence Colombia, as elsewhere in Latin America, the idea of *mestizaje* (racial mixture) came to define national identity in ways that encompassed the multiracial makeup of the country without undermining the core ideology of white supremacy. Mestizaje allowed elites, alongside their darker-skinned compatriots, to rally around the imagined community of Colombia as a mestizo nation while still emphasizing their own whiteness and superiority. By disparaging Afro-descendent and indigenous identities, mestizo nationalism further marginalized spaces, such as Urabá, where these racialized groups formed a majority of the population.[15]

Informed by ideologies of scientific racism from abroad, nationalist discourses turned race and nature into conjoined essentialisms that further exoticized, racialized, and thus produced entire swaths of national territory as unincorporated "savage lands." In Colombia the racialized projection of frontiers as spatial Others was part and parcel of extremely violent forms of resource extraction and the hyperexploitation of their populations—from the genocidal rubber booms of the Amazon to the cattle enclosures of the country's eastern flatlands.[16] In a vicious feedback loop, the racialized poverty and exclusion resulting from these neocolonial projects reinforced the frontier imaginary that helped cause these problems in the first place.

The long history of Urabá's experience with racialized colonial violence could be said to begin with the fact that it was the site of Spain's first colonial settlement on the mainland of the Americas. The indigenous Urabaes put up fierce resistance to the Spaniards.[17] Urabá was also where the Crown sent enslaved Africans to mine for gold along the banks of the Atrato River, giving the region a solid place within the geographies of the Black Atlantic. Many of those who escaped slavery formed autonomous maroon communities in the jungle, setting an early precedent for the region's enduring reputation as a fugitive space. In short, Urabá was an early crucible of colonial violence.

For centuries, however, it remained a sparsely populated region of scattered fishing villages, tiny family farms, and trading posts. It was much more connected to the maritime networks of the Caribbean than to the major cities in the interior of the country. But all this started to change when a confluence of events pushed Medellín to take a greater interest in the region. The city's elites increasingly saw the need for a road or railroad to the coast as a cultural, economic, and geopolitical imperative. One event in particular set things in motion.

Major national attention only turned toward Urabá after the United States engineered the 1903 secession of neighboring Panama, which had until then been a department of Colombia. The Panama debacle was the culmination of a multidimensional crisis. A severe economic depression had deepened age-old political schisms between the Liberal and Conservative parties, plunging Colombia into a bloodletting known as the War of a Thousand Days (1899–1902).[18] The political and economic turmoil had the added misfortune of coinciding with one of the most aggressive periods of U.S. imperialism toward Latin America.

With an eye on U.S. ambitions in the region, a Colombian diplomat passing through the department of Panama in 1902 predicted that its loss was simply a matter of time: "The Isthmus is lost for Colombia; it is painful to say it, but it is true. Here Yankee influence predominates, and all Panamanians, with few exceptions, are capable of selling the Canal, the Isthmus, and even their own mother."[19] With the canal's construction stalled and with the War of a Thousand Days having further stoked preexisting separatist sentiments, Washington seized the opportunity to nudge, bless, and militarily defend Panama's declaration of independence on November 3, 1903.

The loss of Panama left a deeply wounded sense of nationhood along with a serious case of geopolitical paranoia. Rafael Reyes, Colombia's new president, immediately moved to forestall any further dismemberment of the nation. He called for an administrative–territorial reorganization of the country that would centralize power in Bogotá and partition the country's departments into smaller, more manageable units. President Reyes's plans turned into a chance for Antioquia to reclaim its territorial jurisdiction over Urabá, which it had lost to the department of Cauca during a previous national shakeup. As Reyes pushed his reforms through Congress, land-locked Antioquia, led by its capital, Medellín, tapped into the country's lingering geopolitical anxieties to lobby for its repossession of Urabá.

With Panama as the subtext, Medellín's city council implored Congress "to return territory that has always properly belonged to Antioquia, thus placing the area on the road to progress and helping defend our national integrity."[20] After all, went the argument, it was hardy antioqueños who just decades earlier had settled the lands to the south of Medellín, turning them into Colombia's "eje cafetero" (coffee axis). As the creators of the country's mighty coffee boom, antioqueños—or *paisas,* as they call themselves—claimed they had a proven track record of spearheading a successful mission of civilizing untamed lands and turning a profit in the process.

The colonization of Colombia's coffee heartland is one of the founding myths of paisa (pronounced pie·sa) exceptionalism. A play on the word "paisano" (countryman), paisa is, in its ugliest incarnation, a chauvinistic regional–cultural identity assumed by people from the highlands of Antioquia and a few neighboring provinces in which they see themselves as Colombia's most enterprising, pious, conservative, hardworking, light-skinned, macho people.[21] From the perspective of paisa elites in Medellín, Urabá had naturally belonged to Antioquia all along; it was *their* corridor to the sea, and only antioqueños had the civilizational wherewithal for ensuring the region stayed within the national fold.

The paisa dream of linking their capital of Medellín to the sea was an old one, but the loss of Panama gave it new urgency and wider traction. With his thumb on the pulse of the nation's geopolitical fears, a government official in Urabá said the need for a highway or a railroad was strategic "in case of a war with some nation of the North." Only Antioquia, he insisted, could prevent Urabá from being seduced by the "welcoming shade of the colossus."[22] The ominous shadow of U.S. imperialism had turned Urabá's isolation and statelessness into geopolitical liabilities and the need for a road into a strategic requirement. On April 11, 1905, Congress officially redrew Antioquia's borders, restoring its jurisdiction over Urabá. Editorials in Medellín's newspapers celebrated the move: "Let's open up the tangled jungles of the aborigines to make way for the triumphant carriage of commerce and the patriotic defense of our national integrity."[23] On the basis of their sense of racial superiority, paisas cast the "open[ing] up" of Urabá not only as a political and economic process but also as a moral responsibility.

The governor of Antioquia's new officials in the region began sending back letters full of descriptions about the supposed moral and intellectual inferiority of Urabá's mostly black population. "If we want to not just maintain but rather foster the true moral hegemony of Antioquia over this region, then it's indispensable to make sure public instruction here is in the hands of Antioquia's most experienced teachers," suggested one dispatch from the regional prefect. "We need them to come and radically resolve the moral chaos afflicting the region." Giving a hint of self-awareness about his own prejudice, the prefect added, "In this case, it is not so much my regionalism that leads me to speak in this way; it's my firsthand view of the barbarous life being led by the vast majority of the inhabitants of the region.... The teachers of Antioquia must educate this agonizing society ... [which is] one of the most morally and intellectually backward of Colombia."[24]

Explaining this presumed backwardness, a Catholic missionary flatly lamented, "There are blacks, mulatos, mestizos, and Indians, but proper whites are very few."[25] The multiracial composition of Urabá's growing population had been spurred by a succession of early commodity booms, including rubber, tropical woods, ipecac, and ivory palm (*tagua*).[26] Attracted by these commodity cycles, Afro-descendents continued streaming into the region from the south (Chocó) and the east (Cartagena), while mestizo campesinos were arriving from the neighboring Sinú river basin in the present-day department of Córdoba.[27]

The region's mixed racial makeup allowed the incoming antioqueños to reify the myth of their racial purity by contrasting their supposed whiteness against the much darker spectrum of local skin tones. Locals, meanwhile, began using the terms "white" and "antioqueño" interchangeably. For these antioqueños from the highlands of the department, the poverty they encountered in Urabá had nothing to do with local histories of colonial violence or with relentless cycles of resource extraction and everything to do with the combined effects of race, nature, and elevation. Within the context of Colombia's mountainous and equatorial geography, elevation had long bolstered the racist linkages between biological and environmental determinisms.

For instance, judging from the cooler climes of Antioquia's Andean highlands, Medellín's upper crust believed it was only natural that the miscegenated races inhabiting the steamy lowlands of Urabá would be lazy and morally deplorable. The fact that antioqueños could even survive near the scorching shores of Urabá came as a surprise to a government visitor from Medellín who happily reported that "*la raza antioqueña* [the antioqueño race] has acclimated to the region, living with normal conditions and robustness."[28] Even today it is not altogether unheard of for conservative paisas to proudly describe themselves as la raza antioqueña; and throughout Colombia elevation remains a powerful element in the essentialized couplings of race and nature that help prop up the country's social hierarchies.

On April 11, 1905, the same day Congress returned Urabá to Antioquia, President Reyes signed a contract for the construction of a railroad from Medellín to the coast, promising it would open up the "completely abandoned area of rich and fertile lands." Paisas celebrated the move, saying a train would allow them to "antioquianize" the region by "homogenizing [i.e., whitening] the race" and gracing it with their superior "spirit of the mountains."[29] The contract went to Henry Granger, a U.S. expat from Philadelphia who had become a gold baron with several dozen mines in neighboring Chocó. The whitening of Urabá was written into the contract itself through a stipulation in which Granger promised to "foment European and American immigration" to the region.

The contract also called for a new port city at the terminus of the tracks. As the crown jewel of the project, the city by the shore was going to be named Ciudad Reyes in recognition of the president's role in reinstating Antioquia's jurisdiction over the gulf. At a ceremony marking the transfer of jurisdiction, a prestigious judge from Medellín gushed with effusive prose about the planned metropolis: "I can already imagine the future Ciudad Reyes flowering populously with its artistically decorated buildings, its skyscrapers, and its towering streetlights, surrounded by gardens; a portrait of Naples on the shores of the Atlantic slumbering to the cadence of the gulf's lapping waves."[30] Ultimately, however, the U.S. financial panic of 1907 doomed Granger's company, and neither the railroad nor Ciudad Reyes ever materialized.

The aborted railroad project left little more than a paper trail of charts and blueprints, but it helped set in motion other plans. Antioquia's legislative body, the Departmental Assembly, was particularly dead set on making the reincorporation of the gulf mean more than just a few redrawn lines on the map. Legislators decided the grassroots efforts of thousands of antioqueño campesinos driven by paisa perseverance could succeed where the single grand scheme of the railroad had failed. Based on the heroic example of paisas' colonization of the coffee axis, lawmakers entrusted the settlement of Urabá to the bootstrap initiative of campesino homesteaders, or *colonos*. The assembly passed a law in 1913 that stated, "Colonization is of the utmost urgency [*urgentísimo*] . . . as it brings with it the advance of culture and civilization."[31] To entice prospective colonos the assembly would pay for their relocation and give them a six-month living stipend, tools, and a one-hundred-hectare plot, a portion of which they could eventually formalize with legal title. In exchange, colonos would have to clear at least ten hectares of forest, farm the land, and build a house ("with a separate kitchen").

Despite all the incentives the expected flood of paisa colonos was never more than a trickle thanks to a combination of formidable deterrents. To begin with, Urabá's rain-drenched lands were not suitable for coffee, and its dense forests could not be easily burned to make pasture. The region's staunch allegiance to the Liberal Party also made it hostile political terrain for the overwhelmingly Conservative paisas. And finally, unlike the temperate, rolling hills of the coffee axis, Urabá was seen as a hot, low-lying, insalubrious, Afro-Colombian backwater. Antioquia's imagined geographies of race and nature proved insurmountable obstacles—at least, for now. It was in the 1920s, in the wake of the failed railroad project and the floundering colonization scheme, that Gonzalo Mejía, the ambitious paisa businessman and "dream maker," started trying to drum up a *fiebre colonizadora* (colonizing fever). He doubled down on calls for Antioquia's triumphant march to the sea and recruited key figures from Medellín's notoriously tightknit high society. Together, they formed the Junta Propulsadora para la Carretera al Mar, a booster committee tasked with making sure the Highway to the Sea materialized. The junta began lobbying at all levels of government and launched an all-out marketing campaign replete with mass rallies and propaganda.

The junta placed a gigantic map in a plaza of downtown Medellín showing the road's proposed route. One journalist wrote, "Anyone who looks at the map of Colombia will notice Medellín and, in their imagination, will immediately draw a line from our capital to the gulf."[32] For him, as for many other paisas, the highway's route was as natural as it was obvious. The arguments for the highway mobilized the same racist discourses of civilization and barbarism used to justify Antioquia's repossession of Urabá just a few decades earlier.

Paisa commentators again asserted that Antioquia had the moral responsibility to redeem the lesser races: "They have been languishing there in unhappy hamlets, vegetating in indolence and carelessness. They have no ideals or love for work, no aspirations for education and have no ties to Antioquia other than our public officials there." After mentioning the region's abandonment by the state, the same author described Urabá as "a sick patient" in dire need of being "injected with the boiling, moral, and progressive blood of the antioqueño people." Only then, he argued, "will you see the sick patient rise to enjoy all the benefits the Colombian nation has to offer."[33] Once again, propaganda contrasted the "fortune-seeking raza antioqueña" and the racial degeneracy of Urabá.

Mejía and his fellow boosters declared that the Highway to the Sea would be the spearhead of antioqueño civilization's definitive triumph over barbarism in an area they explicitly claimed, in imperial Roman terms, as *mare nostrum*.[34] Reflecting on the fanatical support Mejía elicited for the project, one observer said, "Every antioqueño backed the project with crazy enthusiasm: women offered their jewelry, men offered their work or their money. It was a beautiful moment of our history."[35] While ideology and shrewd marketing played important roles, broader political and economic forces were just as crucial for pushing the highway forward.

Medellín's rise as a financial and commercial powerhouse had been building for a long time, stretching back to the colonial era, when the city became a hub for the export of gold mined by slaves and the import of goods from abroad. Late in the nineteenth century the members of this merchant and banking class became the primary beneficiaries of the coffee boom, using their financial muscle to control the credit, pricing, distribution, and transportation of the crop.[36] They leveraged their excess wealth from coffee remittances toward industrial development, specifically textile manufacturing. The industrial boom eventually earned the city a seven-page spread in *Life* magazine under the headline "Medellín: South American showplace hailed as a 'Capitalist Paradise.'"[37]

For the city's well-heeled families, the construction of the Highway to the Sea was going to solve several problems at once. It would afford them a long-term place to park the large amounts of idle capital they had accumulated from coffee and textile manufacturing. In addition, once finished, the road would ensure Medellín's continued success as a capitalist paradise by granting it better access to global markets, especially via the adjacent the Panama Canal. Finally, it would open up Urabá, a wholly undercapitalized frontier, to lucrative investments in land and agriculture.

In other words, the road project was a textbook case of what the geographer David Harvey calls a "spatial fix," when investors take unproductive surplus capital and make it profitable by shunting it into new spaces and fixed objects, particularly infrastructure.[38] The spatial fix played a fundamental role in shaping the material contours of the frontier relationship: as excess capital sloshed from Medellín to Urabá, it tipped off the back and forth seesaw movements of investment and disinvestment that perpetuate uneven development on an ever-growing scale.

With added help from capital raised through bonds in the United States, Antioquia finally began constructing its long-sought-after Highway to the Sea on June 10, 1926. At the height of construction seven thousand laborers and forty-three engineers were working on the road. By the end of 1929, however, after a mere three years of construction, the Great Depression brought the project to a screeching halt, thereby confirming the spatial fix's structural tendency to leave a skeletal landscape of underdevelopment in its wake. In this case, that meant half-dug tunnels, blown-up mountainsides, stripped forests, and huge tracts of the road still missing.

As the global economy slowly recovered, the project again began inching its way forward, but the outbreak in 1948 of La Violencia, yet another civil war between Liberals and Conservatives, created further delays. The intensity of La Violencia in Urabá, in addition to the endless problems with the highway's construction, reinforced the region's reputation as a stateless and indomitable frontier. La Violencia played a particularly strong role in consolidating Medellín's frontier relationship with Urabá because of the way the conflict became intertwined with the cultural politics of internal colonialism and the ideological struggles of the Cold War.

La Violencia

Although rooted in the long-standing enmities of Colombia's partisan duopoly, La Violencia's definitive spark was the assassination in 1948 of Jorge Eliécer Gaitán, a wildly popular leader of the Liberal Party. Gaitán's rise was buoyed by a wave of popular militancy that began in the 1920s as a countercurrent to the onset of rapid industrialization in the cities and unbridled neocolonial extraction in the countryside. The Liberal Party's most radical wing, which would soon morph into the Partido Comunista Colombiano (PCC), led much of the unrest.[39] The country's various export enclaves, namely, around oil, mining, and bananas, became intense flashpoints of this era's labor struggles.

One of the largest, most notorious of these conflicts was the 1928 banana workers' strike against the United Fruit Company near Santa Marta, on the opposite end of the Caribbean coast from Urabá. Weeks into the strike, the government declared a state of emergency and the military turned its machine guns on four thousand striking workers who had gathered in protest outside a train station. To this day no one knows how many unionists died in the massacre, but one carefree cable from the U.S. Embassy noted, "I have the honor to report that . . . the total number of strikers killed by the Colombian military authorities during the recent disturbance reached between five and six hundred."[40]

Gaitán, then a young congressman in the Liberal Party, catapulted himself into the national spotlight by investigating the massacre and holding congressional hearings on the repression. Drawing on his background as a labor lawyer, he began cultivating a strong image as a defender of the working class, railing against "la oligarquía" in his speeches. A spellbinding orator, Gaitán led huge rallies that attracted an impressively diverse mass of followers into the country's plazas. His popularity set him up, despite stiff resistance from the old guard of his own party, as the likely winner of the 1950 presidential election.

What might have been Colombia's version of the national–populist experiments then sweeping across Latin America was never given a chance. On April 9, 1948, a lone gunman shot and killed Gaitán as he left his office for lunch in downtown Bogotá. Witnesses immediately lynched the shooter, so his motivations or fellow conspirators, if any, remain unknown. But since political violence against radical Liberals and Communists had been building for decades, Gaitán's seething supporters had good reason to blame the Conservative Party. Massive riots erupted in Bogotá and quickly spread nationwide, sending the country spiraling into nine years of vicious partisan warfare.[41]

According to conservative estimates of official census data, Urabá had some fifty thousand inhabitants at the time of the assassination. Although the rest of Antioquia was a bastion of Conservative power, Urabá, overwhelmingly populated by Afro-Colombians, who to this day tend to be anti-Conservative, was dominated by the Liberal Party. Nonetheless, the region's municipal governments were run by Conservative politicians because the Constitution at the time assigned to governors the job of appointing all the mayors in their department. So even before La Violencia, Antioquia's relationship to Urabá was beset by tensions along both racial and party lines.

When news of Gaitán's murder reached Turbo, Urabá's largest town at the time, Liberal leaders dissolved the Conservative municipal government and declared a Revolutionary Junta.[42] Two days later a desperate Conservative sympathizer telegrammed Medellín from Turbo: "Rebels took the town. . . . They armed campesinos and are ready to attack. . . . Please tell Governor of Antioquia if the country's situation worsens we will be in grave danger."[43] The gulf region soon turned into a geostrategic hot spot of the conflict. Besides being a major Liberal enclave and guerrilla haven, it was a busy arms-smuggling corridor for gunrunners supplying Liberals with weapons from Central America.[44] The Conservative leadership in control of both the national government in Bogotá and the departmental government in Medellín desperately wanted to rein in what it saw as a runaway, fugitive space.

From the perspective of Medellín's elites part of the problem with Urabá was that locals did not consider themselves antioqueños. During a trip through the region one paisa traveler observed, "In general, it is populated by blacks that— lo and behold!—do not consider themselves antioqueños. This goes for all of Urabá. They call whites 'antioqueños' and respect them more out of fear than for any other reason." Even worse, he added, "far from considering themselves antioqueños, they actually hate antioqueños."[45]

For proud paisas the issue of locals' lack of identification with Antioquia was not just about wounded regional egos but also had serious security implications.

Urabá's racial and cultural differences were inseparable from the military and political challenges it posed. Since the highway was unfinished it was impossible for the governor to send army soldiers from Medellín; instead he had to rely on troop deployments from army brigades stationed in other parts of the Caribbean. So rather than the white, mostly Conservative antioqueño soldiers based in Medellín he had to count on Caribbean conscripts who, like the restless residents of Urabá, were mostly black and thus probably closet Liberals.

The National Police posed its own problems. Police overwhelmingly came from historically Conservative parts of the country with more indigenous ancestry, so they clashed with Urabá's residents racially and politically.[46] In 1952 a local police captain complained to the governor that "people here harbor special hate for the Police." The captain advised his officers against openly patrolling the streets, lest it incite Liberal unrest and jeopardize "the ongoing construction of the Highway to the Sea, a project of primordial importance for Antioquia."[47]

His choice of troops limited by this regional, racial, and political minefield, the governor started arming antioqueño-born civilians and moonlighting police officers, creating what amounted to paramilitary brigades. Against the Liberal *chusma*—an epithet for guerrillas meaning "rabble"—Conservatives organized private counterinsurgent forces known as the *contrachusma*. Although the notorious brutality of the contrachusma militias sometimes appalled even their patrons in Bogotá and Medellín, the Conservative leadership rarely let that get in the way of the material support it gave these paramilitaries.

Mutual partisan hatred, of course, fueled much of the violence, but the politics of the Cold War also played a role. Although Liberals could be just as virulently anticommunist as Conservatives, only the former were on the receiving end of accusations of communist subversion. Although Liberal guerrilla groups indeed had communists among their ranks, the red-baiting served at least two broader purposes: it questioned Liberals' nationalist credentials by associating them with international communism while also helping the Conservative government in Bogotá curry favor with Washington. Indeed, Conservatives saw Liberal, guerrilla, communist, and bandit as synonymous terms. In Urabá the discursive conflation of communism and criminality became especially pronounced.

In 1950, for instance, a police captain begged his superiors for reinforcements, saying, "The contraband of weapons of all kinds and calibers continues unabated in the gulf, threatening the tranquility of the entire country. The culprits are smugglers who draw inspiration and support from the communist ideologies led by Russia."[48] With Urabá a growing headache for the military, the Highway to the Sea again reentered the geopolitical calculus. Under the sway of the U.S. National Security Doctrine the military brass became so convinced the road would help resolve the local security situation that it took charge of the construction project. Reflecting on this move, a contemporary report by the army notes, "The construction of the road was a medium for pacifying the region, a way of rescuing the sovereignty of the State."[49] Once the military took charge, the road finally started making headway into the region. Alongside it came the long-sought-after colono homesteaders, carving out plots of land along the length of the road. Many colonos were actually Liberal refugees fleeing Conservative persecution or highway workers (also Liberals) who had decided to stay put. With the Cold War in full swing and La Violencia still raging, Antioquia's Conservative authorities started viewing these colonos as well as the unionized highway workers still toiling on the road with growing suspicion.

Accusing them of communist sympathies, an army report from 1950 recommended that "amid the necessity of pacifying the region, it would be advisable to impose a complete change of the highway workers along with the colonos in the region."[50] The governor began receiving blacklists of highway workers with short accusative descriptions next to their names: "unionist and communist."[51] As colonos and workers continued arriving in droves, local officials described an increasingly unruly situation in the region's growing boomtowns.

The mayor of the town of Chigorodó complained that the dramatic influx of people had upended small-town life: "Once peaceful and easy to govern, the population has turned dangerous because of the increased numbers of hard-drinking workers and wanderers."[52] The army, meanwhile, painted an almost Hobbesian portrait: "The region has been totally abandoned in terms of both services . . . and authorities in general. . . . The authorities, from every point of view, are totally deficient and for these reasons, little by little, violence has taken hold of the region, becoming the supreme and absolute law of the land."[53]

By this point the Highway to the Sea, although still under construction, had become a series of long, passable if not altogether connected lengths of road. Once considered the salvation of Antioquia, the highway turned into a criminal thoroughfare. Alarmed authorities telegrammed the governor warning him that the highway had become a corridor where "bandits . . . harass workers and private citizens, interrupt transportation, rob settlers, and maintain a climate of terror."[54] In an effort to crack down on the insecurity, the police controlled traffic on the road by issuing official transit permits (salvoconductos): anyone found traveling without one was arrested. The situation became so unstable that the governor gave up completely and handed over control to the military by declaring a state of emergency. Abandoned by their governor and still distrustful of the army, local Conservatives redoubled their paramilitary contrachusma forces and quickly turned Urabá into one of the bloodiest regions of the country.

The Leaf Storm

In her book on La Violencia in Antioquia Mary Roldán traces a subtle yet pivotal shift in the conflict during these years: by the end of 1952 economic interests, both licit and illicit, had overshadowed partisan divisions in determining the course of the violence.[55] Resource extraction and capital accumulation were now more in lockstep with the violence than the tit for tat political strife. A government forest inspector, for example, reported that a major logging company had "fomented, given aid to, and sustained the reigning state of insecurity in the area in order to monopolize control of the forest products which abound in the region."[56]

The presence of the counterinsurgent contrachusma forces had an especially strong correlation with violent forms of accumulation, especially via land dispossession and speculation. Roldán describes a pattern that precisely foreshadows the workings of Colombia's contemporary paramilitary groups: "What all the towns experiencing the most dramatic increases in average local property values had in common was the presence or operation of well-organized paramilitary forces supported by and deployed in cattle-rustling, theft, worker elimination, and land usurpation by sectors of the economically powerful."[57] In other words, Urabá's economies of violence around land, labor, and capital were most intense wherever the contrachusma militias were most active.

However, the contrachusma and its local patrons were not the only groups preying on peasant landholders. Taking advantage of the surfeit of hired guns, land speculators and regional elites from across the political spectrum began forcing campesinos off their farms. This emergent class of *latifundistas* had the political connections to formalize and legalize their ill-gotten lands. The dispossessed were the informal settlers who over the decades—and in much greater numbers as the highway neared completion—had painstakingly carved their family farms out of the forest. Having few alternatives, many of the landless campesinos became sharecroppers and laborers on the new estates of the local *patrones* (bosses). In her reconstruction of these dynamics, the historian Catherine LeGrande concludes, "This basic conflict of interests between self-provisioning settler families and elite investors intent on controlling the settlers' land and labor was intrinsic to the Colombian frontier experience."[58]

Indeed, for most locals the frontier was a lived experience shot through with multidimensional forms of violence, whether political, economic, or cultural, but it would all reach a whole new order of magnitude in the decades to come. The opening of the Highway to the Sea in 1954—just as La Violencia was winding down—paved the way for the arrival of the United Fruit Company, which would unleash a new wave of dispossession and exploitation. Urabá was about to become a real-life version of Gabriel García Márquez's fictional boomtown of Macondo. Medellín's elites had at one point dreamed of turning Urabá into a massive cotton belt capable of feeding the city's textile industry. Cotton never took off, but the United Fruit Company stepped in at just the right moment. The company had been shopping around for a site to build a new banana enclave. Disease and hurricanes had decimated its plantations in Central America, and its only enclave in Colombia, near García Márquez's hometown, had been restless ever since the massacre of striking banana workers in 1928, an event he immortalized in the climax of *One Hundred Years of Solitude*. After an exploratory visit to the region in 1959 company executives decided Urabá would make an ideal investment.

Absolving itself of the messy entanglements that came with land and labor, United Fruit introduced a then-innovative subcontracting system. The company built the enclave's infrastructure, but the actual plantations were owned and operated by Colombian investors, most of them from Medellín, whom the company enticed with generous financial incentives and technical assistance. In exchange, the company reserved for itself sole purchasing rights on the bananas of its so-called associate producers. The highway again helped turn Urabá into a reservoir for Medellín's spillover of riches. United Fruit's incentives were enough to again tip the seesaw of uneven development back toward Urabá. Overaccumulated capital from Medellín came pouring back into the region in the form of a massive land grab by its soon-to-be absentee landowners. This time the spatial fix materialized into the wholesale transformation of the region, turning it into an endless sea of banana plantations.

International events also played a role in steering the changes afoot in Urabá, not only the global banana industry's struggling operations in Central America but also the Cuban Revolution and the broader politics of the Cold War. In 1963, when United Fruit announced its plans for Urabá, a company executive explained that the new location and its novel subcontracting system would help it avoid the land confiscations it had just faced in revolutionary Cuba. "Turning a bunch of people into capitalists is a way of putting the brakes on communism," said the executive.[59] He also noted that the planned enclave would be an ideal complement to the Kennedy administration's new Alliance for Progress.

As a direct response to the Cuban Revolution, the anticommunist Alliance for Progress was part of a broader Cold War ideology of modernization and nation building that held powerful sway over Washington in the 1950s and 1960s. According to the historian Michael Latham, modernization theorists imagined the United States taking its "nation-building spirit to help Latin Americans complete their own drive toward progress."[60] Colombia quickly became Washington's showcase for the alliance, which, among many other things, helped provide grants and cheap credit to Urabá's new banana growers.

The division of labor for the construction of the banana enclave followed a clearly racialized hierarchy. The mostly white and absentee antioqueño landowners relied on their fellow light-skinned paisas to oversee the operations. These plantation bosses generally hired mestizo campesino-migrants from Córdoba for clear-cutting the forests, while black migrants from Chocó and the eastern Caribbean coast dug the canals and ditches. Landowners' dehumanizing name for these Afro-Colombian workers doing the most backbreaking labor was "black shovels."[61]

The banana boom unleashed what a newspaper at the time called "a massive land-grab," making it a perfect match with what Marx termed "primitive accumulation."[62] Using the example of the enclosure of common lands in England, Marx described primitive accumulation as a process in which powerful elites use legal and illegal means to violently strip self-provisioning peasants of their lands, forcing them to survive by selling the only thing they still possess: their labor. Indeed, primitive accumulation in Urabá pushed many dispossessed peasants to join the region's new agroindustrial proletariat as banana plantation workers. Most of these workers, sometimes with entire families in tow, lived onsite on the plantations themselves, crowded into camps. Labor conditions were ghastly. They worked sixteen-hour shifts or longer, sometimes by torchlight, and often without weekends or holidays off; health or social security benefits were nonexistent. Workers reserved special ire for the abusive plantation bosses, known as *administradores*, who engaged in sporadic arbitrary firings just to keep the labor force in line. Workers' measly wages sometimes took the form of coupons (*vales*), which they could exchange only for basic necessities at overpriced company stores.[63]

In just six years, from 1960 to 1966, land values in Urabá exploded by a factor of ten, which priced most people out of the market.[64] Although the national government's land management agency promised it would distribute unclaimed lands (*baldíos*) to poor peasants, the only group getting any significant amounts of those lands were the private banana companies posing (on paper) as poor campesinos.[65] During a visit to the town of Apartadó in 1967 amid the early stages of the boom, a gringo geographer named James Parsons described its Macondo-like transformation: "It is a vast swollen slum of muddy streets and rough, palm-thatched houses without running water, or latrines. But Apartadó has three banks, a bull-ring, a radio station ('Voz de Uraba'), a newspaper (*Vanguardia de Urabá*), a modern 'subdivision,' and dozens of noisy cantinas (taverns)."[66]

Outside the ramshackle towns the landscape was morphing into a geometric patchwork of properties and crop lines stretching to the horizon in every direction. As in Macondo, the real forces at work in Urabá were not the supernatural powers of magical realism, but the all-too-earthly forces of capitalism: "There was not much time to think about it, however, because the suspicious inhabitants of Macondo barely began to wonder what the devil was going on when the town had already become transformed."[67] The frontier had gained definitive, identifiable form.

From the Panama debacle to the Highway to the Sea, from La Violencia to the United Fruit Company, Urabá took shape as a frontier zone through both the power and the limits of Medellín's neocolonial project for the region. Amid the fits and starts of urban elites' attempts to impose their cultural, political, and economic dominion over Urabá, the frontier effect—expressed through discourses about the region's barbarism and abandonment—conjured all kinds of state projects. Contingent forces operating at wider scales, such as nationwide political violence and Cold War geopolitics, also conspired in the making of this space. Meanwhile, for Urabá's subaltern communities, it was internal colonialism's racialized economies of violence that defined the frontier as a lived experience.

A key point of this chapter is that frontiers, as social spaces, are not so much opened as they are made; or, to use Lefebvre's terminology, they are *produced*. According to Lefebvre, the production of space is always a three-part combination of mutually transformative physical, ideological, and social processes.[68] In the case of Urabá, for instance, the physical transformations sparked by the Highway to the Sea and the banana industry, as forms of uneven development, were inextricably tied to the racist ideologies of paisa regionalism and related spatial imaginaries of Urabá as a barbarous, savage land. In the process, these material and ideological dimensions of spatiality shaped and were shaped by the social struggles and lived experiences of the region's economies of violence and the brutalities of war.

The frontier—again, put into the terms of Lefebvre's conceptual triads—was "at once conceived, perceived, and directly lived."[69] Lefebvre's three-part understanding of space has oriented my attention here to the material, discursive, and quotidian dimensions of the production of Urabá as a frontier zone. Even the failed early schemes like the aborted railroad, the dashed colonization effort, and the never-built Ciudad Reyes, played a role in the production of this space. They laid important material and ideological groundwork for what came later.

No other part of this story illustrates the social production of the frontier as clearly as the Highway to the Sea. The decades-long construction of the road, which threads its way through every episode in this chapter, was achieved not only with bulldozers and asphalt but also through antioqueños' collective imagination and their aspirations of extending their hegemony (a term they used) over the region. As an integral part of internal colonialism, the road was just as much the expression of paisas' cultural politics as it was the outcome of the spatial fix induced by Medellín's cyclical crises of overaccumulation. The highway was also a product of the frontier effect: elites in Medellín and military leaders both viewed it as an infrastructure of integration and state building. Besides describing it as an instrument of political order, one military strategist said the road would be a way of showing "these faraway and completely isolated settlements that Antioquia has not forgotten them."[70] The road was seen as the trunk from which every other strategic objective would naturally sprout. Above all, it was supposed to finally subject the region to the discipline of capitalism and state power.

The banana enclave is another of the frontier effect's enduring material legacies from this period. Executives of the United Fruit Company described the hyper-capitalist enclave as a bulwark against communist influence. Industrial agriculture was also well aligned with then-dominant theories of export-oriented moderniza-tion and with the state-building goals of the Alliance for Progress. For urban elites in Medellín, the banana enclave was the culmination of decades-long efforts to turn Antioquia's repossession of Urabá into a meaningful and profitable reality.

Today, when one flies into the region the Highway to the Sea and the banana enclave are the most prominent physical features of the landscape visible from the air. Even from flying-altitude the vast expanse of verdant banana plantations stretches to the horizon. The only thing interrupting the geometrical grid of banana trees, which from the air look like tiny green asterisks, is the two-lane Highway to the Sea. From high above it is hard to imagine how this rail-thin strip of asphalt aroused such passions and absorbed so much capital over so many decades. At intermittent points along the road one can see the large splotches of orange-brick and gray tin roofs that constitute the architecture of urban settle-ment in the region. The municipal seat of Apartadó, by far the region's largest city, with 150,000 residents, was almost entirely built by banana workers. The handful of other major urban agglomerations along the highway were also estab-lished as (and largely remain) do-it-yourself operations. This process of urban-ization, too, has been part of the production of Urabá as a frontier.

For the workers in these towns and the campesinos in the surrounding coun-tryside violence has been a defining aspect of the frontier experience. This is not to reductively claim that violence has been the only feature of everyday life in Urabá or even the most salient one, but it is to say that violence has, in one way or another, left almost nothing and no one untouched. The banana boom in particular turned the region's already brutal clashes over land and labor into even more violent affairs. As communist rebel groups began sending their envoys into the region in the late 1960s, Urabá's subaltern sectors had no shortage of griev-ances. In fact, the region's history as a guerrilla stronghold during La Violencia, along with the land grabbing and exploitation unleashed by the United Fruit Company, meant that the Communist Party was already thriving in Urabá by the time its armed vanguards arrived on the scene.

TURF WARS IN COLOMBIA'S RED CORNER

Unforeseen catastrophes are never the consequence or the effect, if you prefer, of a single motive, of a cause singular; but are rather like a whirlpool, a cyclonic point of depression . . . towards which a whole multitude of converging causes have contributed.

—Carlo Emilio Gadda, *That Awful Mess on the Via Merulana* (1957)

From the 1970s to the 1990s the whirlwind unleashed by the United Fruit Company converged with the cyclonic forces of insurgency and counterinsurgency. Making things worse, the cocaine boom in the 1980s exacerbated the escalating spiral of political violence. The press started calling Urabá the "red corner" of Colombia, a reference to both the scale of the bloodshed and the unparalleled power of the communist insurgencies. "Urabá, Drowning in Blood" blared a front-page headline of the country's leading newspaper.[1] An article in a newspaper in Medellín decried the "barbarism" that had seized this "faraway land," concluding, "The violence affecting Urabá has exposed something fundamental: the deep vacuum of the State and the total absence of governmental authority in the region."[2]

Urabá's residents made the same diagnosis. The problem, according to a local priest, was "the absence of the state in the area and its abandonment by national and departmental entities."[3] The political violence wracking Urabá had further clinched its position in the minds of locals and outsiders alike as a lawless, stateless frontier zone. While critical of these discourses of statelessness, I show here how they had a powerful effect on local political struggles. The frontier effect enabled the proliferation of competing state projects, turning the region into an even more fractious social space, a jagged mosaic of rival territorialities. But the violent clashes between insurgency and counterinsurgency that made Urabá into the red corner of Colombia were not caused by the absence of the state; they were conflicts over the form and content of statehood itself. None of these struggles played out in the absence of governmental structures and practices.

Even the communist guerrilla movements operated and in some ways consolidated the state as they vied for territorial hegemony in the region. The origins of Colombia's communist-inspired guerrilla groups can be traced back to the political repercussions of La Violencia, which formally ended in 1957 through a power-sharing deal between Liberals and Conservatives. Known as the National Front, the agreement stipulated that the two parties would systematically alternate in the presidency and divide all public offices and bureaucratic posts equally. The Constitution at the time did not subject governors and mayors to popular election. Instead, the president appointed departmental governors, who in turn appointed municipal mayors in their department. The implementation of the accord was thus relatively simple. For elites, the institutionalization of the two-party duopoly had the added advantage of systematically excluding the Partido Comunista de Colombia (PCC) from any meaningful political participation.

The National Front did, however, make one notable reform. It introduced a new feature in the country's institutional–political landscape: Juntas de Acción Comunal (Juntas of Community Action). To this day the *juntas* are a ubiquitous institution of political life in Colombia, especially among rural communities and poor urban areas. Two left-wing intellectuals drafted the decree that introduced the juntas: Orlando Fals Borda, a revered public intellectual who is remembered as the father of Colombian sociology; and Camilo Torres, a radical priest and, years later, guerrilla-turned-martyr of liberation theology.

The two men hoped the juntas would help address some of the root causes of La Violencia by bolstering the social cohesion, political participation, and autonomy of local communities. They envisioned the juntas as an institutional structure for local self-management (*autogestión*) that would also give poor communities a stronger collective voice before government entities. In many ways the juntas were supposed to be the grassroots building blocks of postconflict state formation, but they mainly served the political machinery of the reigning parties as clientelist vote banks. At the same time, however, they were (and still are) a fixture of communal governance throughout the country.

The National Front and its tepid reforms did little for the political prospects of the most radical factions of the Liberal Party. In fact, alongside members of the PCC, left-wing Liberals continued to face violent persecution. Refusing to relinquish their weapons amid the repression, these leftist hardliners banded together and formed a handful of autonomous peasant communities in central Colombia, where they organized armed self-defense groups for their protection. Elites from both of the traditional parties called for the violent elimination of these communist enclaves, which Cold War fearmongers labeled breakaway *repúblicas independientes*.

FIGURE 6.   Manuel Marulanda, one of the founding members of the FARC, with his rebel entourage during peace talks with the government in 2001.

(Credit: Reuters Pictures/José Gómez)

In 1964, with the help of U.S. military advisers, the government carpet-bombed these campesino communities. The surviving ragtag group of peasant leaders became the founding members of what they named the Fuerzas Armadas Revolucionarias de Colombia (FARC). The Cuban-inspired Ejército de Liberación Nacional (ELN), more closely associated with urban intellectuals and liberation theology, followed soon after. The other rebel group that formed at this time was the Ejército Popular de Liberación (EPL), which initially followed a Maoist line. Although more guerrilla organizations emerged in subsequent years, these three would remain the country's largest—and only the EPL and the FARC ever gained a major presence in Urabá.[4]

"Zone Breaking" the Banana Enclave

Several circumstances made Urabá perfect terrain for the insurgencies. To begin with, the rapaciousness of the landowners and the subhuman conditions of the banana plantations meant the region had an exploited rural proletariat and an impoverished peasantry. Its residents were, to say the least, receptive to the guerrillas' revolutionary message. For related reasons the region already counted on a strong presence of the PCC. Urabá also had a negligible army presence, well-established smuggling routes, and mountainous jungle ideal for guerrilla warfare. Despite all these factors working in its favor, however, the business of clandestine armed struggle was slow-going, laborious work.

Colombia's combatant groups have a name for the methodical work involved in building up their presence in a new area: *rompiendo zona* (zone breaking). The mechanics of zone breaking were explained to me by Elda Mosquera, a former FARC commander better known as Karina. Raised in Urabá, she served in the FARC for almost thirty years, gaining a reputation as a fearsome military leader. She surrendered in 2008 and was still being detained at an army base in Urabá when I interviewed her in 2013.[5] Karina explained that zone breaking was about securing strategic corridors. She described the corridors as the logistical lifelines of any armed group because they ensure the safe passage of troops, contraband, and basic supplies. Zone breaking, she added, has a double meaning: on the one hand, it refers to physically cutting paths in the jungle—"rompíamos trocha" (we broke trails), said Karina—but it also refers to breaking new ground socially.

"We could spend one or two weeks breaking those trails," she said, referring to the physicality of the process. "But the other part of zone breaking was the work with the civilian population. It was about winning over the people." At a minimum their work sought to, as she put it, "make sure they wouldn't rat us out." But under ideal circumstances the "organizing commissions" she deployed would succeed in cultivating genuine political–ideological support, a process Karina described with a metaphor from her peasant upbringing: "Es como abonar el territorio" (it's like fertilizing the territory).

Put into Lefebvre's theoretical framework, a combatant group's strategic corridors and territories are not just physical spaces but eminently social spaces; they must be actively produced and maintained. Colombia's irregular armed groups create and sustain their territorial hegemony by, in their words, cultivating "una base social"—that is, building a degree of civilian support or collaboration. They seek out this civilian cooperation through the painstaking labor of what they describe as their "political (or social) work."

For armed groups, a strong social base and the resources, intelligence, and recruits that tend to come with it make for strong territorial control; a weak social base means little material support, loose lips, few recruits, and a territory likely to be lost. As particular kinds of social spaces, territories arise when a political authority of some kind stakes out or lays claim to a specific geographic area. The political authority in question, however, does not necessarily have to be what we commonsensically call a state.[6] Territory is a political technology, both the result of and an instrument for the spatialization of power.[7] But since territories are fundamentally dependent on civilian cooperation, they can never be held by force alone and are always fluid mixtures of coercion and consent. The strategic social–spatial relations that constitute a territory must be maintained, therefore, through the workings of hegemony.

In Urabá the FARC was the first rebel group to make meaningful headway in building their territorial hegemony. The FARC first gained traction in the late 1960s by sponsoring peasant land colonizations beyond the property frontier on both sides of the Highway to the Sea. By leading the settlement of these unclaimed lands the FARC effectively terraformed its first territories in the region. After securing a foothold among these campesino homesteaders the rebels increasingly turned to organized labor.

The FARC, as the armed wing of the PCC, counted on the organizing prowess of the party. The PCC gained converts to the rebel cause by helping the nascent banana workers' union, Sintrabanano, which became an organic extension of the party. While the labor organizing helped build up the FARC's political clout, it also elicited a violent backlash from landowners, who responded with firings, blacklists, and, aided by the government security forces, violent repression. The banana union barely survived the 1960s. But in the following decade, through an expansion of its political work, the FARC began gaining momentum.

A close observer of those early efforts describes the FARC's new repertoire of tactics: "They put a lot of importance on supporting cooperatives and community self-management [*autogestión*]. In fact, they had been doing a lot of political and electoral work through the municipal councils—institutional work—around very specific grievances. I remember that in 1978 there was a general strike over the lack of public services and they used those types of grievances to work with the people."[8] In other words, the FARC's growing influence was the result of political work that targeted multiple political fronts all at once: campesino cooperatives, community organizing, municipal offices and elections, and mass protests. The most pivotal aspect of the FARC's growing territorial hegemony turned out to be the quasi-governmental Juntas de Acción Comunal that had been introduced after La Violencia. The FARC coopted these organizations of community governance enthusiastically.

Now, as then, legislation allows any rural or urban community to create a junta where one does not exist. A junta must undergo an approval process with their respective departmental government, and their leaders are democratically elected, but they are legally defined as nonstate "civil society" organizations. Communities mainly use the juntas as vehicles for resolving internal disputes, organizing local improvement projects, and maintaining basic infrastructure. As

Colombia's most subsidiary institutions of local governance, the juntas are especially active in underserved areas like urban slums and impoverished rural areas. For the FARC, the juntas were a ready-made institutional structure for organizing and governing local communities. While the FARC was finally making headway by means of its multipronged political work, its comrades in the Maoist-inspired EPL were close to total annihilation. Of all the guerrilla organizations that sprang up in Colombia after the Cuban Revolution the EPL was the most doctrinaire. As a Maoist offshoot of the pro-Soviet PCC, the EPL sought out some of the country's most remote and abandoned rural hinterlands. Indeed, the absence of the state loomed large in the EPL's political imaginary. By the late 1970s the military had decimated the group. Its last remaining battalion was holed up in the steep jungle headwaters of the San Jorge and Sinú Rivers in western Córdoba, just over the border from Antioquia's slice of Urabá. According to Mario Agudelo, a former commander of the EPL, the group never quite got its footing in Córdoba.

I first met Mario in 2012 at a leafy outdoor café in downtown Medellín next to the courthouse plaza where, several years earlier, El Alemán's supporters had cheered him on at the start of his trial.[9] Having previously spoken to Mario only by phone, I remember being surprised when the ex-rebel commander I had heard so much about turned out to be a short, fifty-something man in glasses, khakis, and a short-sleeved oxford shirt. Appropriately, however, his appearance reflected the distance he had traveled since his days of toting rifles *en el monte,* in the bush, as guerrillas say.

Recalling the EPL's early days in the 1960s and 1970s, Mario described how the government's military offensive had reduced them to a few dozen malnourished diehards. Regrouping, they focused all their efforts on an area of the country they affectionately called *el noro*—for *el noroccidente,* the northwest. Reciting their Maoist recipe for revolution, Mario told me that, from their base in el noro they had hoped to build revolutionary momentum among Córdoba's rural masses, creating liberated zones until they managed to surround the cities in their final march to victory. He chuckled over almost every word of their heady revolutionary vocabulary. "It wasn't just schematic," he admitted. "It was a total caricature, and we believed it for many years."[10]

Mario reflected critically on those early experiences. Most cartoonish of all, in his eyes, were what they called Juntas Patrióticas. The EPL imagined the Juntas Patrióticas, he said, as organs of popular power and embryos of the socialist state. "But they were completely quixotic. Sure, we were 'the state,' but the state of what? Of maybe five families. You're not building up the revolutionary masses when you have to trudge almost four hours from one campesino's house to the next." Part of the problem was the EPL's abstentionist political culture. While the FARC worked by coopting preestablished state institutions like the Juntas de

Acción Comunal or municipal offices, he went on, the EPL avoided any dealings with the tainted institutions of the bourgeois state. Instead, the rebel group tried creating its own parallel structures like the Juntas Patrióticas.

As the first president of a Junta Patriótica the EPL chose Julio Guerra, a veteran of La Violencia who had led a famously disciplined and radicalized group of Liberal guerrillas. The local concentration of former Liberal guerrillas—a handful of whom joined the EPL—in el noro was one of the reasons they had chosen it as the staging ground for their protracted people's war. The concentration of landownership caused by La Violencia also meant that this part of Córdoba had a strong tradition of radical agrarian struggle. In Mario's view, the importance of Guerra and his fellow veterans was not so much their military experience, though that was welcomed. Their primary value for the EPL was the rapport and prestige they enjoyed with Córdoba's local peasantry. With these old-timers in its ranks, the EPL could essentially revive the territorial hegemony—that is, *la base social*—that had sustained its predecessors during La Violencia. At a time when the EPL was in desperate need of momentum, the ex-guerrillas and el noro's sedimented territorialities proved to be invaluable lifelines.

By the late 1970s, however, it became painfully obvious that in such a sparsely populated area the EPL's quixotic armed struggle, as Mario called it, was tilting at windmills. With their organization going nowhere, the EPL leadership dropped, or, in its words, corrected, its orthodox Maoism and settled on "a Marxist-Leninist interpretation of the Colombian situation." The neighboring region of Urabá was an obvious and enticing option for rebooting their revolution. After some brief reconnaissance they set their sights on a small rural area of Urabá called Tulapas. Roughly three times the size of Manhattan, Tulapas contains about fourteen *veredas*, Colombia's rural equivalent of neighborhoods or districts. Most of its campesinos arrived decades ago from Córdoba, some as refugees from La Violencia. Tulapas is a mix of forests, croplands, and pastures spread out over low-lying mountainous terrain dotted by tiny villages. It lies along the left bank of the Mulatos River in the middle of the triangle formed by the municipal seats of Necoclí, San Pedro, and Turbo. Although it's strategically located about midway between the Gulf of Urabá and the Antioquia–Córdoba border, the rebels chose it as their beachhead for a more coincidental and, ultimately, fateful reason.

Rival Guerrilla Territories

At the time, Tulapas was solid FARC territory and was controlled by a charismatic commander named Bernardo Gutiérrez. In the years before the EPL's arrival Gutiérrez and his troops had grown disgruntled with the FARC. They criticized the organization for neglecting labor struggles and complained that it had fallen for the "bourgeois trap" of letting the electoral efforts of the party take priority over the armed struggle. The brewing dissent within the FARC being led by Gutiérrez gave the more doctrinaire EPL an opening. "The situation obviously fit us like a glove," Mario said.[11] As Mario and his comrades began trickling into Urabá, Gutiérrez defected and formally joined the EPL, a betrayal the FARC would neither forgive nor forget; it widened the growing rift between the two guerrilla groups.

The number of guerrillas Gutiérrez brought to the EPL was welcome but negligible. Again, as in the case of Guerra and the ex-guerrillas of La Violencia, the social–territorial implications of Gutiérrez's defection far outweighed what the EPL gained militarily. Gutiérrez and his troops had forged close ties with the campesinos of Tulapas, so much so that his faction's defection to the EPL was ratified by a community assembly. Mario recalled that "at the assembly we had a debate, and Bernardo publicly announced that he and his group were leaving the FARC. And the majority of the campesinos voted in support of the decision."[12]

With Tulapas as its new home base, the EPL began elbowing, or zone breaking, its way into the rest of Urabá. The FARC saw this as an unwelcome trespass on its territory. The EPL further inflamed tensions by promoting its own parallel banana workers' union. The FARC saw this too as an intrusion on its turf. As each guerrilla organization backed its own union the banana enclave turned into a competitive patchwork of territorialized worksites. Locals described particular banana plantations as belonging to either the EPL or the FARC, depending on the union affiliation of its workers. In 1985 the rivalry escalated into a bloody proxy war in which the guerrillas engaged in tit-for-tat assassinations against each other's union members.[13] The unions were also hit by a vicious wave of labor repression at the hands of landowners and the military. Surprisingly, however, neither the left-on-left violence nor the government-backed crackdown dampened union activity and militant labor actions; in fact, throughout the 1980s they actually increased.

In addition to gains on the labor front, the two guerrilla groups won sympathizers by supporting other popular struggles, particularly those arising from the breakneck speed of the region's urbanization. When the banana boom took off in the 1960s Urabá had about 50,000 mostly rural residents; by 1980 its population had quintupled to 250,000. Although a majority of the residents lived in the region's growing urban areas, Urabá did not yet have a single electrical hookup, sewage line, or water pipe.

Besides the ceaseless cycles of violence it was the complete lack of infrastructure, adequate housing, and basic public services that locals most often cited in their complaints about the absence of the state. In response, officials from Bogotá repeatedly promised, as in the vague words of the minister of the interior, to "bring a greater presence of the state in Urabá." But the national government dragged its feet until the EPL and the FARC began supporting the local clamor for public services. In the 1980s a slew of protests, including marches, general strikes, and occupations of government buildings, pressured departmental and national agencies into undertaking a widespread program of infrastructure construction across the region.[14]

The guerrillas helped address the regional housing crisis by backing massive *invasiones,* or land occupations, of urban and periurban properties. Land invasions became especially common in the municipal seat of Apartadó, which had become Urabá's largest city. Political parties of all stripes along with their acting public officials lent their support to the land occupations as a way of securing future votes. In one case Apartadó's municipal council was sufficiently supportive of a land occupation by twelve hundred families that the neighborhood to this day is named El Concejo (The Council).

A land occupation led by the PCC in league with the FARC settled fifteen hundred families. Eventually residents gained formal title thanks to an initiative cosponsored by the national government and the UN Development Program (UNDP). Today, Policarpa, as it's known, is one of Apartadó's largest neighborhoods. The land-titling program was part of a larger foreign aid project that, according to one of its reports, was aimed at "the creation of a state presence in critically isolated regions and the promotion of new kinds of relationships between the State and civil society."[15] The UN-backed projects sought to convert the frontier effect's contentious struggles over land into conduits of state formation.

More than once when I asked former guerrillas how they managed such huge land occupations I got the same answer: "It was the easiest thing in the world!"[16] In light of locals' desperate desire to live a more dignified, urban life, the rebels won massive support through the land occupations. Guerrillas thus actively produced their urban territories, in Lefebvre's elaborate sense: ideologically by winning residents' political loyalties, materially through the built environment, and socially through everyday forms of assistance and the lived experience of the occupations themselves. As a result Urabá's working-class cities, like the banana fields surrounding them, turned into rival archipelagos of insurgent territorialities. Whether through the FARC's multipronged political organizing or via both rebel groups' involvement in struggles over land, labor, and urbanization, guerrillas' territorial hegemony was not built in a vacuum of the state or even through the production of breakaway or interstitial spaces. Guerrilla-controlled territories were not antistate or states in waiting. They were intricately intertwined with well-established, formal governmental practices and institutional formations.

The process demonstrates what Lefebvre described as the "hypercomplexity" of space, by which he meant the fluid tendency of social spaces to overlap, fuse, and interpenetrate. Each fragment of space, he wrote, "masks not just one social relationship but a host of them that analysis can potentially disclose."[17]

In the case of Policarpa, for instance, the FARC produced its territorial hegemony alongside and, arguably, through a government-backed program explicitly aimed at state building and fostering stronger ties between "the state and civil society." The territory produced by the FARC via its political work and the land occupation in Policarpa ultimately overlapped, intertwined, and worked in tandem with governmental practices aimed at state building; in fact, rather than supplanting guerrilla hegemony the land-titling project consolidated it.

The quasi-governmental Juntas de Acción Comunal are another case in point. The FARC may have been pulling some strings behind the scenes, but the juntas nevertheless governed day-to-day affairs based on their state-sanctioned legal mandate. And they still served as an institutional articulation between a municipal government and local constituents. The FARC could certainly be an overbearing presence, but the juntas always asserted at least some degree of autonomy. During elections, for instance, most juntas reverted back to the role of vote banks within the clientelist networks of the traditional parties, which still dominated public offices at every scale.

In short, the state, as an effect and instrument of governmental practices and power relations, operated through many of the same practical and institutional channels as the guerrillas. Far from undermining state power or forming a parallel insurgent state, Colombian guerrillas have, to a surprising degree, worked well within the country's formally recognized ensembles of government.[18] And this was just the beginning of their political forays. When the government opened the door for guerrillas' incorporation into official electoral politics in the 1980s, the rebels became even more entangled in the meshes of state power.

After his election in 1982 President Belisario Betancur, an uncharacteristically progressive Conservative, began peace talks with the country's various guerrilla organizations. As a peace offering he introduced two far-reaching political reforms. Although the talks ultimately failed, the reforms of the *apertura política* (political opening), as he called it, stayed on the books. One reform changed the law so that mayors and governors would be elected to office rather than appointed. The second reform allowed guerrillas to form legally recognized political parties and participate in elections without first laying down their weapons.

In 1985 the FARC created the Unión Patriótica (UP) party; a year later the more institutionally reticent EPL followed suit with its own party, the Frente Popular. In Urabá the lull in fighting during the failed peace negotiations had allowed the guerrillas to consolidate their political work. The banana unions now represented almost the entirety of the sector's workforce. Occupations of both urban and rural land had increased. In just two years, between 1984 and 1986, with the EPL taking a notable lead, Urabá had forty-nine major union actions and thirty-six large-scale land invasions.[19]

The guerrillas' political work had become distinctly specialized: the EPL flexed its muscle mainly via the labor unions and the land occupations, while the FARC's efforts were more concentrated on its new political party, the UP.[20] Urabá became an electoral bastion of the UP, which far outperformed the Frente Popular. The more abstentionist EPL had come late and reluctantly to the electoral game: its aversion to dirtying its hands with the structures of the bourgeois state meant it lacked the dense social–institutional networks the FARC had built up over the years. Through its long-standing political work with the PCC, the peasant organizations, the cooperatives, and the Juntas de Acción Comunal, the FARC was far better positioned to achieve electoral success.

For a brief moment in the late 1980s the EPL and the FARC temporarily set aside their bloody history and forged an alliance between their parties; they even coordinated some joint military operations. Though fleeting, the rapprochement had one lasting result: their two rival banana unions united into a single entity called Sintrainagro. As a combined force, the new union arm-twisted the banana companies into signing an industry-wide collective contract, turning Urabá's banana proletariat into the best-remunerated agricultural workforce in the country.

Gerardo Vega, who worked for the EPL as a labor lawyer in those days, told me these victories, though unprecedented, were minor. "I mean, imagine having to 'enter into negotiations' just to guarantee an eight-hour workday. These were not revolutionary victories," he said. "More than anything, what we did was simply help enforce the laws that already existed." Gerardo, as I noted earlier, insisted that "in Urabá *we* were the ones who built the state! *We* were the ones who brought the labor code. . . . *We* made it respected, and it was thanks to *us* that there's now an Office of Labor Affairs and Social Security in the region."[21] Apparently, on the question of labor relations the guerrillas were decidedly on the side of law and order.

The two political parties, the EPL's Frente Popular and the FARC's UP, sometimes engaged in case-by-case electoral alliances, but on this front the EPL was the junior partner. The UP, by contrast, was a genuine radical-left coalition that included active members of the FARC, the PCC, unionists, community leaders, students, peasant leaders, and others. Reaping the fruits of the FARC's meticulous political groundwork, the UP won dozens of municipal council seats and several mayor's offices in Urabá, including that of the city of Apartadó.

According to Gloria Cuartas, a social worker who served a stint as mayor of Apartadó in 1994, "The life of the UP was critical in opening up an alternative *production of space* in the region."[22] When we met in 2013 Gloria was getting her master's degree in geography, so her use of Lefebvre's notion of the production of space was deliberate. When I asked her to explain, she responded, "What I mean is that the UP created and left behind a whole infrastructure that fortified popular organizations through cooperatives, clinics, schools, and Juntas de Acción Comunal." By wielding the power and the coffers of local government the UP used municipal administrations to formalize and institutionalize much of the political work started by the FARC.

After it won a critical mass of local offices the UP began coordinating its efforts across the region by creating an alliance of municipal governments called the Urabá Association of Municipalities (MADU). The UP's local mayors and municipal councilors used the MADU as a vehicle for pooling resources and coordinating local development projects across the region. Gloria described the alliance by referring to the feminist geographer Doreen Massey's concept of "power geometries," which describes how space and scale are integral to the workings of power. According to Gloria, "The MADU helped the UP build its geometries of power" by connecting its political work across communal, municipal, and global scales. It was all part of the FARC's doctrine calling for "the combination of all forms of struggle," meaning the fusion of armed insurrection with electoral politics and community organizing.

The combination of all forms of struggle proved so successful that between 1984 and 1988, as the UP surged in the polls, the FARC's combatant force doubled in size. Over the same period the army reported a fivefold increase in skirmishes and battles with the rebels.[23] The FARC bankrolled its military expansion through a major new stream of revenue: it had started protecting and taxing the first few stages of the cocaine commodity chain—that is, coca leaf cultivation and processing.[24] In short, by the end of the decade the FARC was deep in the throes of a nationwide politico-military offensive.

As a key site of the FARC's power Urabá became ground zero for the explosive blowback that ended in the UP's total annihilation. The incipient paramilitary movement in league with government security forces mounted a vicious dirty war against the UP. Nationwide, over the course of the party's ten-year life span the dirty war killed around five thousand members of the UP, including the assassination of eleven mayors, seventy municipal councilors, twenty-one members of Congress, and two presidential candidates.[25] Among those leading the slaughter was a young antioqueño landowner and drug trafficker named Fidel Castaño.

The Paramilitary Conjuncture

Fidel Castaño's name began making news in early 1988, when gunmen under his command killed more than eighty defenseless civilians in a spate of four back-to-back massacres in Urabá. Terrified locals dubbed Castaño's group *los mochacabezas* (the decapitators), a reference to the gruesome way they dismembered their victims' bodies. Castaño, or Rambo as his men called him, had launched the opening salvos of what would become a broad-based counterinsurgency that eventually spread nationwide. It coalesced with particular force in Urabá, but it grew out of a much broader conjuncture of events, including the cocaine boom, neoliberal restructuring, and the intensification of U.S. military intervention in the country.

In the 1980s Medellín's economy was again riding high: this time, on cocaine profits. Pablo Escobar and his partners in the Medellín Cartel had started investing and laundering their drug profits through rural real estate and agribusinesses. Urabá turned into a major site of these financial operations. In some parts of the region drug traffickers, or narcos, snatched up as much as two-thirds of all arable lands—yet another of Colombia's many agrarian counterreforms.[26] Following the well-worn path of antioqueño investment, the cocaine boom again sent capital flooding from town to country, reinforcing historical patterns of uneven development between Medellín and Urabá and unleashing a narco land rush in the region.

Landed elites responded uneasily to this newly ascendant class of narco estate owners, who were grudgingly dubbed the *clase emergente* by their blue-blooded counterparts. But agrarian crises in the late 1980s and early 1990s gave the clase emergente a fortuitous entrée into agrarian society.[27] Under pressure from the World Bank and the International Monetary Fund (IMF) Colombia had started a process of neoliberal restructuring that began with the slashing of agricultural supports, a move that exposed its previously cushioned producers. In 1985 the country's tariff barriers averaged 83 percent, giving it the highest tariff rates in Latin America, but by 1992 they had plummeted to less than 7 percent, the second-lowest in the region.[28]

The economist José Antonio Ocampo notes that the reforms caused "the massive redistribution of income between the city and countryside. The biggest winners were high-income sectors in urban areas, while the biggest losers were high-income sectors in rural areas."[29] Urabá's high-income agrarian sectors, namely, cattle ranchers and banana growers, also faced diminishing returns from the liberalization of foreign exchange controls (another neoliberal stricture) alongside plummeting commodity prices. Bananas lost a third of their value by 1994, marking a twenty-five-year low, and beef prices also crashed, losing nearly half their value from 1993 to 1995.

In Urabá the economic crisis arrived on the heels of guerillas' politico-military offensive, so rebel violence, mass labor strikes, and peasant land occupations were still fresh in the minds of local agrarian elites. From their perspective the state not only had failed to protect them from the insurgencies and working-class militancy but also exposed them now to the vagaries of the global economy. "We felt totally abandoned by the state," said one landowner.[30] The arrival of the land-hungry narcos was yet another indication that their world had come unglued.

One old-guard landowner from the ranchlands of Córdoba, which would soon become the epicenter of the paramilitary movement, recalled that the narcos arrived with "unlimited ambition."[31] The situation echoed the shifts identified by E. P. Thompson in early eighteenth-century England: "We appear to glimpse a declining gentry and yeoman class confronted by incomers with greater command of money and influence, and with a ruthlessness in the use of both."[32]

Castaño was especially ruthless. The way he wrested a twenty-one-hundred-hectare estate called Las Tangas from a well-established ranching family in Córdoba attests to how the initial encounters between landowners and narcos were, in some cases, quite violent. In 1983 Castaño and the owner of Las Tangas cut a deal in which Castaño agreed to pay for the ranch in two installments. He made the first payment, but then, instead of handing over the rest of the money, he kidnapped the rancher's son. In exchange for the boy's life he collected a ransom that more than covered what he had spent on his one and only payment for the land. Obviously, not all or even a majority of the dealings between landowners and narcos were this violent, but neither was the class alliance that ultimately emerged between them completely seamless.

Class alliances are always rocky affairs, but a common enemy can quickly smooth them out. Indeed, the split between landowners and narcos might have continued apace had it not been for the guerrillas. The rebels started subjecting the narcos, as the newly minted agrarian elite, to the kind of extortive kidnappings they had once reserved for the established landowners. The agrarian economy's decline coupled with guerrilla aggression made natural allies of the clase emergente and the reticent rural oligarchy. In Raymond Williams's words, the "overreachers" and the "wellborn" in Colombia made common cause.[33]

Together, the narcos and landowners, with crucial assistance from the military, began organizing private militias to fend off the rebel offensive. Paramilitaries, or *paras* as they are commonly known in Colombia, began cropping up all over the country. Politicians and business owners also played a role in the creation of the paras, but it was the narco–landowner alliance that most defined paramilitary groups' dual role as the private armies of drug traffickers and government-backed counterinsurgent death squads. In Urabá they had an additional particularity: much more than in other parts of the country, the paras in Urabá had a notable proportion of ex-guerrillas in their ranks, especially from the EPL.

The contradictory conversion from left-wing guerrillas to right-wing paramilitaries was the result of the final, bloodiest chapter of the EPL–FARC rivalry.

In 1991 the EPL accepted a government peace deal and demobilized, reinventing itself as a political party with the same initials.[34] A holdout faction of dissidents, however, refused the deal and returned to el monte, where they teamed up with the FARC. Together, the two groups began slaughtering the EPL's demobilized ex-guerrillas, labeling them traitors to the revolution. Castaño seized the opportunity and, citing their mutual hatred of the FARC, wooed many of the besieged demobilized fighters to join his growing paramilitary war machine.[35]

By now, Castaño had amassed even more lands throughout Córdoba and turned Las Tangas into the military headquarters of his growing personal fiefdom. In the early 1990s he dabbled in trying to build up a grassroots base of support by parceling out eighteen thousand hectares of land to local campesino families, including some demobilized EPL rebels. He billed this venture an agrarian reform and assigned the management of the land-distribution program to his family's newly created NGO, the Foundation for Peace in Córdoba, known as Funpazcor for short. (A few years later Funpazcor took back the lands by displacing the campesinos it had helped settle.)

FIGURE 7.   Sor Teresa Gómez, a major player in the paramilitary movement, at the moment of her arrest in 2013 for the murder and displacement of campesino farmers.

(Credit: Publicaciones Semana SA/Guillermo Torres)

Castaño appointed a close family friend, Sor Teresa Gómez, as the director of Funpazcor. Doña Tere, as most people knew her, was named after Mother Teresa of Calcutta ("Sor" being the title for nuns in Spanish). Despite her saintly name she became one of the paramilitary movement's shadiest operatives. As the director of Funpazcor, which doubled as a money-laundering front, Doña Tere was also the unofficial treasurer of Castaño's narco-paramilitary empire. At one point the NGO was raking in and laundering an estimated US$5 million a month in cocaine proceeds alone.[36] With Doña Tere at the helm, Funpazcor also handled the paperwork and legal machinations for laundering the family's ill-gotten landholdings—often by leaving the properties in the NGO's name. Funpazcor's other role was bankrolling philanthropic projects like schools and clinics as a way of shoring up the paras' territorial control over strategic areas.

By the time the paramilitary movement entered the fray of the conflict, Colombia's passage of a new Constitution in 1991 had just transformed the country's political–institutional landscape. Reformers hoped a new Constitution would help pull Colombia out of the profound political crisis it faced in the run-up to the 1990 presidential elections. Besides the guerrillas' ongoing nationwide political–military offensive and the paramilitaries' rampaging from massacre to massacre, Escobar had launched an all-out war against the Colombian government's capitulation to U.S. pressure for his capture and extradition. He lashed out by blowing a passenger plane out of the sky, detonating huge car bombs in urban areas, murdering his high-profile critics, and launching a killing spree against police. The assassination of three presidential candidates running in the 1990 elections, including the clear favorite, sank the country deeper into the abyss.

Colombians overwhelmingly recognized that the situation had spun far out of the government's control and doubted anything could be done about it. The country faced a full-fledged "crisis of authority," which Gramsci defined as "precisely the crisis of hegemony, or general crisis of the State," in which even the total use of force is incapable of guaranteeing the stability or even recognition of its rule.[37] Or, more succinctly, as then-president César Gaviria put it in a recent television interview: "The country was fucked."[38] On the bright side, the prospect of participating in the drafting of a new Constitution was what had finally convinced the EPL and a handful of smaller guerrilla groups to lay down their weapons; the FARC and the ELN, however, remained at large.

Ratified in 1991, the new Constitution introduced far-reaching reforms. One of the most profound was a nationwide territorial restructuring through political, administrative, and fiscal decentralization.[39] The reforms consolidated the political opening that began with the popular election of mayors and complemented it with administrative and fiscal decentralization. The Constitution turned municipalities into the main protagonists of the new territorial order. Administratively, they gained a host of new responsibilities, including the provision of public services, health care, and education. Fiscally, municipalities could now count on mandatory budget transfers from Bogotá giving them the means for carrying out their new duties.

At the time decentralization was the policy darling of the global development community, and it was well aligned with the country's ongoing neoliberal restructuring. But Colombian reformers' primary rationale was that they expected it would help address the underlying political roots of the armed conflict; their goal, as one motto had it, was "decentralize to pacify." One of its proponents claimed "decentralization . . . will one day allow us to say that we have as much territory as we have a State, because until now the expanse of the first has been far superior to the authority of the latter."[40] The territorial restructuring was aimed at extending the state's presence into the furthest reaches of the nation—that is, into its most conflictive frontier zones.

Reformers reasoned that decentralization would give insurgents and other excluded social groups in these areas, especially peasants and ethnic minorities, more immediate and consequential forms of political participation along with a greater stake in the country's political life. It was also supposed to make local governments more responsive and accountable to their constituents. In sum, the overarching goal of decentralization was to make the state a more meaningful presence in people's lives, particularly in the most war-torn parts of the country; it was supposed to finally resolve the absence of the state.

The Paramilitary Backlash

Already disgruntled for the reasons mentioned above, regional elites balked at the reforms. A banana company executive expressed an opinion I heard in almost identical terms from other landowners in the region: "For years the state had totally abandoned us, but now we had been betrayed."[41] In their eyes the new Constitution opened the way for subversion by the guerrillas, allowing them to institutionalize the "combination of all forms of struggle." Landowners saw the reforms as undue concessions to rebel groups that had incessantly victimized them for decades.

Castaño was among those feeling the sting of betrayal. He was one of the eldest brothers of a stereotypical antioqueño family: large, patriarchal, conservative, and religious. Since the family patriarch had died during a botched kidnapping by the FARC, the Castaños were also vehemently anticommunist. Fidel and two of his brothers, Vicente and Carlos, had had stints in the Medellín cartel, which gave them the money and the contacts they needed to raise a private paramilitary army. In 1994, with the help of a retired army officer nicknamed Doble Cero, as in 007, James Bond's license to kill, they formed the paramilitary Autodefensas Campesinas de Córdoba y Urabá (ACCU).[42]

FIGURE 8. Together with his brothers, Carlos Castaño was a founding member and a nationwide leader of the paramilitary cause.

(Credit: AP Photo/File)

FIGURE 9. By the time he became a paramilitary commander Vicente Castaño was one of the country's leading drug traffickers.

(Credit: Publicaciones Semana SA/León Darío Pelaez)

Fidel died under mysterious circumstances just months after creating the ACCU, leaving Vicente and Carlos to take control of the organization.[43] Carlos, the youngest of the three, handled most of the military operations alongside Doble Cero, while Vicente handled logistics and the business side of things. Although the public came to know their paramilitary group by its acronym, the ACCU, insiders referred to it with the more intimate- and regal-sounding name of *la Casa Castaño* (the House of Castaño).

The Casa Castaño immediately popped up on the radar of U.S. intelligence services. A classified report from 1996 described the paras in Urabá as "a law unto themselves."[44] Another noted that growing paramilitary dominion over entire regions, especially Urabá, had led to the establishment of "quasi-independent states" in a process the report likened to the "feudalization of Colombia."[45] From their headquarters in Córdoba the Castaños turned Urabá into a laboratory for perfecting their model of armed colonization, which they later exported by helping establish local paramilitary franchises all over the country.

Colombia's security forces, aided by billions of dollars in U.S. military assistance, played a crucial role in the paras' creation and proliferation. Across the ranks the military encouraged, protected, and aided paramilitary networks. They collaborated so closely with each other that Human Rights Watch described the paras as the army's "Sixth Division."[46] Among themselves they referred to each other as *primos* (cousins). The paras did much of the army's dirty work—the massacres, assassinations, and mass displacements—giving the military brass a degree of plausible deniability.

The paramilitary movement also spread thanks to a 1994 presidential decree that sought to beat back the FARC's offensive by allowing the creation of Cooperatives of Private Security and Vigilance, which were known as the Convivir.[47] The decree essentially deputized civilians by allowing them to organize not-for-profit private security organizations. In a prescient cable the U.S. ambassador in Bogotá wrote Washington with the concern that "there has never been an example in Colombia of a para-statal security group that has not ultimately operated with wanton disregard for human rights or been corrupted by local economic interests."[48] Three years later, as predicted, a follow-up cable reported that the military was using the Convivir for "illegally authorized weapons sales to suspected paramilitaries and narcotraffickers."[49]

The most enthusiastic supporter of these so-called security cooperatives was then-Governor of Antioquia Álvaro Uribe, a rising figure in the most reactionary sector of antioqueño politics. Uribe would later serve two terms as president in the 2000s. His family history closely parallels that of the Castaños: he grew up in a traditional antioqueño family; like the Castaños, the Uribes were heavily invested in Córdoba's cattle lands; and Uribe's father also had died in a failed kidnapping by the FARC. Uribe's critics have long accused him of having collaborated with drug traffickers and paramilitaries, accusations he categorically denies.

FIGURE 10.   Álvaro Uribe was the governor of Antioquia in the mid-1990s and later was twice elected president (2002–10); behind him is Juan Manuel Santos, then-minister of defense and Uribe's successor as president.

(Credit: AP Photo/Fernando Vergara)

As the governor of Antioquia from 1995 to 1997 Uribe approved the permits of at least sixty-seven separate Convivir groups totaling six thousand members, many of whom were simply paramilitaries dressed as civilians.[50] In Urabá the Convivir effectively became a legalized armed wing of the banana industry. The Chiquita banana company (formerly the United Fruit Company), for example, used the Convivir as a way of secretly contracting the security services of the Casa Castaño. Chiquita made a total of US$1.7 million in payments to the Convivir between 1997 and 2004. Claiming extortion, Chiquita said it made the payments out of a "good faith concern for the safety of our employees." But testimonies by paramilitary chiefs suggest otherwise. As one confessed, "We forced the [striking] workers to go back to work on the plantations. Those who disobeyed the order and didn't work knew what would happen to them."[51] A lengthy investigation by the attorney general's office corroborated the accusations, concluding, "This was a criminal relationship. Money and arms and, in exchange, the bloody pacification of Urabá."[52] With the help of the Convivir the paras wiped out the weakened militancy that remained in Urabá's banana union, which was already a shell of its former self.[53]

By 1997 the paras were a fully nationwide phenomenon, so Carlos Castaño called a meeting in Tulapas, which the paras had recently seized. He convinced the country's paramilitary commanders to unite their blocs under a single umbrella organization, which they named the Autodefensas Unidas de Colombia (AUC). The AUC would never be more than a loose federation of paramilitary groups, but Carlos hoped it would help them coordinate their actions. He also suspected the organization could serve as an institutional vehicle for eventual negotiations with the government. When Álvaro Uribe, the former governor of Antioquia and anti-FARC hardliner, successfully ran for president in 2002, the paras openly supported his candidacy. Since they shared such close ideological affinities, he was their best bet for a favorable way out of the conflict.

Uribe took office just as the implementation of the U.S. military aid package known as Plan Colombia was gaining momentum. Plan Colombia ultimately pumped about US$10 billion in mostly military aid into the country. U.S. military assistance gave the Uribe administration everything it needed to turn the tide against the FARC: elite military training programs, a fleet of combat helicopters and other advanced hardware, real-time intelligence, aerial fumigation of coca crops, a stepped-up CIA presence, and several hundred U.S. military personnel and private contractors.

Already the most abusive security force in the Western Hemisphere, the Colombian military drew increasing scrutiny from the international human rights community. Instead of cleaning up its act, however, the military simply outsourced the abuse to its paramilitary proxies. The FARC had reached the zenith of its military strength with eighteen thousand fighters, but it was no match for the combined force of paramilitaries and a U.S.-backed military. During Uribe's two terms as president (2002–10) the Colombian military almost doubled in size and decimated the guerrillas, pushing them deeper into the jungle. With the insurgencies on the run, Plan Colombia in full swing, and an ally in the presidency, the paras had a window of opportunity for exiting the conflict. As a candidate Uribe had sent them clear signals he was willing to negotiate; exploratory talks began shortly after his election.

The result of the negotiations was a controversial law that dictated the terms of the paramilitaries' demobilization.[54] The law set an eight-year maximum jail sentence for top and midlevel paramilitary commanders as long as they confessed to the full extent of their crimes. The rank and file, meanwhile, would begin a process of disarmament, demobilization, and reintegration.[55] The last paramilitary group to demobilize under the deal was the bloc led by El Alemán. When his hearing began he said, "Reconciliation and reparations in this country should be that the state finally arrives to its territories, so that civilians will never again have to take up arms to defend themselves. . . . [F]or this, we give back the monopoly of force."[56]

Wars tend to make geography obvious. They not only make the intimate ties between people and space self-evident, the conduct of warfare—particularly so-called irregular warfare—is also in many ways premised on a conflation of people and space. When Colombian combatant groups talk about territory, they have in mind something similar to Lefebvre's understanding of "social space." For the armed groups a territory is not a lifeless geometric area but a set of social relationships formed between combatants and civilians. They know that a territory is not a preexisting empty patch of land or a hollow container to be filled at will. An armed group's territory can really be said to exist in any meaningful sense only insofar as it is produced and reproduced, materially and ideologically, through everyday relationships between combatants and communities. The fact that territories depend in such fundamental ways on the cooperation of a social base is why civilians so often suffer the brunt of violence.

Torn asunder by the forces of insurgency and counterinsurgency, Urabá became a field of violently clashing territories; not so much because of the absence of the state but because the state was precisely what was at stake. Despite their diametrically opposed political projects, guerrillas and paramilitaries both saw Urabá as a place of statelessness; they were both under the powerful spell of the frontier effect. For the rebels, the absence of the state posed an opportunity, a breach in which a revolutionary project could assert itself; for the paras, state absence was what most needed remedying. In the process, the war reinforced the idea, locally and nationally, of Urabá as a lawless, violent no-man's-land, the red corner of Colombia.

In both popular and scholarly discourse insurgencies are supposedly the antithesis of the state. But, as we have seen, the EPL and the FARC, albeit in different ways, were not anathema to the consolidation of formally established practices and institutions of rule. Whether by working through the Juntas de Acción Comunal or via their support for mass protests demanding public services, the insurgencies were surprisingly conducive to the establishment and routinization of certain institutions and practices typically associated with the state. The role of the FARC in strengthening the juntas could be interpreted even in terms of what the development industry calls local institution building. Both guerrilla groups helped direct Urabá's process of urbanization by helping working-class residents gain access to land, housing, and public services. The rebels' territorial hegemony worked alongside government initiatives that sought to build, as in Policarpa's land-titling program, a state presence by fostering stronger relationships between the state and civil society.

Another way the guerrillas strengthened locals' relationship to the matrices of state power was by consolidating the channels and institutions of collective representation: not only through the juntas but also through their labor unions and political parties. Only when the guerrillas flexed their political muscle through these organizations did government agencies and international aid finally respond to locals' long-standing grievances around land, labor, housing, and public services. Once the FARC's political party, the UP, won mayors' offices and municipal council seats across the region, it leveraged the formidable power geometries of its alliance of municipal governments toward consolidating these gains by pooling resources and coordinating development projects.

All of these frontier state formations—that is, the unruly political assemblages produced at the imagined limits of the state—sprang up out of the social relationships involved in the production of guerrillas' territorial hegemony. Paradoxically, the rebels' territorial imperative made their relationship with official government structures quite direct and even generative: from helping consolidate municipal administrations and the juntas to the consolidation of basic state practices like the delivery of public services and the enforcement of labor law.

In some ways the frontier effect turned the EPL and the FARC into vanguards of state formation. The strongest indicator of the growing power of the insurgencies' state projects was the fierceness of the blowback by the paramilitary movement. It was as soon as the insurgencies began unmooring the region's established regimes of accumulation and rule in the late 1980s that the counterinsurgency led by the paramilitaries erupted in such furious form.

The frontier effect also played a role in drawing Plan Colombia into the conflict. The aid package emerged at a moment between the Cold War and the War on Terror when the U.S. security establishment had started eyeing the failed state as a potential new threat paradigm of the twenty-first century. One U.S. security expert claimed Plan Colombia would target a "Hobbesian trinity" of narco traffickers, guerrillas, and paramilitaries. A senator from Ohio justified his vote for the aid package by warning that "the balkanization of Colombia into politically and socially unstable mini-states is a significant threat. . . . Colombia is shaping up to be the Balkan problem of the Americas."[57] The failed-state paradigm was why Plan Colombia included billions in aid explicitly destined for state-building projects.

The Convivir security cooperatives, which helped lay the groundwork for the military success of Plan Colombia, arose from a similar problematization of statelessness. As governor, Uribe justified the Convivir by citing the "weakness of the state."[58] More recently, the former president has said that as conduits for "citizen collaboration with the security forces" the cooperatives had helped build "citizens' confidence in state institutions."[59] In reality, however, the Convivir perpetuated and operated within a vast, nebulous gray area between the legal and illegal, the state and the nonstate. Indeed, a characteristic feature of the frontier as a lived experience is the way in which, in Walter Benjamin's words, the "state of emergency" is "not the exception but the rule."[60] The permanence of the exception, however, stems not from the frontier existing outside the law but from the way it is a space in which the putative insides and outsides of the legal order are blurred and indecipherable.

Frontiers exemplify what Giorgio Agamben called a "zone of indistinction," a space where "the normative aspect of law can thus be obliterated and contradicted with impunity by a governmental violence that—while ignoring international law externally and producing a permanent state of exception internally—nevertheless still claims to be applying the law."[61] Explaining to me how the Convivir worked, a paramilitary summed up the same idea in much simpler terms: "In Urabá we constantly legalized the illegal."[62]

THE PARAMILITARY WAR OF POSITION

Whether gifted mimics or unwitting apprentices, conservatives glean from the Left and the world it creates nothing less than a recipe for making a new old regime.

—Corey Robin, "You Say You Want a Counterrevolution" (2010)

For a poor village in Córdoba's western cattle lands, the school in Villanueva is impressive. The grounds of the small campus are impeccably well kept. A tidy hedge runs alongside a sturdy wooden fence that lines the entire perimeter of the school's property. It is the kind of enclosure that more commonly surrounds the wealthy estates of the local ranchers for whom high-quality fencing is both a point of pride and a status symbol. At one side of the main entrance is a white, podium-like structure made of concrete with a large cast-iron plaque that reads "The Villanueva School Founded in 1988 by Fidel Castaño."

The school was a pet project of Funpazcor, the paramilitary NGO directed by Sor Teresa Gómez, known as Doña Tere. Funpazcor took charge of the school in the 1990s, coordinating everything from staff and curricula to the free uniforms and supplies doled out to students. Tuition was also free. Doña Tere kept the school's paperwork up to date with the governor's office and successfully petitioned for its incorporation into the national public school system in 1998.

Besides being the Castaños' first major populist gesture, the school was also the birthplace of a broader political initiative, one with nationwide repercussions. In 1998 Carlos Castaño hosted a week-long retreat at the school attended by about 150 paramilitary delegates from across the country. The event was more of a workshop than a meeting. Through a series of panels, lectures, and training exercises Carlos sought to push the paramilitary movement beyond the military aspects of the war and into the realm of politics and community organizing. No one took the retreat's lessons more seriously than Carlos's rising protégé, El Alemán.

El Alemán described the purpose of the event during his trial: "We realized guns were never going to be enough. As a political–military movement, we also had to think about the social and political front."[1] In Gramscian terms, the paras decided that the brutal "war of maneuver" against the insurgencies needed to be complemented with a subtler "war of position" on the politico-ideological front. As Gramsci formulated it, the war of position is about much more than a simple campaign for hearts and minds: it is a struggle for hegemony pressed into the service of state formation.

"In politics," wrote Gramsci, "the 'war of position,' once won, is decisive definitively."[2] As the political counterpart to the paramilitaries' military efforts, their war of position was an effort to reconcile the extralegal violence of primitive accumulation and counterinsurgency with Colombia's liberal-democratic order. The paramilitaries fought their version of the war of position through what they called, borrowing from the guerrillas, their social or political work. In fact, the paras' war of position borrowed more than just words from the rebels; they copied and repurposed the guerrillas' entire political playbook. And ultimately the paras beat the guerrillas at their own game.

The paramilitary war of position was a revanchist political–economic project aimed at decisively and definitively turning the tide against the insurgencies through state building. The paras' efforts to cultivate a social base, control their territories, and "create a state presence," as they described it, were integral and practically indistinguishable parts of the same process. The Castaños' school in Villanueva is a good example of how these practices of the war of position overlapped: the school was a way of winning grassroots support and bolstering their territorial hegemony; simultaneously, it was a deliberate form of state building and explicitly described as such. The school's incorporation into the formal networks of government solidified the paras' popular interpellation as state builders, which was, in turn, a pivotal part of their ability to win grassroots support. Indeed, the incredible power paramilitaries attained in Colombia was in no small part due to the way campesinos hailed the paras and the way they positioned themselves as state makers.

The construction of schools and other populist actions were not simply smoke screens for the paramilitaries' drug-fueled criminal economies, nor were they just the egotistical self-indulgence of a few charismatic commanders, as some scholars and journalists have argued.[3] Or rather they were those things but also much more. The war of position was a genuine state project; it was a deliberate attempt to create a durable new regime of accumulation and rule. And for the most part it succeeded. Paramilitary statecraft, however, was not the mechanical imposition of a preexisting blueprint; the war of position was a contingent, negotiated process that proceeded (had to proceed) through a mix of coercion and consent among rural communities. Most of the scholarship on the Colombian conflict has neglected this aspect of the paramilitary movement.[4] The paras' links to political and economic elites and their litany of atrocities against campesinos have been well established, but scholars have largely overlooked the cooperative relationships forged between paramilitaries and grassroots communities. The production of paramilitary territory followed a distinct arc: the violent seizure of guerrilla-controlled areas slowly transitioned, through the war of position, into a more affirmative and fulsome form of territorial control.

Zone Breaking Tulapas

The paras' takeover of the rebel stronghold of Tulapas is a revealing example of the foundational violence upon which the paras would build their territorial hegemony. When the Castaños' paramilitaries moved into Urabá from Córdoba, Tulapas once again became a flashpoint of the war. In Tulapas, as in so many other parts of the country, the opening salvo of paramilitary zone breaking was a mass slaughter: the massacre of forty-two villagers from the small town of Pueblo Bello in 1990.

Like the EPL decades before them, the Castaños saw Tulapas as a stepping-stone for their wider conquest of Urabá. It not only offered ideal military terrain in terms of topography, resources, and location but also had been the site of the EPL's rebirth and its historical refuge, so its value for the paras was as symbolic as it was strategic. In addition, the EPL had long used Tulapas as a staging ground for its relentless attacks on the wealthy cattle ranchers of Córdoba who formed the Casa Castaño's organic social base. In fact, a cattle-rustling operation by the EPL was what ultimately incited the paramilitaries' bloody march into Urabá.

In December 1989 EPL guerrillas attacked the Castaños' Las Tangas estate and brutally murdered its foreman. On their way back to Tulapas they stole forty-two head of cattle from one of Fidel Castaño's landholdings near Pueblo Bello.[5] Rambo, as his troops called him, quickly retaliated by sending sixty heavily armed men into Pueblo Bello on the night of January 14, 1990. As they strafed the darkness with machine-gun fire, they barricaded the residents inside the town, blocking its main exit points. With a list in hand, the paras began breaking down doors and pulling people from their homes, forcing their soon-to-be victims to lie facedown on the floor of the village's central plaza.

Town plazas throughout the nation would become a main venue of paramilitary butchery. As the first move in seizing guerrilla territories, the spectacle of wholesale massacre in the most public of public spaces became a hallmark of paramilitary terror, marking an unforgettable before and after in people's memories. Like the raising of a new flag, the bloodied plaza dramatically and unmistakably announced regime change. Brutalized bodies lying lifelessly on the plaza floor were a visceral display, physically and symbolically, of how terror and territory in the Colombian conflict worked through an intimate conflation of people and space.

In the case of Pueblo Bello, rather than kill their victims on the spot, as would become their custom, the paras packed them into two trucks and took them back to Fidel's ranch. The victims spent the rest of the night digging their own graves and lining up to be executed. Shortly after sunrise a single shot to the head claimed the final victim, a sixteen-year-old boy. Throughout the ordeal the victims endured violent interrogations and torture (eyes gouged, ears cut, genitals mutilated) until finally being killed, in some cases by Rambo himself.

According to a police report, when the families of the missing victims sought help from the local army base the next day the commanding officer's response was chilling: "Don't come here looking for answers. Or don't you remember that when the cows were stolen you all said nothing? You traded your lives for cattle."[6] Fidel reportedly killed one person for each of the forty-two head of cattle the EPL had stolen (a truck driver killed on the road made the final tally forty-three). The massacre also had clear political motives: most of the victims were members of the EPL's political party.

The paras made no distinction between civilians and combatants in the process of zone breaking. As in Pueblo Bello, they designated entire towns as *pueblos guerrilleros*, so their brutality tended to be both collective and indiscriminate. Alongside the terrifying spectacle of mass murder, the amazing efficiency of rumor in the countryside multiplied its effects. The circulation of terror through what the anthropologist Michael Taussig once described as the "coils of rumor, story, gossip, and chit-chat" was as integral to paramilitary zone breaking as the physical violence itself.[7] In fact, it was a deliberate tactic. In Pueblo Bello, for instance, Fidel gave his troops a hit list identifying purported guerrilla collaborators, but he also instructed his men to choose a few people at random so as to sow doubt and confusion.

After the massacre, villagers reeled in fear, unsure about the ultimate fate of the victims, the true reasons for the attack, the real identity of the perpetrators, or who might be next. Next came a steady progression of selective assassinations. The Casa Castaño was chipping away at the guerrillas' social base. "Pueblo Bello is when the disorder started," a resident of Tulapas remembered. "That's when everything went to hell."[8]

Salvatore Mancuso, a wealthy rancher who became a national paramilitary leader, recalled the takeover of Tulapas during his trial. He said that when full-blown combat operations began there in 1995 the paras and the army worked

FIGURE 11.   Salvatore Mancuso, a wealthy rancher and member of Córdoba's elite circles, became a powerful paramilitary commander.

(Credit: Publicaciones Semana SA/León Darío Pelaez)

jointly as a single military force in routing the guerrillas. "The combat that displaced the guerrillas from those territories lasted like a month and a half," he said. "And from beginning to end, from the moment we planned, executed, and finalized our military operations, during all that time, we were buying up lands in Tulapas."[9] Mancuso said the Castaños chose him as their envoy for "buying up" as much land in the area as he could because he was a respected cattleman at the time whose links to the paras were not yet public.

Mancuso's comments attest to how "from beginning to end" the violent dispossession of campesino communities was a crucial part of paramilitary zone breaking. The displacement of civilians was both a political imperative and a form of violent land speculation: mass dispossession destroyed guerrillas' support networks, and by neutralizing the rebel threat the Castaños ensured that the value of their newly seized lands would soon shoot up. The paras also guaranteed their future profit margins by forcing peasant landholders to sell at rock-bottom prices or by simply never paying the coercively "agreed-upon" price.

The paras forced some four thousand campesinos from Tulapas. After emptying the area of the real-and-imagined social underpinnings of guerrilla territoriality, the paras confidently described the area, using medicalized metaphors, as sanitized or cleansed of subversives. "They said they came here to clean out the guerrillas," observed one displaced peasant, "but it was us, the campesinos, they cleaned out."[10] All told, the Casa Castaño ended up with about twenty-two thousand hectares of land in Tulapas, much of it acquired through shady deals cut by Doña Tere and Funpazcor. Property registries show the majority of the coerced sales took place between 1998 and 2002.

When prosecutors asked Mancuso why this area was so important to the paras he replied, "Why Tulapas? Because Tulapas is far from everything." Tulapas is actually, at least on the map, only about a fifteen-mile beeline from Turbo's municipal seat, whose sixty-three thousand residents make it Urabá's second-largest urban center. However, the frequent rains and the ruggedness of the terrain in Tulapas—the mud, jungle, and mountainous topography—has complicated the construction of roads into the area, so the circuitous route from Turbo (via Necoclí) can take three to five hours by motorcycle. The geographical paradox of being close and yet distant is one of the things that makes Tulapas such an ideal spot for the armed groups.

The violence of paramilitary zone breaking stands in stark contrast with the guerrillas' entry into Tulapas two decades earlier.[11] Whereas the guerrillas engaged in painstaking political work among the local communities, the paras at first simply wiped them out without a shred of concern for civilian support because, initially at least, the paras had no need for civilian cooperation. As government proxy forces, the paras moved their troops, supplies, and contraband with impunity. And since they counted on wealthy backers and a bottomless, cocaine-funded war chest they were never short of resources, and thus material support from the rural masses was irrelevant.

Paramilitaries' concern with building *una base social* came only after the guerrillas had been defeated militarily and their alleged civilian collaborators "cleaned" out and displaced. For the paras, the war of position was an entirely retroactive endeavor aimed at shoring up their territorial hegemony and building a state presence. Only after they had gained almost total control of Urabá did they make the shift. Explaining the transition, a paramilitary soldier said, "We realized we could do more by working in an organized way through the law and what was legal than we could with ten thousand armed men."[12]

Promoters of Social Development

All of Colombia's paramilitary groups adopted aspects of the counterinsurgent war of position, but it gained its fullest expression in Urabá, especially in the territories controlled by Freddy Rendón, aka El Alemán. Freddy was an early convert to the paramilitary cause. After growing up in Medellín, where his family had moved after being displaced from the countryside by the FARC, he made his first visit to Urabá in his early twenties as part of his job as a truck driver. His route took him over the Highway to the Sea, meaning that as he shuttled between Medellín and Urabá he experienced constant harassment from the FARC at its impromptu roadblocks and tolls.

During one of Freddy's stays in Urabá a friend introduced him to Carlos Castaño. As they talked, Carlos laid out a long, elaborate impromptu manifesto. "He said it was our urgent duty to defend the institutions of the established democratic order," recalled El Alemán. "[He said] the country's chaotic situation obligated us as citizens to defend the state's institutional integrity even if doing so meant breaking the law."[13] Freddy was so struck by his future mentor's political vision that he joined on the spot. With a handshake, Carlos said, "Welcome to the *autodefensas*," using the paras' preferred name for themselves.

Carlos instructed Freddy to join a small band of autodefensas that was just getting off the ground in the town of Necoclí on the northeastern shores of the gulf. As he helped the new outfit amass men and weapons, Freddy quickly rose to the top of its command structure. As commander, he was so strict his troops began calling him El Alemán (The German). In 1997 the group rechristened itself the Bloque Elmer Cárdenas (BEC) in honor of a fallen comrade. Although the BEC functioned mostly as an autonomous group, it sometimes received its marching orders from the Casa Castaño.

FIGURE 12.   El Alemán with troops from the Bloque Elmer Cárdenas (BEC) in 2006.

(Credit: Jorge Matos/Surimages)

During his ten years as the commander of the BEC (1996–2006) El Alemán turned what had been a scrappy gang of gunmen into a disciplined army of almost seventeen-hundred battle-hardened paramilitaries. The bloc quickly won a well-deserved reputation as an expert counterinsurgent force, with a specialty in zone breaking. On multiple occasions when the Castaños opened a new front in their war against the FARC they asked El Alemán and his troops to spearhead its initial stages. The Castaños also entrusted him with control over nearly the entirety of Urabá, including the all-important territory of Tulapas.

Several years after the 1995 mass exodus from Tulapas, peasants from other parts of Urabá, with the authorization of its new paramilitary overlords, started trickling into the area and slowly began resettling the deserted farmlands. The transplants arrived for a variety of reasons: some were displaced from elsewhere, others came at the express invitation of the BEC, and still others were simply campesinos looking for work, land, or opportunities. One of the new settlers was Víctor Martínez. He arrived in Tulapas in 2002 after hearing that the paras were hiring *macheteros* to hack away at the overgrowth that had consumed the abandoned farmlands.

"In those days, you never would've come here without the paramilitaries' permission," he told me.[14] By the time we met in 2012 Víctor, a jovial, charismatic campesino in his fifties, had become a respected community leader in Tulapas. He recalled that when campesinos first started resettling the lands the paras were so desperate for more people that "they brought in maybe thirty or forty families and gave them parcels to work."

"Why did they want more people?" I asked.

"I guess they needed workers, and they just had way too much land. There was also the issue of the coca, so they also needed people to work that too," said Víctor. The EPL had left behind several coca plantations in Tulapas. Another new arrival remembered being shocked at the size of the coca bushes, which he said had grown "trunks practically the size of trees."[15] The paramilitaries eagerly incorporated the coca left behind by the guerrillas into the social and economic structures of their own territorial control. As Víctor explained, "I had El Alemán's permission, and I started growing coca, but the condition was that I could sell the product only to them."

It was among these new coca-growing campesinos and at the intimate scale of their communities that the BEC began the social and political work of its war of position. El Alemán began the process by setting up an extensive training program aimed at turning a retinue of his soldiers into expert community organizers. He envisioned them as the paramilitary counterpart to the so-called political commissars that guerrillas deployed for their own political *trabajo de masas* (work among the masses). El Alemán even adopted the same name for the operatives he tasked with this community organizing: political commissars. At his trial El Alemán explained, "We sent them out to do community work— initially, as liaisons between the communities and the different local commanders of the BEC."[16]

He soon rechristened them with the loftier title of Promotores de Desarrollo Social (Promoters of Social Development, or PDSs). Dressed in civilian clothes and armed with only a radio or cellphone, the PDSs became the foot soldiers of the BEC's war of position. "Our PDSs would go out and do community work," said El Alemán. "They had a degree of knowledge of cooperativism, so they knew something about how to create a junta and how citizen oversight worked, empowering the presidents of the juntas, giving them juridical life in all our municipalities."[17]

The PDSs gave "juridical life" to the juntas either by helping communities create a junta in places that did not have one or, as was more often the case, by assisting communities in the legal–bureaucratic process of formally registering a preexisting junta. The BEC even bankrolled community leaders' trips to Medellín to complete the registration process with the governor's office. The Juntas de Acción Comunal, just as they had been for the FARC's political commissars, became the cornerstone of the political work conducted by the PDSs.

The paramilitary war of position learned and borrowed heavily from the political cultures of its sworn enemies, the EPL and the FARC. And since the BEC had an extraordinarily high number of former rebels in its ranks it was well equipped for repurposing the political tactics pioneered by the guerrillas. Aware of this advantage, El Alemán purposely tapped the ex-rebels in his army to fulfill the role of PDSs because they had the necessary experience and skill set for the job. Hence the paras recycled the tried and tested methods and even the personnel of the guerrillas' political work, thereby enabling the BEC to create its territories through the use of proven, locally familiar political practices. Paradoxically, the deep-seated sedimentations of guerrilla territoriality, like the coca fields, the juntas, and the political commissars, ended up facilitating rather than disabling the paramilitaries' war of position.

At the height of its power the BEC had more than one hundred PDSs deployed across its territories. El Alemán had formalized their training process by creating a special academy called the Simón Bolívar Social and Political Training School. He even brought in conservative professors from the University of Córdoba to conduct legal workshops. The professors made sure the PDSs were especially well versed in the legislation passed after the decentralization reforms of the 1991 Constitution that governed the relationship between municipal administrations and the juntas.[18]

Since the decentralization gave municipalities greater political, administrative, and fiscal power, it indirectly turned the juntas into much more important institutional interlocutors between communities and municipal government structures. After the new Constitution was passed, local communities increasingly turned to their juntas as vehicles for lobbying the newly empowered municipal administrations to deliver things like roads, clinics, schools, and other vital improvements. The juntas had also gained a stronger political footing because the decentralization had eroded the Liberal–Conservative duopoly. While they remained firmly ensconced in Colombia's patron–client networks, the juntas now had a wider menu of patrons to choose from, giving them more leverage over local politicians. In short, the juntas had become much more pivotal and powerful institutional hubs than they had been when the guerrillas controlled Urabá.

In interviews former PDSs' favorite term for describing their relationship with the juntas was that they "accompanied" them. The BEC "accompanied" an astonishing proportion of the juntas in the territories under its control: in Necoclí alone, for example, the paras worked with 110 of the municipality's 121 juntas.[19] By giving "juridical life" to the juntas and accompanying them in their daily activities, the BEC saw itself, in El Alemán's words, as creating the conditions "for the state to gain a presence in those areas."

Although they are defined by the law as "civil society" organizations, the juntas are state-sanctioned, legally regulated, and democratically elected bodies of community governance; each has a president, vice president, treasurer, and so on. In other words, they are effectively, if not officially, the Colombian state's most subsidiary administrative unit. The PDSs helped not only to establish and manage the juntas' relationships with municipal entities but also to "thicken" the intensity and significance of those local political relationships. By working through the juntas the PDSs wedded together the networks and social relations of Colombian statehood at their most localized scale.

Everyday State Formation

It took over a year for the campesinos of Tulapas to open up to me about the nature of their relationship with the paras during the height of their rule over the area in the early 2000s. A community's association with a particular armed group carries a heavy stigma. But slowly they began painting a mixed portrait with divergent opinions about the role of the PDSs and the juntas in those years.

One campesino described the communities' relationship with the paras in authoritarian terms. He became the president of a junta in Tulapas after being

actively recruited by the paras from another part of Urabá. "They came looking for me because they wanted someone who knew how to work with communities," he said. "And since I had helped manage a community organization
where I was from, they brought me in."[20] He soon discovered his position was
not outside the paras' strict chain of command. "As the president of the junta,
when I gave an order . . . you knew it was coming from the boss [*el patrón*]. If the
president of the junta said it, you knew El Alemán had said it. . . . The junta was
the one who was given the power, and the community was expected to fall in line.
So, of course, all of this worked to perfection for El Alemán."

Eventually, disgruntled with his figurehead status, this campesino ran afoul
of the PDSs after trying to rally community members who, like him, wanted to
change the terms of the arrangement. "The problem I had with the PDSs was that
I wanted to work with the people in the community who were really interested
in working for the community," he said. "And those kinds of divisions were not
convenient for them." After his run-in with the PDSs he fled Tulapas for fear the
paras would kill him for stirring up trouble.

Most of the stories I heard about the PDSs, however, describe a far more amicable situation. A story from a campesina who served as the president of a different junta in Tulapas demonstrates the complexity of the relationships between
locals, municipalities, and the PDS.[21] It also shows the subtleties of the paramilitary war of position as a form of state building. The story centers on a formal letter she wrote to her municipal government requesting more information about
a stalled road construction project. In writing the letter she was exercising her
constitutionally protected *derecho de petición* (right to petition), which legally
obliges the entity being petitioned to respond in a timely manner.

She wrote the letter at the prodding and with the help of one of the PDSs
keeping tabs on her community. Directed to the mayor of Turbo, the letter sought
documentation that might indicate whether the funds for the road project were
being well spent—exercising yet another constitutionally enshrined right, that of
veeduría ciudadana (citizen oversight). The PDSs trained the juntas on the legal
process for exercising this oversight as a way of promoting transparency and
good governance. Although cognizant of those loftier goals, she admitted to me
that in her mind the letter had a more immediate purpose. She saw the letter as
being less about fighting corruption than about pressuring the mayor into actually building the road.

"Corruption?" she said. "There'll always be corruption!" The real purpose was
to show the mayor that, as she described it, the "community had its eye on him" in
the hope this would force his hand and "poner a funcionar el estado," which can
be translated as "make the state work," as in both putting it *to work* and making it
work properly.[22] Even though the road never materialized, the episode highlights

how junta members navigated the networks of local governance by drawing on the counsel and training they received from the PDSs. In the process, they were able to make the state "work" for their communities. "Our reelection depended on it," she finished.

Another campesino, still the vice president of a junta in Tulapas when we met in 2013, said, "As the Junta de Acción Comunal, we'd tell the PDSs if we felt the bloc was doing something we didn't like. And in general that was respected," he said. "We were very direct with them, and them with us—upfront like."[23] It would be a gross exaggeration to say they were on equal footing, a point he conceded, but civilians were never passive subjects entirely sapped of their political agency.

Indeed, communities sometimes secured noteworthy concessions from the paras. One junta succeeded even in pressuring the BEC into introducing an agrarian reform, albeit a very meager one and on lands that had been stolen. In 2002 the president of this junta convinced El Alemán to cede a small parcel of a paramilitary estate known as La 24, a four-thousand-hectare spread made up of properties stolen from the original inhabitants of Tulapas. Working through the local PDSs, the junta president succeeded in acquiring three hundred hectares for sixteen families, who to this day openly proclaim their allegiance to El Alemán as someone "who did a lot for the community."[24]

The general coordinator of the PDSs was Secretario, a paramilitary operative who went from being El Alemán's personal assistant to one of his most trusted confidants. Initially, Secretario's job was a series of mundane tasks: managing emails, updating the group's website, coordinating meetings, and keeping El Alemán abreast of reports about the bloc's relations with communities. Through this last responsibility, said Secretario, he "got involved with the PDSs and became interested in," as he described it, "the social side of the BEC."[25]

Secretario understood the "social side of the BEC," which included the work of the PDSs and the juntas, as a hands-on form of state building. He explained his view via a revealing metaphor: "We [the PDSs] were in charge of organizing the communities, organizing them as units, as the base of power in Colombia. The state in Colombia is like a pyramid with the communities at the bottom. At the top are the president, the Senate, and then [the lower house of] Congress with the Juntas de Acción Comunal at the very bottom with the communities. Every community has a junta, so our job was to organize those juntas, train them, and show them how to do their work."

El Alemán used the same metaphor, describing the juntas as the building blocks of the state: "Training the juntas was really important to us because they are the first step in the pyramid of democratic participation, so our objective was for them to be mechanisms of social participation, as legislated by Law 743."[26] The law he referred to was passed after the decentralization to regulate the juntas' relationships with municipalities. According to a BEC training manual, the work of PDSs in the juntas was supposed to "promote social and community development in geographic areas characterized by state abandonment and high levels of unmet basic necessities through the consolidation of basic state structures."[27]

The social side of the BEC's work—to continue the architectural metaphor—was supposed to help fill in the "basic state structures" at the base of the pyramid so as to strengthen the foundations on which the larger edifice of Colombian statehood rested. As Secretario explained, the "consolidation of basic state structures" encompassed "all kinds of community work: creating the Juntas de Acción Comunal; training the juntas; creating their dispute resolution committees; organizing and motivating work brigades to improve bridges, roads, community centers."[28]

The building and maintenance of roads and bridges were especially important. The lack of a road or the terrible state of an existing one almost always tops the list of grievances expressed by campesino communities throughout the country. In Colombia roads have a powerful capacity to invoke the presence or absence of the state; they are both symbolic and material indices of statehood.[29] For the paras, besides valorizing their stolen lands, the construction of a road was a surefire way of winning local approval and consolidating their territorial control.

A former PDS explained that road building worked through a consistent division of labor: "The organization [i.e., the BEC] would pay for the bulldozers and fuel, while the juntas were in charge of organizing the community—food, manual labor, and the rest. That's how we worked hand in hand in making the roads, leaving everything nice and organized."[30] He looked down at the map I took with me to interviews and circled his index finger around Tulapas. "You see all those *carreteras* [roads] here," he said, "that bunch of internal *carreteritas*? Ninety-eight percent of them were done by the autodefensas." It was the third time an ex-member of the BEC cited this statistic to me as concrete evidence of their contribution to materializing the presence of the state.

Paramilitary road building brought together a diverse assemblage of actors: besides the paras themselves and the juntas, road projects often enlisted government entities from all scales, including the military. The army unit in charge of Urabá, the 17th Brigade, was the only government institution in the area with its own heavy machinery. Since wealthy landowners reaped economic benefits from improved access to markets for their products and the valorization of their properties, El Alemán said he usually convinced them to chip in funds as well. Through these joint efforts the construction of roads in paramilitary territories was something of a public–private partnership.

The paras cast campesinos as the ultimate beneficiaries of the road projects. "We would sell [the road] to the communities as something entirely for their social welfare, but the benefit was really for us," admitted one paramilitary chief.[31] Locals were by no means naïve about the paras' ulterior economic and military motives, but if it meant they would finally get their long-sought-after road they dutifully played the role of grateful supplicants.

The BEC had other everyday forms of shoring up its territorial hegemony. Locals in Tulapas said that whenever anyone became gravely ill the family would simply call one of the local PDSs, who would get on his radio and within minutes a late-model SUV would pull up and drive the patient to the hospital hours away. The paras donated things like generators, water pumps, pesticides, seeds, and other basic necessities. Large community events and festivities were also all-expenses paid. And every Christmas the PDSs made sure every child under the age of ten received a toy, a task enabled by the population censuses the PDSs conducted in their jurisdictions.

When I asked Cocinero, a former PDS, about the Christmas gifts, he rummaged through his house and came out with a Barbie doll, a plastic tool set, and a toy truck. The toys were in their original, now-yellowing plastic packaging like collector's items. "See, we gave them nice Barbies, not some little ugly thing—the latest models," he said. Looking over the toys, I told him it was almost comical to think that Barbie had helped them keep their territories intact. With his usual macho bravado, Cocinero joked in return: "Well, she's a hot little lady."[32]

Cocinero was the former PDS I got to know best during my fieldwork. Before joining the BEC he had done stints in both the FARC and the EPL. He turned to the paras not out of political conviction but for entirely practical reasons, namely, unemployment and fear of rebel reprisals. But within weeks of his enlistment he contracted a severe respiratory problem while slogging through the swamps of Chocó. El Alemán reassigned him as a PDS, a job that fit him well thanks to his experience with the guerrillas and his gregarious personality.

Cocinero claimed the PDSs were completely nonviolent operatives. El Alemán similarly maintained that the BEC maintained a strict firewall between its social–political work and its military operations. But plenty of incidents suggest otherwise. A PDS, for instance, was responsible for the high-profile assassination in 2005 of Orlando Valencia, a beloved Afro-Colombian activist. The PDSs may have fulfilled a primarily nonmilitary role, but they still formed part of the paras' ecologies of violence.

As we sat on his porch one day I shared my skepticism with Cocinero about the rosy descriptions he was giving me of BEC's social work. Unfazed, he replied, "One of these days, if you want, I can give you a tour of some of our projects." It

FIGURE 13.   The leftover toys Cocinero showed me to prove his paramilitary bloc gave out gifts during Christmas.

(Credit: Author)

would later become clear that by "our projects" he meant the communities the BEC had not just supported but actually created. He cited the projects as examples of how the paras had "brought the state to the communities." He wanted me to see for myself. "I can take you to talk to them. I want you to see that I'm not talking about some utopia," he insisted. "This was something that was actually done and achieved. I can take you on the roads and the bridges we built and show you the clinics that are still there. All that is still there."[33]

From his perspective, not only had the paras "brought the state to the communities," but also the state was "still there," something that could be seen, touched, and experienced. With a clear sense of pride, he added, "We did some very elegant things," the same words he always used to brag about the bloc's social and political work: "unas cosas muy elegantes." A few weeks later, having accepted his invitation, I was riding on the back of his motorcycle heading into the mountains toward Tulapas.

Paramilitary Land Redistributions

Over the course of two days Cocinero took me to two separate communities. In yet another example of how the paras copied the guerrillas' political and territorial practices, the communities were the product of paramilitary-sponsored *invasiones de tierras,* or land occupations, that took place in the early 2000s. We stayed in each place only long enough for me to do a handful of interviews.

The simple fact that I had arrived with a former paramilitary—who, I would learn, was under strict orders from El Alemán—obviously meant that my conversations with locals took place in a controlled environment, but they nonetheless revealed a lot about the imaginaries and practices of paramilitary state building. The trip was by no means an objective stroll through the local histories of paramilitary–civilian relations. It was a guided tour, and Cocinero was my handler.

Cocinero arrived at my hotel in the municipal seat of Necoclí, and I climbed on the back of his motorcycle. From the shores of Urabá's coastal flatlands we headed east toward the mountains into an undulating green expanse of huge cattle estates. These ranchlands were the regional epicenter of the narco land rush in the 1980s. As we gained elevation we zipped past humped-back zebu cattle and entered a jungle landscape interrupted intermittently by neat rows of plantation forestry: teak, melina, and acacia trees. After almost three hours we sped past a sign that read Hacienda Tulapas. This was the main entrance of a huge estate of stolen properties owned by a paramilitary-backed cattle company. We had reached Tulapas. At the terminus of the hacienda's fancy fencing we reached our destination, a tiny village called El Olleto.

Day 1. El Olleto

A woman emerged from the largest house bordering the dirt road and effusively greeted Cocinero.[34] "Reina, I brought a friend," he said.[35] She invited us to take a seat around a billiard table under a tin roof adjacent to her house, a space that served as the village cantina. After about ten minutes of chitchat and catching up Cocinero began explaining the purpose of our visit. He said El Alemán had asked him to show me around.

"He already talked to El Alemán, who mentioned everything. So he's here to hear your testimony because he's interested in—what was it you're interested in?"

Timidly, I offered, "Well, I was hoping to learn more about what the relationship was like between the bloc and the community."

"Right," continued Cocinero, "so he's here to hear about everything—the bad as well as the good. He knows the autodefensas were no little angels. As I said, El Alemán already told him everything." He repeatedly assured her she could be honest without getting into trouble with either El Alemán or the authorities.

She calmly replied, "Sure, of course, at your service. Nothing to hide, nothing to fear." Cocinero excused himself. After a few more minutes of small talk I asked if I could use my audio recorder. "You better!" she said laughingly. "It's a long story!"

"Okay. Maybe you could start by telling me where we are."

"Well, El Olleto, the place you see here, is mostly made up of people brought by the Bloque Elmer Cárdenas," Reina began. "Imagine, before the bloque brought them, we barely had enough people to make up a Junta de Acción Comunal, at least one with all the proper committees."

Before the paramilitaries Olleto was controlled by the EPL. Reina had only bad things to say about the rebels. "It was terrible. . . . They wouldn't let people in or out of Olleto because they said you were giving information to the government," she recalled. "If you wanted to leave, you'd have to leave forever, leaving everything behind. And that's what a lot of people did. They never came back."

The sporadic displacements by the guerrillas turned into an exodus when the paramilitaries arrived. "They came in raining down blood and fire. Everyone had to leave. Everyone was afraid of being killed, so some fled to San Pedro, others went to Necoclí."[36]

Reina and her family fled to the town of San Pedro and lived there for the next several years. Eventually they began hearing that the paras were allowing people to come back: "It was through gossip. You know, like a broken telephone. We heard it was safe, and people, at first, just peeked in to see if it was true. And it was, but there was nothing left. A whole lot of work to do—that was all that was left." In 1999, almost five years after their displacement, she returned with her family. "And that's when the Bloque Elmer Cárdenas started supporting us."

Tired of living with her father, Reina joined a few other locals who had moved onto a string of small, abandoned properties lining one side of the road that bisects the village. She built her house on one of these lots. From where we sat she pointed to the opposite side of the road. "The lands over there" she said, "belonged to a single person who bought them from the owners when we were displaced. You could say that this señor took advantage of them. They sold to him because, you know, people will do whatever it takes to save their life."

"You can recover land, but not your life," she said. Then, paraphrasing the Old Testament, she added, "Your life is not a tree that sprouts up again when it's cut down. But this señor didn't care about the *parcelitas* on this side of the road; he only cared about his huge farm."[37]

Following up later, I tracked down the property's publicly registered documents. The unscrupulous buyer was Roberto Ojeda, a rancher from Córdoba who in the 1990s led a small group of hired guns that eventually joined the Casa Castaño. Ojeda combined the stolen properties into a single two-thousand-hectare spread, which he later sold to a member of the Mafioli clan, another of Córdoba's elite families. Famous for breeding champion gamecocks, members of the Mafioli family have also been dogged by allegations about their involvement in the drug trade.

"So I built my little house on one of these *parcelitas*," said Reina. "No one bothered me about it. No one said, 'This is mine' or told me to leave or anything like that, so along with some neighbors we organized a Junta de Acción Comunal."

Soon afterward El Alemán paid a visit to the community. It was the early 2000s. He announced he was bringing a teacher back to the local schoolhouse. The village had been without one for more than a decade. A few months later he called a community meeting through the Junta de Acción Comunal, which was led then by a respected campesino leader named Alberto Jiménez.

"And that's when Alberto told us that El Alemán was bringing all those *desplazados* [displaced people] from over there, from Chocó. These were very needy people."

"Why did he bring them?" I asked.

"I don't know exactly what happened. But they had been practically imprisoned by the FARC in the Chocó. They had been stuck there, forced into collaborating with the guerrillas, growing their food, and all that."

Alberto announced that El Alemán was taking control of the Mafiolis' estate and parceling out the land to current members of the community and to the incoming desplazados from Chocó. The older residents got a ten-hectare plot, while the newcomers got five hectares. In court El Alemán later claimed he had seized the Mafiolis' property by force with the intent of helping the campesinos. But I heard gossip that the Mafiolis had actually handed it over to settle an old debt with the Castaños.[38]

"Now that we had land," Reina continued, "El Alemán saw that we were really hardworking people, so he sent in the PDSs like [Cocinero], and they began doing workshops with the community. They trained us and taught us how to work through the juntas and its committees. We even had a committee in charge of reforestation. All the teak and melina you see planted here in this area is because they always brought very good development projects." The forestry project was part of a government coca-eradication program.

"Very good projects," she reemphasized. "Because as long as you get well trained you learn how to work and get in with the state [*aprendes a trabajar y a como entrarle al estado*]."

Reina mentioned that El Alemán sent several community representatives to Córdoba for leadership workshops. "They came back very well trained," she said. "Politicians could no longer come to us and say, 'Oh, the thing is that the law says such and such.' No, now we were much better informed. None of us were buying those stories anymore."

According to Reina, Alberto Jiménez, the respected leader of Olleto's junta, was a product of one of those workshops. After successfully overseeing the Mafioli land redistribution, Alberto got the BEC's blessing to run for mayor of Turbo. After losing the election he made a bid for the lower house of Congress as part of a slate of candidates backed by El Alemán but again failed to be elected. In 2010 police arrested Alberto in a mass roundup of local politicians for their links to paramilitaries.

Reina and the other residents of Olleto were incensed over his arrest. "It was the most unjust thing that could've happened," she said. "Because he was working just for the community, not for the paramilitaries. But things need to be said exactly how they are: he was a very good leader, a very good leader. Alberto always let the communities know exactly what was going on. He was very loved."

Toward the end of our conversation she reiterated that the BEC had empowered the community in its relationships with the state in lasting ways. "I'll say it again: the bloc helped us immensely as campesinos. Before, the state always had its back turned away from us, but now the state more or less sees the campesino."

"And the experience we gained still works for us," she continued. "Now, we all know what to do with the state, exactly where to complain, how to do things right, and how not to get tripped up [*no enredarnos*]. The bloque made that bridge for us with the state, and we crossed it."

Day 2. Galilea

The next day Cocinero took me to a community called Galilea near Arboletes on the Caribbean coast in Córdoba just a few miles beyond the Antioquia border. I first heard about this land occupation from Secretario, El Alemán's general coordinator of the PDSs, who had said, "That was our biggest land invasion; it was a beautiful thing." As in Olleto, the land was an idle property that had once belonged to a narco. But in this case the property had been languishing for years as a seized asset under the custody the national drug enforcement agency.

According to Secretario, "The day of the invasion [in 2003], the bloc ordered that every bus, truck, or jeep in the area be commandeered for the invasion. We put families onto that property by the truckload." He also mentioned that the governor of Córdoba at the time, Jesús María López, prevented the police from forcibly evicting the occupiers and even provided wood, tarps, and other supplies for the effort. Secretario said Governor López "was a big friend of the invasion."[39] The governor, a member of one of Córdoba's elite families, later ended up in jail for being elected with the help of the paras.

When I arrived at Galilea with Cocinero a few dozen community members were in the middle of a workshop being led by an agronomist from Incoder, Colombia's rural development and land management agency. As the workshop wrapped up, a campesino named Roberto introduced himself to me as "one of the original leaders of the invasion" and agreed to tell me his story. Roberto began by explaining that Galilea had been the ranch of a drug trafficker: "I think his name was Matta Ballesteros."[40]

The Honduran-born Juan Ramón Matta Ballesteros had an infamous career in the transnational cocaine underworld until his capture in 1988. He not only helped broker a working relationship between the Mexican and Colombian cartels but also ran the private airline that shipped cocaine and brought back arms shipments for the Contras in Nicaragua under the watch of the U.S. State Department and the CIA. He is currently serving consecutive life sentences in a high-security prison in Pennsylvania for the kidnapping and murder of a U.S. federal agent.[41]

"The land had belonged to this trafficker," said Roberto, "but here we're in a territory that belonged to the autodefensas and so the land occupation all happened hand in hand with them." Justifying the collaboration, he pointed out that "campesinos are stuck in the middle of the armed conflict with a sword at their throats and their backs against the wall. You always end up having to tend to one group or another."

"The abandonment of the state gives rise to those things," Roberto continued. As examples, he claimed some villages in the area had never seen a policeman. "Who do you think controlled stealing and those types of things in the area? The autodefensas! Who else can you turn to?"

"But the absence of the state was not only in a military sense," he added. "There was no presence of the state in the sense of public works. It was the autodefensas that were out there building the roads and bridges. With what money? I don't know, but they'd do it. The roads back then were in even better shape than they are now," he assured me. "Of course, with Galilea, the only reason we dared with the invasion—it must be said—was because we were backed by the autodefensas. They said, 'Go for it. Relax, no problem.'"[42]

As a gentle provocation, I asked, "Does that make you part of the autodefensas in some people's eyes?"

"I was never a part of the autodefensas, but I have a lot of experience doing the kind social work that was done here. I've always lived in places in the middle of the conflict."

"And how did you end up here?" I wondered.

"I was one of the leaders of the whole process." He had been living in the town of Bajirá on the Antioquia–Chocó border, a place where the paras with Doña Tere had carried out a similar land "redistribution." He said the BEC had sought him out: "They found me and said, 'Hombre, way over there people are going to do this and that. And, *hermano*, there are some lands over there that the people could get for themselves. We need people who can help organize the communities.'"

"It attracted me," Roberto explained. "I wasn't even thinking about having my own *parcelita*. My objective was just to help people. That's what really brought me here, because I've had a long trajectory as a leader."

Roberto got his start in the EPL's banana union, which he said gave its labor militants "a very solid political education." Working his way up the union ranks, Roberto helped lead some of the EPL's land occupations. He also served multiple times in the junta of his community and ultimately won a seat on Apartadó's municipal council. "During all these processes," said Roberto, "I got to know the laws: like 136 on how municipal government is supposed to work, 743 about the juntas, Law 80 about [municipal] contracting—all those rules."[43]

Working with the paramilitaries, however, he "gained much more experience with all the mechanisms related to citizen participation." As examples he cited the process for filing an injunction, the right to petition and redress, and citizen oversight, all in relation to municipal government.[44] "I learned all those types of things," he said. "I'm really good at talking with people, organizing them, approaching organizations and saying, 'Okay, these are the mechanisms we can use for enforcing what's in such and such law.'"

Roberto's experience made him an ideal candidate for working on the BEC's planned invasion of Galilea. It took almost a year for Roberto, the other community leaders, and the PDSs to prepare for the land occupation. On the night of September 23, 2003, under cover of darkness, around five hundred families scrambled on to the property. The overseer of the entire process was a recently formed organization called Asocomún, an NGO established by El Alemán's brother, who went by the name Germán Monsalve.[45] Asocomún, which publicly presented itself as an alliance of Juntas de Acción Comunal, took charge of all the training workshops offered by the BEC. Besides leading the training efforts, Don Germán, as he was reverently known, also supplied the land occupants with meat, rice, and vegetables grown by what Roberto called their "sister communities in Tulapas." The BEC's territories had turned into an archipelago of mutual aid.

"One of the first things we did was choose our representatives and organize an assembly. It was all coordinated by the PDSs and Asocomún." The NGO also helped them craft a "manual of coexistence." According to Roberto, "These were the norms we had to abide by inside Galilea. Everyone had to volunteer for community work and guard duty. If you left for town, you had to give notice to the guards and sign a paper, saying at what time you left and at what time you were coming back." He said it also included things like "no drinking, smoking, gambling, prostitution, or shacking up [*meterse al cambuche*] with another person's wife."

Many of the first settlers did not last long: "They got tired of the rules and the sanctions." Other participants left after it became clear they faced a year-long trial period before receiving an individual parcel of land. Today, Galilea has 350 families spread over almost eleven hundred hectares of land. "Those of us who stayed are very happy," said Roberto, "because the Incoder gave us a certificate that shows we're registered with them, so we can get loans. It's not a title yet, not like when the land is totally yours. But at least we know that we have a paper with the state."

The increasing security of their tenure has also opened doors for national and international sources of financing for agricultural projects. The workshop underway when I arrived in Galilea, for instance, was part of a larger, US$1.5 million-dollar plantain project backed by the Ministry of Agriculture. The community also had a microcredit fund backed by the Rotary Club. Roberto said Galilea's success is largely thanks to Asocomún: "These are all things we've been doing because of the social development and training we got from Asocomún."

With genuine curiosity, as our conversation began winding down, I asked him, "Why do you think the autodefensas were so good to Galilea and so violent with other communities?" He began by pointing out that the paras' control over the area was undisputed. "So, logically, in places where they have control, they have no reason to be abusive with the people." Roberto cited the massacre in Pueblo Bello as a counterexample: "In Pueblo Bello, they did *una limpieza* [a cleansing], as they call it, and killed something like fifty people. In those days, they would show up with all their force but without any ideology. It was just an organization of extermination against the guerrillas." In fact, as mentioned earlier, the Pueblo Bello massacre had clear ideological dimensions, as most of those killed were EPL sympathizers.

"They killed a lot of people. One can't deny that. . . . There's no justification," he lamented. But then Roberto repeated the story of Fidel Castaño's stolen cattle, suggesting that the townspeople brought it on themselves: "Sometimes people create their own problems. If I go out and steal, then I can't be surprised if something happens to me."

"But what happens is that the state's abandonment means there's no justice for that theft. Hombre! If there had been real justice, then there would have been no need for the autodefensas." He then slipped into the default Hobbesian thesis: "Around here we often say that the problem behind the violence is not the armed groups; the real problem, we say, is the absence of the state. The absence feeds the violence."

The land occupations in Olleto and Galilea reveal the rich nexus of political practices, institutional formations, and power relations that materialized out of the frontier effect in the BEC's territories. Through the war of position, both places became productive and lasting sites of the paras' frontier state formations. As El Alemán's trusted PDS, Cocinero, assured me, "All of that is still there." The juntas they created, the community leaders they trained, the roads and bridges they built, the land occupations they sponsored, the laws they put into practice, the submunicipal political relationships they established, the development projects they secured, "all of that is still there." One of El Alemán's fellow paramilitary commanders in Urabá described this elaborate mix of tactics as a lesson they had learned from the guerrillas' doctrine calling for "the combination of all forms of struggle."[46]

One of the foremost architects of U.S. counterinsurgency campaigns in Latin America once noted the military importance of winning civilians' hearts and minds by saying, "The only territory you want to hold is the six inches between the ears of the campesino."[47] El Alemán said as much when he noted, "We realized guns were never going to be enough. . . . [W]e also had to think about the social and political front."[48] The paramilitary war of position was as much of a struggle for territorial hegemony as it was a revanchist project of state building against the political–military power of the insurgencies.

Military thinkers have always seen state building as a key part of counterinsurgency.[49] David Kilcullen, the influential counterinsurgency guru described by some as a "modern-day Sun Tzu," has criticized the U.S. wars in Iraq and Afghanistan, noting the ineffectiveness of their narrow "focus on top-down, state-centric processes that have a structural focus on putting in place the central, national-level institutions of the state." Future efforts, he suggested, should "focus on local-level governance" and "bottom-up, community-centric approaches" to state building.[50]

In Colombia El Alemán implemented these tactics intuitively and with astonishing precision. By dispatching the PDSs, setting up and consolidating the juntas, training their leaders, and marshaling the law, the paramilitaries solidified the social relations of statehood in their territories. In the technocratic terms of development professionals, paramilitary state building was both decentralized and bottom-up. In fact, the paras even became the on-the-ground handmaidens of the 1991 constitutional reforms legislating the state's decentralization. In Reina's words, the BEC served as a "bridge" that helped them "get in with the state," so that now "the state more or less sees the campesino."

In Urabá paramilitaries' transition from the violent terror of zone breaking to a more fulsome and lasting production of territorial control was more than a simple ploy for winning hearts and minds. The paramilitary war of position was a sophisticated, wide-ranging effort to, in El Alemán's words, "create a state presence in those areas." The paras' ability to credibly position themselves as state builders was a key part of their appeal and an integral part of their identity and mission as the extralegal restorers of the established political order. The process involved an incredible amount of coercion but also a good measure of consent. As the historian Greg Grandin has noted, "Counterinsurgency, above all else, is choreography."[51]

In the case of Colombia one of the most overlooked aspects of this violent choreography is how the counterinsurgent paramilitaries sought out and earned a notable degree of cooperation and support from subaltern campesino communities. The war of position enabled paramilitary dominion through the state structures it helped materialize. One paramilitary operative, looking back on these efforts, said, "It was a movement that sought to bring the campesino masses closer to the autodefensas."[52] Indeed, the war of position was a pragmatic outgrowth of the paras' need to secure their hold over strategic areas by building *una base social* among real communities made up of real people with real problems. But the war of position and the forms of state building it engendered were a far more nuanced process than that suggested by the hearts and minds cliché.

Campesino communities were not mindless dupes seduced by the empty rhetoric of charismatic paramilitary leaders, nor were they passive subjects devoid of political agency. The paras' sophisticated territorial practices, from the juntas to the PDSs, from the Christmas toys to the road projects, are proof of civilians' agency. Their cooperation was conditional. Whether in the case of the land redistributions or that of the PDSs, civilians banked on the paras' need for consent and leveraged it to reach their own goals. In these ways, too, despite the overwhelming power imbalance, campesinos retained a degree of agency. The relationships they forged with paramilitaries were complicated, varied, and fluid. Although campesinos are often cast into narratives of Colombia's armed conflict as either powerless pawns or heroes of subaltern resistance, most of the time they simply made do.

4

PARAMILITARY POPULISM
In Defense of the Region

If we want things to stay as they are, things will have to change.
—Giuseppe Lampedusa, *The Leopard* (1958)

In 2010 the Colombian attorney general's office ordered the arrest of more than two dozen local politicians in Urabá. They stood accused of having won their elections with the covert financial and logistical backing of the paramilitaries. Although the politicians' collusion with the paras was an open secret in Urabá, a widely circulated flyer denounced their arrests, arguing they were simply committed public servants who had worked tirelessly for "the identity, dignity, and political unity of the region."

Beneath the title "In Defense of the Region of Urabá," the long preamble of the anonymous flyer read in part: "We have always dreamed of organizing a regional political project for Urabá . . . to obtain the representation we deserve and so badly need. . . . We cannot depend on other regions and leaders who are not our own to end this forgotten land's abandonment by the state." The "regional political project for Urabá" was the reason the politicians were arrested. They all belonged to Urabá Grande, an electoral coalition secretly organized and managed by El Alemán and his Bloque Elmer Cárdenas (BEC).

From 2000 to 2006 the Urabá Grande coalition stacked elected offices at every scale, from municipal governments to the halls of Congress, with politicians approved and supported by the BEC. The effort was part of a broader, nationwide process of clandestine electoral collusion between paramilitaries and politicians that came to be known as the *parapolítica* scandal. Many of the parapolítica deals were formal, written agreements like the pact signed by several paramilitary bosses and nearly two dozen politicians who vowed that together

83

they would "refound our country" and "sign a new social contract" to "build a New Colombia."[1]

Eventually, judicial investigators discovered that at least four hundred elected officials across the country, including a full third of Congress, had secured their positions with the paramilitaries' assistance.[2] Carlos Castaño had first called for the paras' to enter electoral politics in 1998 at the schoolhouse retreat in Villanueva, but it was not until the run-up to the 2002 presidential and congressional elections that the alliance between paramilitaries and politicians became nationwide and systematic. The victory of Álvaro Uribe, the former governor of Antioquia, as president in those elections gave the parapolítica alliances another burst of momentum as the paras scrambled to lock their deals into place before their definitive demobilization.

Within the paramilitary movement, the BEC's version of parapolítica was unrivaled in its ability to capture elected offices at every scale of government. El Alemán's efforts began in 2000 when he supported a few local candidates in Antioquia. He soon expanded his influence into several municipalities in Chocó and Córdoba, which is why he named the coalition Urabá Grande, or Greater Urabá. Across its life span (2000–2006) Urabá Grande helped elect dozens of city councilors and mayors throughout the region, governors and departmental assembly members, and, at the national scale, six congressional representatives and three senators.[3]

Urabá Grande formed the electoral wing of the paras' state-oriented war of position. As an extension of BEC's methodical community organizing, Urabá Grande was an effort to give lasting institutional form to the political, economic, and military power the bloc had gained on the battlefield. Urabá Grande also reflects the broader way in which the paras and their allied politicians all over the country presented themselves as the defenders and saviors of Colombia's supposed forgotten regions, promising to bring an end to what they called the regions' abandonment by the state. The paras built a powerful brand of agrarian populism by fusing the discourse of state absence with the politics of Colombian regionalism.[4] As an instance of the frontier effect, paramilitary populism turned statelessness into an affirmative political project of regional affirmation and state formation that tried to reconcile their narrow self-interests with practices of grassroots political participation.

One of the most sophisticated articulators of the paras' regionalist politics was Ernesto Báez, a commander and national ideologue of the paramilitary movement. In 2004, a year into the demobilization talks with the Uribe administration, Báez published a book titled *Scenarios for Peace Through the Construction of Regions* (*Escenarios para la paz a partir de la construcción de regiones*). In the book Báez called for a "debate between the State and society over the urgency of

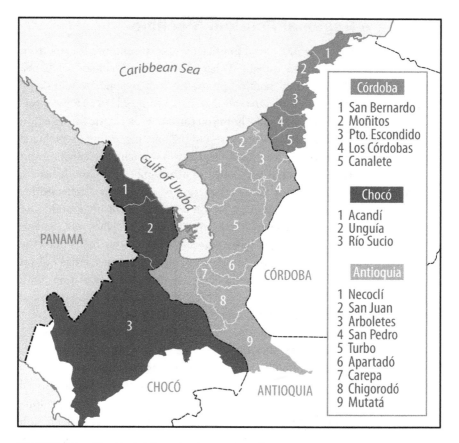

FIGURE 14. The Urabá Grande electoral coalition supported politicians elected to seventeen municipal governments in three departments.

(Credit: Author)

constructing regions, politically, economically, and socially."[5] He added, "Only the arrival or return of the State will incorporate these marginalized regions, socially and economically, into the body politic of the nation."

In more dramatic terms El Alemán described the state's abandonment of the regions as what had forced him and his troops into their life-or-death struggles as *autodefensas*: "If the state's reach had extended across its territory, then we wouldn't have turned into arms-bearing citizens to *defend the regions*—to defend our very lives."[6] In its mission statement the BEC listed even the "regional integration and consolidation of Greater Urabá" as one of its primary "politico-military" objectives. For paramilitary leaders like Ernesto Báez and El Alemán, the construction of "regionhood" and statehood were complementary, if not synonymous, endeavors.

Building a Regional Political Machine

At a meeting between the BEC, local politicians, and community leaders from across the region El Alemán explained that the "uniting ideology" of Urabá Grande was "the defense" and "political progress of our region." He told them, "Instead of seeing me like this *comandante* that makes you come to all these meetings, I want you to see me as a friend whom you can count on for the construction of regionhood."[7] The attendees spent the rest of the meeting setting up thematic working groups on everything from media strategy to women's participation and deliberating on the best potential candidates for achieving Urabá Grande's goals.

El Alemán's comment about the "construction of regionhood" reflected his view of Urabá as a work in progress, a region still in need of integration and consolidation. Even critical scholars like María Teresa Uribe, who published an exhaustive history of Urabá in 1992, have expressed similar views. In her book she argued that Urabá was still a region "under construction, because it has not yet achieved internal and organic cohesion." She continued, "Its articulations with Antioquia, with neighboring departments, and with the Nation are still weak and conflictive. Urabá, then, does not yet constitute a real region."[8]

From her perspective, Urabá fails to meet this narrow definition of "region" as an internally cohesive and outwardly integrated social space. Internally, it has been ripped apart by violent political conflicts and class divisions, and its settlement by multiracial waves of migration means it lacks a strong, unitary social identity. Outwardly, Urabá has stood at rather awkward angles, racially, culturally, and politically, to the rest of Antioquia; and even its allegiance to the nation has been questioned, as happened after the loss of Panama in 1903. For antioqueños, in particular, the consolidation of Urabá's regionhood has been something of an obsession for more than a century.

Anthropologists like Margarita Serje and Julio Arias have shown how discourses about *las regiones* in Colombia are contemporary reformulations of older frontier narratives about the duel between civilization and barbarism.[9] Dominant discourses in the present-day perpetuate this dualism via the prevalent idea of *las dos Colombias* (the two Colombias): one is urban, civilized, and peaceful, while the Other Colombia ("*la Otra Colombia*," another common trope) is rural, savage, and war-torn. The juxtaposition of las regiones, which are undoubtedly the Other Colombia, to major metropolitan centers like Bogotá and Medellín creates the same Manichaean division of the country as civilization and barbarism. As in the past, race, violence, and statelessness remain defining features of the ongoing production of many regions as frontier zones.

The combined workings of these discourses were starkly reflected in comments I heard made by the former head of the Colombian Army in Urabá.

Nicknamed the Pacifier of Urabá, General Rito Alejo del Río led the army's 17th Brigade in the region during the height of the paramilitary onslaught in the late 1990s. When we met in 2013 he was under house arrest at an army base in Bogotá, serving out a sentence for war crimes committed during his purported pacification of the region. After recounting the history of Urabá's early settlement by Afro-Colombian and mestizo peasants, the general claimed, "And, well, from out of that mixture come a bunch of degenerates, and they're the ones who have promoted the illegal armed groups in the region. Eighty percent of those migrants to Urabá had criminal records when they arrived. They were completely rootless people without any sense of belonging."[10] In his mind Urabá's racial and criminal mélange of rootless migrants made any genuine sense of regionhood a biological impossibility.

Even those who did not hold the same blistering degree of racism as the general made comparable assumptions. El Alemán, for instance, linked Urabá's conflictive history to its multiracial composition. He cited its racial diversity as one reason the BEC's community work involved "a lot of workshops and awareness-raising among the mass of campesino leaders with the goal of creating a stronger *sense of belonging to the region*."[11] The BEC's mission statement made clear the bloc's deliberate and racially inflected goal of producing a wider and deeper sense of collective regionhood: "The Bloque Elmer Cárdenas operates in areas with very diverse sociocultural characteristics, such as those of the south of Córdoba or the north of Urabá—or those of the campesinos from the mountains of western Antioquia or the indigenous and Afro-Colombians of Chocó."

After this inventory of spatial–racial essentialisms, the statement continued, "But what all these areas fundamentally share is a common inventory of unmet basic necessities. By implication, they also share an immense potential that could be unlocked through the region's integration and consolidation." The BEC's mission statement pointed to Urabá's "agroindustrial expertise, infrastructure, export experience, and its [free trade] Special Economic Zone" as examples of its untapped potential.[12] This was not the first time nor would it be the last that Urabá's political–economic integration was infused with the cultural politics of race and regionalism.[13]

Regional integration was a major topic of debate at a campaign event sponsored by Urabá Grande in 2003 that featured all the main candidates running for governor of Antioquia. At a large auditorium in Apartadó the gubernatorial contenders gave their speeches from a stage above which was a huge yellow banner that read "*¡Qué Bueno!* Urabá Grande United and in Peace!" The Conservative Party candidate, an aging man with white hair named Álvaro Villegas, was the first to speak. He was a Conservative Party bigwig and titan of Medellín's industrial sector who had helped launch Uribe's political career, giving the president his first major political appointment back in the 1980s.[14]

Villegas, the patriarch of an elite family in Medellín and a prominent member of its political class, self-consciously acknowledged the city's long history of internal colonialism toward the region. "The banana miracle and the Highway [to the Sea] that unites this region with the center of Antioquia created a lot of prosperity," he began. "But the model of development Antioquia has used for the last one hundred years is completely exhausted. It was a centralized model in which the totality of the department's wealth was sent to and concentrated in Medellín."

Continuing his description of uneven development, he said, "The result of this exhausted model is, on one side, a region in which people's only common denominator is poverty and, on the other side, a grandiose city with high levels of development, wealth, and services." True integration, said Villegas, would connect the region in a way that generated more wealth for its local inhabitants. If elected, he promised to end "the state's abandonment of Urabá" with a burst of infrastructural development and a new industrial park—which is to say, low-wage *maquiladora* factories—"turning it into a genuine pole of development for Antioquia and for the country."

In the end Urabá Grande threw its weight behind one of the other candidates on the stage: Aníbal Gaviria of the Liberal Party. He was not only the clear favorite in the gubernatorial race but also had a much more elaborate platform of regional integration. Yet his victory was a striking continuity rather than a break with Urabá's history of uneven development and internal colonialism. Gaviria is the scion of one of the wealthy Medellín families that established the banana enclave back in the 1960s alongside the United Fruit Company. Nonetheless, much more so than the other candidates, he shared Urabá Grande's elaborate vision for the construction of regionhood.

The "economic, political, and social consolidation of the region," as El Alemán envisioned it, was as ideological as it was material: Urabá Grande was as concerned with creating a stronger sense of regional identity and belonging as it was with constructing infrastructure and promoting capitalist development. He described Urabá Grande as a "process of restoring the dignity and legitimacy of the state."[15] He saw the consolidation of regionhood and statehood as working hand in hand. And, as was true of almost everything encompassing the BEC's political work, the Juntas de Acción Comunal became the building blocks of this process. El Alemán officially launched Urabá Grande in 2001 with the help of Jorge Pinzón, a wealthy and politically well-connected rancher from the town of Necoclí. By then the BEC had gained valuable expertise in working with the juntas, and it had dabbled in fielding candidates for local municipal offices. But what Pinzón and El Alemán now planned was a much more systematic electoral initiative with national aspirations: a genuine "regional political project," as they called it. (Urabá Grande's full name was Regional Political Project for the Peace and Unity of Greater Urabá.)

They began by setting up a new NGO that would serve as the central node of Urabá Grande's elaborate institutional network. Although the organization was effectively the BEC's political action committee, its status as an NGO gave it an innocuous institutional façade. They even put the Spanish acronym for "NGO" in the name of the nonprofit: Corporación ONG: Democracia, paz y desarrollo del Urabá Grande" (Corporation NGO: Democracy, Peace, and Development for Greater Urabá). The NGO immediately established local branch offices in all of the municipalities where the BEC maintained a presence. Each municipal office was led by a coordinator who answered directly to Pinzón.

El Alemán's community organizers, the Promoters of Social Development (PDSs), not only helped set up the branch offices but also delivered monthly wads of cash to cover their expenses. The PDSs played an additional role as the primary liaisons between Urabá Grande's municipal coordinators and the Juntas de Acción Comunal. The juntas, in turn, became political incubators for the BEC's local candidates. As El Alemán explained, "We trained leaders who carried out their work in the Juntas de Acción Comunal, so that they would then go out and become municipal council members and so that they'd work for the communities in which combat operations had ended and a state presence was needed." From the intimate scale of community, Urabá Grande sought to build up that state presence *desde la base*—literally, "from the base," or, from the ground up.

As the frontline troops of the BEC's war of position, the PDSs once again did the heavy lifting of paramilitary statecraft. They ensured that all of Urabá Grande's moving parts—the NGO, its branch offices, the candidates, the juntas, and the communities—worked as coordinated parts of a whole. The PDSs also took charge of the more mundane tasks during election season; for instance, they organized cattle auctions to finance candidates, delivered SUVs to the campaigns for transportation, ordered refreshments for events, and arranged buses for voters on Election Day.

The candidates running for municipal council seats faced an extensive vetting process jointly overseen by the BEC's commanders and Urabá Grande's NGO. After reviewing their options, they passed on a list of approved candidates to the PDSs. With this list in hand, the PDSs held community assemblies to determine the most popular candidates and further whittle down the list. The few remaining candidates would then face off at the polls on Election Day, when voters decided the winners. When he described this process in court El Alemán said, "That's why there's not a single municipal councilor in Urabá from the last three administrations who can say they didn't know me or was unaware of the social work carried out by the PDSs with the communities."

In fact, the BEC recruited many of its local candidates from the community leaders it had meticulously groomed in the juntas, so most of the municipal councilors elected with Urabá Grande's help—80 percent by El Alemán's estimate—hailed from the rural areas of Colombia's county-like municipalities. Urabá Grande thus helped reverse the traditional overrepresentation of urbanites within municipal administrations by bringing in more rural residents. El Alemán claimed this change meant not only the direct participation of grassroots campesino leaders in municipal government but also closer ties between neglected rural communities and their local representatives.

For the election of mayors the BEC devised a slightly more elaborate process. "The idea was to have two candidates per municipality: a preferred candidate aligned with the social work of the autodefensas and another candidate with little political weight," said El Alemán. But even with a handpicked paramilitary-backed candidate running against a strawman, things did not always go according to plan, especially in Urabá Grande's early days. In 2000, when Urabá Grande was still in its formative stages, the BEC held a meeting in Tulapas to winnow the field of candidates running for mayor of Necoclí. The meeting was organized by a young PDS known as Slimy (El Escamoso). Slimy, who became the BEC's most active intermediary between local politicians and the juntas, said, "We had our candidate and we had the puppet candidate—you know, for quote-unquote 'Democracy.'" But the plan backfired.

On Election Day the BEC's preferred candidate, a community leader who had worked his way up from the juntas, lost big. The intended strawman candidate, a respected member of the evangelical Christian community, received three times as many votes by drawing on his ties with the churches. Once in office, however, the devout Christian mayor developed excellent relations with the paramilitaries.[16] After some of these early mishaps, however, Urabá Grande soon became more precise in its orchestration. The paras began leaving almost nothing to chance. As Slimy recalled, "Since we weren't really sure who was going to win, we began working with all sides to keep control after the elections, making sure all the candidates were implicated in the project, whether they liked it or not."[17]

Despite Slimy's ominous phrase "whether they liked it or not," El Alemán emphatically denied Urabá Grande involved the coercion of candidates or the intimidation of voters. But paramilitary terror had already accomplished its work. Landslide victories in the pivotal 2002 elections were tightly correlated with four years of paramilitary savagery: in districts where candidates won with the unusual margin of 70 percent or more of all votes, paramilitary massacres had increased by 664 percent and homicides by 33 percent. In any case, by 2002 voters' choices were already limited to candidates handpicked by the paras, making continued coercion unnecessary.

However, in parts of Urabá where the FARC still maintained a strong presence, which was mainly limited to pockets of Chocó, the paras' control over candidates was not as solid. In these areas, as one paramilitary lieutenant put it, elections had to be more "carefully managed." The 2000 mayoral race in the Chocó municipality of Río Sucio demonstrates what careful management meant in practice.[18] The local PDS organized an informal primary in which local community leaders would decide the BEC's main candidate for the race. The winner of the secret ballot, by a margin of five votes, was a popular indigenous leader whom the paras suspected of having sympathies for the FARC, so the PDS carefully managed the results by pocketing six ballots, giving the BEC's preferred candidate a one-vote victory. The indigenous leader's complaints and calls for a revote received a curt reply from the PDS: "We don't have time for that." Since Río Sucio was still disputed territory, it was especially important for its elected officials to be solidly in the paramilitaries' camp. The nature of the relationship between the BEC and local elected officials stunned prosecutors during El Alemán's trial. At one point they cited a letter El Alemán had sent to several other paramilitary chiefs in which he announced he was handing these commanders control over seven of "his municipalities" in Córdoba.[19] The prosecutors pointed out the alarming list of public officials copied on the letter: all seven mayors of the municipalities in question and the governor of Córdoba as well as the local heads of police, the army, and the Catholic Church. One of the prosecutors asked, "In handing over territories like that was it normal to issue these sorts of announcements?" Astounded, he added, "It's shocking. It just doesn't seem like the most normal thing to go and say to a governor: 'Look, from this point on we're handing control over to this other [paramilitary] group.'"

El Alemán explained the letter by situating it within the broader context of the BEC's "social and political work." He pointed out that his bloc had forged "excellent relations" with the grassroots leaders, communities, and elected officials of the area, adding that he had even personally hand delivered the letter to the seven mayors at a meeting. The prosecutor cut him off: "So the mayors knew they were meeting with the commander of an armed group behind the state's back?" El Alemán patiently continued: "What you have to understand is that in the case of the autodefensas *we* filled the role of the state in those places.... [W]e were *states in formation*." Offering examples, he said they resolved local disputes, fixed bridges and roads, and built schools and clinics. "We made sure, through the PDSs or through the community leaders, that the mayors made those investments in the communities. So, yes, sir," he finished, "the mayors knew exactly what was going on."

What the prosecutors found so shocking was that a paramilitary chief had seemingly imposed his authority "over and above" all the government officials copied on the letter: the governor, seven mayors, the security forces—and with their full knowledge, no less. But El Alemán's reply described a far more fluid, organic set of relationships. The BEC's excellent relations with community leaders and elected officials in the area stemmed from the fact that they owed their positions and in some cases their training to the bloc's meticulous social and political work. He described this work as part and parcel of their role as "states in formation," which implied carrying out and routinizing the everyday work of the state, from resolving local disputes to promoting public investment in badly needed community improvements. El Alemán saw the paras' collection of territories (hence the plural *states* in formation) as a holding pattern or as prefigurative and decentralized incubators of statehood.

The campesinos I spoke with who lived in the BEC's territories had varying opinions about the bloc's machinations. At one extreme was the campesino who described the BEC's political interventions as outright "administrative terrorism," while at the other extreme was the campesina who said they were more participatory than "the usual crooked politicking."[20] But most campesinos were far more ambivalent. They generally described their political relationships with the paras in pragmatic and paternalistic terms—and, in the case of the latter, not necessarily in a disparaging way.

One campesina, who admitted that her tiny farm had been personally gifted to her by El Alemán, looked back favorably on the "political counsel" (*asesoría política*) that her community received from the BEC. She said, "Because, you know, sometimes mayors show up, leaving everyone all tied up in knots, so [the paras] counseled us about who would bring the most benefits."[21] She saw the BEC as a buffer that protected the community from the predations of local politicians by assuring or at least improving the chances that campaign promises materialized into concrete benefits. Since Urabá Grande was a multiply scaled process, it positioned the paras as political brokers who both established and mediated the power-laden relations between communities and local government.

The coalition's politicians, however, did not always march in lockstep with the BEC. Sometimes the PDSs had to keep mayors and city councilors in line by reminding them who ultimately called the shots. When stationed in the town of Acandí Slimy intervened at a public meeting during a dispute between local schoolteachers and the mayor. The teachers had not received a paycheck in weeks and had suspended classes. When the mayor openly objected to the PDS's interference at the contentious public meeting Slimy lost his temper: "You talk too much! Keep it up and I'll drag you out of here by your feet." After a somewhat bucktoothed municipal councilor seated next to the mayor chuckled at the reprimand, Slimy snapped, "And you, too! Shut up, toothy [*muelón*]! Or you're next."[22]

Once the meeting settled down Slimy promised the BEC would pay the teachers, but he also made clear the paras would not tolerate any legal actions, called *tutelas*, from the disgruntled schoolteachers or anyone else. Tutelas are constitutionally enshrined legal motions through which citizens can demand the timely fulfillment of basic rights; in this case, for instance, the teachers could have filed tutelas for their paychecks (the right to work), and the students' parents could have filed for the resumption of classes (the right to education). Instead, Slimy reminded the community that any and all grievances should be taken up directly with him. Rather than risk drawing unwelcome attention from outside its territories— that is, from beyond its meticulously maintained spheres of hegemony—the BEC preferred to handle these kinds of problems in-house.

The PDSs may have trained the juntas in things like civilian oversight (*veeduría ciudadana*) of budgets and contracting, as discussed in the previous chapter, but publicly airing dirty laundry through official judicial channels was a dangerous transgression. It is a revealing juxtaposition of how the paras' authoritarian populism worked in practice: they banned legal motions for the protection of basic rights while at the same time encouraging civilian oversight to rein in corruption. Oversight aimed at the efficient operation of bureaucracy was one thing, but a clamoring for justice and rights was beyond the pale. Unlike rights and social justice, anticorruption was a crucial part of the paras' self-proclaimed role as defenders of the regions.

The Politics of Anticorruption

Paramilitaries' critiques of corruption bundled together the guerrillas, the metropolitan oligarchy, and the central government as all part of the same broken system. All three were equally to blame for the marginalization of the regions and the related absence of the state. Carlos Castaño, for instance, once said the reason Colombia had suffered decades of war was "because *la subversión* [i.e., the guerrillas] and government corruption have formed a symbiosis that ensures their mutual coexistence, so the war enriches the few and impoverishes the many." In even bolder terms his brother Fidel claimed to be fighting "a military struggle against the guerrillas and an economic struggle against the oligarchy."[23]

The Castaño brothers leveled their critiques of corruption within a broader set of grievances and resentments held by regional elites against their metropolitan counterparts. Dominated by urban elites, the national political class had abandoned large landowners in the regions to the kidnappings and extortion of the insurgencies and had sacrificed their economic interests on the altar of neoliberal restructuring. Through this "corruption talk," as the anthropologist Winifred Tate has called it, paramilitaries and their allied politicians positioned themselves alongside the subaltern campesinos of the country's beleaguered regions as the aggrieved victims of an uncaring, dysfunctional, and absent state controlled by a faraway, greedy, and arrogant ruling class.[24]

El Alemán framed corruption as part of a broader rural–urban split that had long structured the spatial division of bloodshed in the country. Drawing a parallel between La Violencia and the contemporary conflict, he said, "Both happened under the indifferent gaze of an inept and corrupt upper class who have looked on at the bloodletting as if watching it on television in a soap opera. The only things that have mattered to this corrupt class are its own interests, divvying up bureaucratic posts, and lining its pockets through the clientelistic distribution of public funds."[25] Under this analysis, since the regions had suffered the brunt of Colombia's histories of violence, it was all the more insulting that urban elites treated their agrarian counterparts as primitive, petty tyrants whose only role in the nation's political life was delivering the votes of their rural fiefdoms on Election Day.

As a check on municipal corruption the BEC was an especially burdensome presence for local officials. The bloc's PDSs had helped turn the juntas into demanding, meddlesome counterweights that obstructed local politicians' desires for business as usual. With the paras' help, many juntas had gained formal legal status (*personería jurídica*), meaning they could now bid for minor municipal contracts, a practice encouraged by legislation promoting the 1991 decentralization reforms. With the BEC's support the juntas sought contracts for small construction jobs and rudimentary services, cutting into politicians' sweetheart deals and kickbacks with the private sector.

"The mayors didn't like the juntas," said El Alemán. "Because the Constitution says they are supposed to play a transcendental role in making public administrations in the countryside stronger and more participatory. So if a school is going to be built in a community, then the first one offered the construction contract should be the junta, not the mayor's contractor-buddies."[26] Although municipalities did contract the juntas for some small jobs, the larger, more lucrative projects still consistently went to private companies run by, as El Alemán put it, "the mayor's contractor-buddies."

Secretario, the general coordinator of the bloc's PDSs, gave the example of a road-construction project. He said the normal custom was for the mayor to award the contract to the company of a close business associate. In return, the mayor would receive a kickback for as much as 10 or even 20 percent of the contract's total value. "And so we'd watch over things to make sure it wasn't like this," said Secretario. Noticing my skepticism, he hedged: "Or at least if it was this way, if it *had* to be this way, then we'd say, 'Please, *hermano*, take a bit less, don't take such a huge chunk of the community's money for your pocket. Take a little bit less, invest the rest.'" Secretario said these interventions helped ensure the job actually got done: "It was us who made sure the engineers finished the job. We intervened in everything. We were without a doubt the absolute power in the area. There was no state there."

Despite his claims about the absence of the state and the "absolute power" of the BEC, his story contains nuanced indications about how paramilitary populism worked in practice. For one thing, it shows how the assumed absence of the state underwriting the bloc's political interventions was a generative and yet inherently contradictory discourse: the story includes a mayor, a municipal public works project, the investment of government funds, and a legally binding contract, and nonetheless concludes, "there was no state there."

Contrary to Secretario's claims of the bloc being the "absolute power," the story also shows that the paras were not such omnipotent rulers. Corruption "*had* to be" and it put them in a predicament. They had to weigh the private interests of the mayor and the contractors against winning the community's loyalty by ensuring the construction of the road. They navigated the situation by enforcing the contract and reducing the kickback as a way of improving the chances of the road ever materializing. The paras were pinned between the interests of the road-desiring communities, the municipality's money-hungry politicians, and their own political imperatives. In this, as in many other cases, the paras' hegemony was a negotiated process of juggling all the contradictory political forces that constituted their territories. In relation to corruption, paramilitary populism worked by regulating graft, not eliminating it.

One of the reasons paramilitaries' anticorruption work was such an effective and convincing form of populism was that it simultaneously functioned as a performative critique of the state. Salvatore Mancuso, the wealthy rancher and paramilitary commander whom the Castaños tasked with buying up lands in Tulapas, noted that the paras frequently outperformed the state. "We are more efficient because the state has more bureaucracy, more limitations. We have the advantage because we don't have to deal with the bureaucracy. We can just solve problems," said Mancuso. Citing the vast resources at their disposal from the drug trade, he added, "When we get involved, things get done."[27] As a counterpoint to the corruption-induced dysfunction of the state, the paras could actually "get things done" and "solve problems" without all the usual bureaucratic runaround and endless delays.

The BEC even made the politicians that joined Urabá Grande sign a pledge of allegiance committing them to observe several anticorruption clauses. Printed on the bloc's letterhead and titled "Declaration of Programmatic Agreements," the pledge required its signatories to govern "with pluralism, equality, transparency, and without corruption in accordance with the policies of the BEC." Another clause called for strictly merit-based appointments of public officials who would in any case be subject to the BEC's approval. The paras also reserved the right "to approve all projects coming [to the municipality] from departmental, national, or international entities." In 2003, at a small ceremony captured on video, the future mayor of Arboletes appears on camera signing the pledge.[28] As the video zooms in on his pen scribbling his signature on the page, Doña Tere's voice sounds off-camera loudly telling those in attendance, "Anyone who really has democracy in their blood doesn't even expect an *empanada* (beef pastry) in exchange for their vote." The paras' stance on clientelism and corruption was, to say the least, hypocritical.

After Urabá Grande stacked its anointed politicians into the mayors' offices and municipal councils of the region, some of them began steering funds to the BEC's various front-companies through contracts for local projects and services. The decentralization reforms of the 1991 Constitution had indirectly made subcontracting into an integral part of the devolution of government responsibilities and resources to municipalities. Local contracts for community development projects and public services, including health care and education, proved particularly enticing for the BEC.

The bloc secured minor contracts by creating a handful of NGOs that became the official on-the-ground operators (*operadores*) of the municipally funded projects. For larger contracts the BEC had a series of private companies, some of which existed only on paper. An investigator from the attorney general's office discovered that one of them, a health care firm founded by one of El Alemán's PDSs, helped the paras siphon off more than 40 percent of one municipality's public health budget. The same investigation found that the BEC's business outfits were involved in all kinds of public works projects from street lighting and water services to sewage treatment and (in the ultimate irony) the construction of a Park of Non-Violence.[29]

Corruption maintained a semiautonomous existence outside the BEC's carefully curated political control. The case of Unguía, a town in Chocó, shows how Urabá Grande could get derailed when it butted up against the interests of powerful landowners, demonstrating once again that relations between the paras and local elites were not without their tensions and contradictions. In 2003 Unguía's most powerful landowner, a rancher and business owner known respectfully as Don Dago, defied the BEC by bankrolling the mayoral campaign of his own candidate against the BEC's handpicked choice. Apparently Don Dago wanted a mayor beholden to him alone.

On the day of the election he shipped in more than one hundred voters from outside Unguía. Showing their forged credentials, the extra voters tipped the scales in favor of Don Dago's candidate. Once in office, the new mayor paid back his patron with hefty payments for goods and services rendered only on paper. Don Dago's business also became the sole supplier of construction materials, at enormously inflated prices, for the municipality's other private contractors.[30] Don Dago's local clout and his personal connections to the Casa Castaño meant El Alemán had to tolerate these indiscretions. In any case, Don Dago's minifief-dom was not obstructing the BEC most ambitious plan of all.

Urabá Grande's ultimate aspiration was to gain a presence in the national legislature. The most the coalition could hope for was winning a single seat in the lower house of Congress, but this was a particularly tricky political feat. To begin with, since Urabá Grande consisted of a coalition of politicians from differ-ent political parties, the process of choosing a single candidate for Congress was bound to stoke partisan divisions. In addition, the choice of a candidate hailing from one municipality of Urabá would inevitably alienate politicians from the other towns. The BEC had to triangulate between the mayors, councilors, and juntas of the region while also contending with the broader political party struc-tures at the departmental and national scales. After intense jockeying by all the stakeholders El Alemán struck a compromise.

Instead of a single candidate, he proposed four politicians who became known as *Los Cuatrillizos* (The Quadruplets). Each represented a different party and hailed from a different area of Urabá. Through a loophole in Colombian electoral law, the plan was for each candidate to serve one year of the single seat's four-year term. For the Quadruplets to win, however, they needed the sponsor-ship and national political weight of higher-profile politicians. With the help of a banana company executive El Alemán contacted Rubén Quintero, a machine politician, incumbent senator, and former chief of staff for President Uribe. After El Alemán made about US$100,000 in donations to Quintero's campaign, the senator agreed to support the Quadruplets. With the paras' financial and logisti-cal support Quintero ended up doubling the number of votes he had won in his previous senatorial campaign.

The Quadruplets, too, won easily. Although it took a few nudges from El Alemán to enforce the rotation, as planned, they each took turns serving a quar-ter of the four-year term. The Quadruplets were the BEC's only wholly owned members of Congress, but the bloc also played a role in the successful campaigns of a handful of other congressional representatives and three senators. All told, from 2002 to 2006 the BEC's clandestine congressional caucus sponsored or cosponsored several dozen pieces of legislation. Although most of these bills never made it out of committee, they give an indication of Urabá Grande's vision of state building and regional integration. The bills also show how, within the war of position, the BEC created a circular feedback loop between its community-scale organizing and its capture of national offices.

One bill cosponsored by the BEC's para-politicos, for instance, was aimed at making it easier for juntas and NGOs to win local government contracts. The goal of the law, wrote one of the Quadruplets, was to generate more "interdependence" between "the state and civil society."[31] In a similar vein a piece of legislation drafted by one of the BEC-supported senators sought to restructure "the relationship between the state and associative labor cooperatives."[32] The paras used agricultural cooperatives as a means of local institution building and as a vehicle for laundering the illicit origins of their landholdings. In both cases the laws indicate how the BEC used its congressional power to reinforce its community-scale political work. They also suggest how the paras understood state formation as a process of fomenting more frequent and substantive ties between government institutions and civil society organizations. Overall, the legislation supported by the BEC's politicians reveals how Urabá Grande and the war of position fit within the larger political economy of the paramilitary movement.

Most of the laws sponsored by the BEC's politicians that focused more narrowly on Urabá itself reflect a neoliberal and capital-intensive vision of regional integration. One bill would have given more power to Urabá's regional development corporation, Corpourabá, which oversees environmental licensing for infrastructure development, resource extraction, and agribusiness projects.[33] Another piece of legislation was about upgrading the Highway to the Sea and other economically critical transportation infrastructure, including ports.[34] A third bill would have enlarged Urabá's export-oriented, duty-free Special Economic Zone. The lawmakers introduced this last bill just as the BEC was beginning its demobilization talks with the Uribe administration, so they pitched the expansion of the free-trade zone as a way of settling the nation's "social debt with the frontier area of Urabá by helping the peace process."[35]

Ultimately, the Quadruplets never followed through on their proposed bills, and they were never signed into law. El Alemán was proud that Urabá Grande had gained national representation, but he was disappointed with the politicians themselves, especially with the Quadruplets. "All they did was shine for their absence," he lamented. One of them did, however, push through an act that awarded the Order of Democracy, Colombia's version of a Congressional Gold Medal, to Asocomún, the NGO run by El Alemán's brother, "in recognition of its work promoting community development in Urabá."[36] Although Urabá Grande did not live up to his expectations, El Alemán said that "the most important thing about it, as a political process, was that it proved the region's growing power."[37] The region, as he imagined it, was taking shape.

Colombians frequently describe their nation as a country of regions. This discourse imagines the nation's territory as a motley patchwork of discrete, precariously connected, often opposing spaces called regions, a fractiousness echoed by the subtitle of the most famous book on Colombian history: *A Nation in Spite of Itself*.[38] Through deeply essentialized conceptions of race, nature, and culture, the idea of a country of regions usually assumes a spatial hierarchy in which some regions, namely, the highlands around Bogotá and Medellín, are better than all the Others. Often the subtext of these narratives is that Colombia's violent history and the patchy presence of the state across its national territory are the inevitable by-products of its balkanized cultural and biophysical geography.

This hierarchy of regions has been an integral part of the violent exploitation and marginalization and thus the production of Colombia's frontier zones. They have been on the losing end of that spatial hierarchy. Urabá Grande demonstrates how the paras harnessed the bitter frontier histories of what are called the forgotten regions and molded them into a broadly appealing populist project of regional affirmation and state building. The paras call for the defense of the regions was strategic but it was also sincere; and it was one of the few genuine areas of common ground they had with subaltern campesinos who felt a relatable sense of regional abandonment by a corrupt and indifferent political class.

Urabá Grande harnessed this sentiment and converted it into an impressively well-oiled machine driven by an elaborate institutional structure, meticulous community organizing, and a sophisticated political pitch—it also had a brutally violent army behind it. Without disregarding the coercive foundations of paramilitary rule or discounting the coercion at the heart of their electoral scheming, my discussions here help explain why the paras' discourses and practices of delivering *las regiones* from the absence of the state had such popular resonance and appeal.[39] As part of the paras' broader war of position, Urabá Grande was a project aimed at setting the terms of regional integration and state formation. Its national importance may have been of little significance, but within the region Urabá Grande was a smashing success. The paras operationalized their state project by working across multiple scales: from the communities to the juntas; from the juntas to the municipalities; from the municipalities to the region; and, finally, from the region to the nation.

The paramilitary war of position was as dynamic and forward looking as it was contradictory and incoherent. Urabá Grande exemplifies what the political theorist Corey Robin has described in appropriately paradoxical terms as "democratic feudalism."[40] The paras' territorial control rested in the last instance on violent force, but they maintained it by using the trappings and, in many ways, the practices of liberal-democratic political participation. As the armed forces of political restoration, the right-wing paras never abandoned conservatism's core belief, which, according to Robin, is that "society is and must remain a hierarchy of personal rule."[41]

As the electoral wing of the paramilitaries' war of position, Urabá Grande institutionalized the power the paras had won on the battlefield by capturing and, in some ways, manufacturing the grassroots support of peasant communities. However, as I keep emphasizing, campesinos were not duped by a populist political charade. They leveraged their role in Urabá Grande, as best they could, toward retaining a degree of political agency and securing some material benefits from local governments. Within these political relationships campesinos were conscious, which is not to say wholeheartedly willing, participants in the paras' frontier state formations.

Urabá Grande was as much an instrument as it was a product of the complex, contradictory forces crosscutting paramilitary territories. Sometimes the paras found it necessary to discipline both communities and politicians if they stepped too far out of line ("Shut up, toothy!"). In other cases, as in the kickbacks on the municipal contract for the road construction project, the paras mediated between the opposing interests of stakeholders ("Please, *hermano*, take a bit less, don't take such a huge chunk of the community's money. . ."). At times powerful local elites simply thumbed their noses at the paras, as in the case of Don Dago's transgressions, which El Alemán was simply forced to overlook.

Urabá Grande, like the broader paramilitary movement itself, was never an omnipotent, all-encompassing force capable of coopting or neutralizing every last inkling of political agency. The paras' relationship to corruption, for instance, shows how they often found themselves reconciling their lofty political goals with the grubby real-world of local politics. Still, the paras' discourses about the absence of the state, anticorruption, and the defense of the regions went a long way toward the consolidation of Colombia's democratic feudalism. In the end, however, paramilitary populism never fully managed to resolve its central contradiction: how to reconcile violent plunder and the maintenance of elite power with broad-based political participation.

THE MASQUERADES OF GRASSROOTS DEVELOPMENT

What hegemony constructs, then, is not a shared ideology but a common material and meaningful framework for living through, talking about, and acting upon social orders characterized by domination. That common material and meaningful framework is, in part, discursive: a common language or way of talking about social relationships that sets out the central terms around which and in terms of which contestation and struggle can occur.

—William Roseberry, "Hegemony and the Language of Contention" (1994)

The long strip of beach called Playona in the municipality of Acandí, Chocó, is a famous nesting ground for the critically endangered leatherback sea turtle. Playona's six miles of pristine beachfront are postcard perfect. The only break in the verdant jungle and the picturesque canopy of coconut trees lining the full length of the beach is a cluster of palm-thatched roofs belonging to five small ecolodges. The rustic structures are part of a thriving ecotourism project that features the sea turtles as its main attraction. What visitors to the project probably do not know is that it began in the early 2000s with the help of a violent right-wing paramilitary group, the Bloque Elmer Cárdenas (BEC).

Playona had once been a recreational refuge for the FARC, and it has long served as an illicit entrepôt for the cocaine streaming out of the country and the black market weapons flowing back in. According to El Alemán, when his paramilitaries seized Playona in 1996 "it was totally abandoned by the state, and combat with the guerrillas was so intense that a lot of residents fled the area."[1] Locals lost everything during the paramilitary takeover. "We had to leave the lands just lying there. We had to abandon our farms," said a campesina from the area. "I grabbed my eight kids and a few things and left. . . . I thank god I left because [the paras] massacred my neighbors and my friends."[2]

Several years later, once the paramilitaries' demobilization was clearly on the horizon, the BEC's troops began concocting the ecotourism project as a source of income and employment for their expected transition into civilian life. El Alemán said he organized the project, which included a few local families who had been displaced by the fighting in the 1990s, into a cooperative as a way of "helping mend the community's social fabric." He dispatched the bloc's Promoters of Social Development (PDSs) to "work with the local campesinos, teaching them not to eat the turtle eggs or bother *los animalitos* [the hatchlings]."[3] This from one of Colombia's most notorious mass murderers.

El Alemán denied he profited from the ecotourism venture, but he admitted it had grown out of one of the BEC's flagship demobilization initiatives called Guardagolfos (Guardians of the Gulf). Guardagolfos was a collection of fishing, ecotourism, and handicraft cooperatives that provided livelihoods for demobilized rank-and-file paramilitaries. Guardagolfos became a darling of both the UN Office on Drugs and Crime and national development agencies, both of which showered praise and awards on the project. They even tried replicating it in other coastal areas, making Guardagolfos one of several grassroots development projects pioneered by the BEC that became integrated into the official programming of these agencies.

The turtle ecotourism project in Playona was not the only paramilitary-linked enterprise in Urabá drawing on similar discourses of grassroots development. The paras also pitched some projects as being tailor-made for "ethnic communities." But how could anything tied to this violent paramilitary group be associated with grassroots development ideals of local participation, environmental sustainability, and ethnic empowerment? Paramilitaries' use of grassroots development went beyond simply whitewashing their plunder with fashionable, politically correct development-speak. The discourses, institutions, and practices of grassroots development formed an integral part of the paras' extralegal political economy. In the context of the frontier effect, grassroots development made their economies of violence surprisingly compatible with formal projects of liberal state building, by which I mean government programs aimed at promoting institution building, political participation, good governance, and the rule of law.

The paramilitaries turned grassroots development into a vehicle both for executing their massive land grabs and for promoting, in their words, the "arrival of the state." As a strategic assemblage of discourses, practices, and institutional formations, the grassroots development apparatus did more than simply give the paras' economic ventures a veneer of symbolic legitimacy; it also enabled and worked in conjunction with the concrete practices of paramilitary rule. Grassroots development was thus both a means of state building and a way of laundering their violently and illegally accumulated landholdings.

The synergies between illegality, capital accumulation, violence, and state formation are not unique to Colombia. Scholars have exposed similar dynamics in various other parts of the world, from the former socialist bloc to sub-Saharan Africa and beyond.[4] This literature has conclusively shown that illegality and violence are not aberrations but constitutive parts of actually existing democracies and free-market economies the world over. In Urabá grassroots development helped the paras reconcile their violent, extralegal political–economic project with government-led initiatives aimed at the consolidation of state rule. Discourses of political participation and subsidiarity, environmental conservation, ethnic rights, and women's empowerment were the foundational elements for the way paramilitaries put the grassroots development apparatus to work.

Discourses are not just words. They are the socially produced and historically situated representations we use to make sense of the world. The French theorist Michel Foucault argued that the power of discourses stems from their ability to identify problems in specific ways, enabling some understandings and courses of action while limiting others. For instance, Foucault tracked the way discourses around crime and criminality in eighteenth-century France emerged from the identification of problems caused by demographic growth, the hardening of private property relations, and intensifying capitalist accumulation.[5] The outgrowth of this "problematization" of crime and delinquency was a mushrooming strategic ensemble—an apparatus (*dispositif*), as he called it—of punishment. An apparatus is a strategic assemblage made up of disparate discourses, policies, institutions, practices, tactics, and forms of knowledge that emerge around a particular problem.

Applying Foucault's ideas, scholars have analyzed and critiqued development as an apparatus that emerged after the Second World War around efforts to solve the problems of Third World underdevelopment and poverty.[6] Here, "grassroots development" refers to the apparatus that arose as a bottom-up alternative to the problems and perceived failures of the top-down development initiatives sponsored by national governments and international organizations.[7] The grassroots development apparatus gained definitive form in the wake of the neoliberal, one-size-fits-all structural adjustment programs that were met with so much popular resistance in much of the world in the eighties and nineties.

A World Bank report from 1989, for instance, argued that the failures of top-down development and neoliberal adjustment called for a fundamental course correction. "Alternative paths have been proposed," the report reads. "They give primacy to agricultural development, and emphasize not only prices, markets and private sector activities, but also capacity building, grassroots participation, decentralization and sound environmental practices. So far, such ideas have been accepted and tried only halfheartedly, if at all. The time has come to put them fully into practice."[8] Although grassroots development gained clear, identifiable form during these years, it grew out of a much older lineage that can be traced back to the problematizations of development during previous historical junctures. The genealogy of grassroots development is a global story, but it can be told from the standpoint of Urabá, beginning with the United Fruit Company in the 1960s.

Birth of the Grassroots Development Apparatus

The 1950s and 1960s were the golden age of the developmentalist state, import-substitution industrialization, and the Green Revolution throughout the Third World. In Latin America the 1960s were also the years of the Kennedy administration's anticommunist Alliance for Progress (AFP). The modernization theorists at the helm of the program wanted to make Colombia into a showcase for the AFP. They hoped the country would "demonstrate to all of Latin America that a resolute, competent, reform-minded government with vigorous U.S. assistance can fulfill the hopes of the Alliance for Progress within a reasonably brief period."[9]

In preparation for the AFP's promised assistance, the governor of Antioquia sent an engineering mission to Urabá in 1962. José María Isaza, the head of the mission and the governor's main liaison with the AFP, reported back: "Antioquia has in Urabá an exceptional area thanks to its geographic position, excellent soils, hydrographic richness, hot and tropical climate. It's well suited for large-scale, export-oriented cultivation, which would be a source of foreign exchange."[10] But first, argued Isaza, the region needed a regional development corporation in the mold of the U.S. Tennessee Valley Authority. It would get such a corporation six years later with the creation of the Corporation for the Development of Urabá, or Corpourabá, in 1968. In fact, the introduction of regional development corporations throughout Colombia was one of the AFP's most enduring legacies. Isaza claimed, "Such an entity would be indispensable for channeling all funds from the Alliance for Progress that will bring the region out of its underdevelopment." Medellín's main newspaper published Isaza's entire report as a two-page spread with the headline "Urabá: A Promised Land."

The modernization needed to bring Colombia out of its underdevelopment required diversifying its export portfolio. In 1964 the *New York Times* reported on a promising "banana program" under way in the far northwest corner of the country. "Taking considerable stride away from Colombia's one-crop export economy—coffee—Colombians foresee success for a banana development project in Turbo [Urabá]," read the article. "As a private-enterprise program within the Alliance for Progress, the venture is expected to increase Colombia's banana exports. . . . The Project is considered a shot in the arm for the whole backward region."[11] It was through such assistance that the AFP was supposed to turn the "backward" regions of the country into launchpads for the Colombian economy's takeoff, the term for the self-perpetuating cycle of growth at the center of modernization theory's elusive endgame.

Walt W. Rostow, the godfather of modernization theory, had hoped the AFP, as part of Washington's broader Cold War counterinsurgency strategy, would help keep the underdeveloped areas of Latin America "off our necks as we try to clean up the spots of bad trouble."[12] In Urabá, however, as in many other agrarian locales around the world, the large-scale rural projects implemented in the name of modernization via initiatives like the AFP and the Green Revolution were fodder for rebellion given that they devastated poor farmers. Indeed, the capitalist transformation of already impoverished countrysides created a host of new hardships that problematized development in new ways.

The development industry's focus began shifting away from the problematic grand schemes of the developmentalist state and toward more socially oriented and smaller-scale approaches based on peasants' basic needs. Through the lens of Cold War counterinsurgency, the discontent of Third World peasantries was obviously still a major concern for development institutions, so attending to campesinos' basic needs was both a political and an economic necessity. In the 1970s more holistic programs of "integrated rural development" emerged and became all the rage in Africa, Asia, and Latin America.[13] In contrast to the past these new integrated approaches sought to alleviate rural poverty by promoting small-scale production, peasant cooperatives, credit programs, and local political empowerment. Colombia was the first country to implement an integrated rural development program on a nationwide scale.[14]

As a hotbed of radical agrarian politics, Urabá became a major site for these projects, especially once the banana boom started to wane in the late 1970s. One plan drafted by the Organization of American States, the Darién Project, became the basis for a series of integrated rural development initiatives led by an infusion of Dutch aid and technical assistance. Working in tandem with the new TVA-style Corpourabá, Dutch aid workers helped produce an alphabet soup of regional development initiatives in the seventies and eighties: Integrated Agrarian Assistance Program (PAAI), Integrated Rural Agricultural Development Program (DIAR), Campesino Economy Project (PEC), and the Urabá Rural Development Program (DRU). Corpourabá explained that the purpose of these projects was to distribute more widely "the benefits of the State at all levels, helping campesinos' social cohesion and bolstering their organizations so they are better able to cope with the various needs of their daily lives."[15] Focused on local institution building, peasant cooperatives, community cohesion, and local political participation, these programs were the direct predecessors of grassroots development in Urabá.

Grassroots development began gaining worldwide traction when a slew of international summits, reports, and treaties began articulating development through new discursive registers. The UN Conference on the Human Environment in 1972, the Brundtland Report on "sustainable development" in 1987, and the UN Conference on Environment and Development (the Rio Earth Summit) in 1992, among others, all helped frame a redemptive vision of development as both local and green. A growing global consensus was calling for development to become more "environmentally sustainable" and more "empowering" of local communities, who were encouraged to take "ownership."[16]

Cultural and ethnic rights were also integral parts of the new grassroots ethos, particularly when coupled, as they usually were, with concerns about biodiversity conservation.[17] Signatories to the 1992 Convention on Biological Diversity, for instance, agreed to preserve "knowledge, innovations, and practices of indigenous and local communities . . . relevant for the conservation and sustainable use of biological diversity." The new model recast ethnic, minority, and local communities, once seen as the primary "victims of progress," as romanticized stewards of nature and kinds of knowledge that could now be harnessed rather than bulldozed by the development apparatus.[18] The International Labor Organization's Indigenous and Tribal Peoples Convention (No. 169), ratified by most signatories in the 1990s, brought local development, environmental conservation, and ethnic rights into closer association. Women, too, were now not just targets of development policy but privileged conduits through which many development goals were to be achieved.[19]

A global army of NGOs positioned within vague notions of civil society emerged in conjunction with this expanded conception of stakeholders. The increased role of NGOs in managing development projects was reinforced by critiques across the political spectrum that railed against the heavy-handed, top-down, overly centralized dealings of the clunky developmentalist state. NGOs were supposedly closer to communities and thus more aware of their true needs and desires. Moreover, since neoliberal structural adjustment programs had wiped out the state's delivery of basic and affordable public services, NGOs picked up the slack, becoming crucial agents of development's new-and-improved, decentralized, grassroots vision.

This is not to say that grassroots development was some kind of preconceived secret plan hatched in a smoke-filled room by conniving global elites. Social movements of all kinds, from radical to reformist, were determinant forces in problematizing development in ways that propelled these shifts. It was largely thanks to the critiques and struggles of these new social movements and their transnational alliances that grassroots development discourses gained traction in the first place. The twists and turns of the development apparatus were also linked to structural changes in the evolution of global capitalism, from the exhaustion of import-substitution models and the debt crisis to the neoliberal turn.[20] In short, grassroots development was the product of a converging set of historical events, problematizations, and processes.

By the 1990s the grassroots development apparatus crystallized around four key discursive practices: political subsidiarity, environmental sustainability, women's empowerment, and ethnic rights. In other words, grassroots development was supposed to be, respectively, local, green, gendered, and multicultural.[21] Environmental concern is a revealing proxy for gauging the broader grassroots turn. In just ten years, from 1985 to 1995, the number of environmental specialists on staff at the World Bank went from 5 to 162, while the bank's loan portfolio for "environmental management" ballooned from $15 million to $990 million.[22] The nonprofit sector also reflected this trend: in Colombia, for example, the number of environmental NGOs skyrocketed from just twenty-six in 1990 to more than four hundred just four years later.[23] In 1993, Corpourabá added "sustainable" to its name, becoming the Corporation for the Sustainable Development of Urabá. The convergence of NGOs, experts, community groups, activists, government officials, and aid workers under the banner of grassroots development has produced dramatically contradictory results.

Scholarship in Colombia has been well aware of these contradictions. Some researchers have highlighted the ways in which the use and abuse of these discourses have helped reconstitute state authority and capitalist development through destructive land grabs by paramilitaries.[24] Other scholars contend that social movements have strategically used grassroots development as a stepping-stone to more radical, even emancipatory political ends.[25] Certainly grassroots development has cut both ways in Colombia: it has served both the interests of historically marginalized groups and the strategies of state-backed paramilitaries. The fact that such disparate groups have mobilized ideas about development as local, green, gendered, and multicultural indicates the extent to which these discourses have become powerful. They also signal precisely what have become the most politically contentious issues around which struggles over development have occurred, namely, race, gender, local politics, and the environment. From this perspective, it makes sense that paramilitaries would put grassroots development to work for constructing their frontier state formations and laundering their ill-gotten lands.

Oil Palms Make the State Arrive

Paramilitaries did more than simply describe their agribusiness projects as local, green, gendered, and multicultural. The discourses at once accompanied and made possible a set of concrete practices and institutional formations through which they executed and ratified their land grab. In the case of the paras, grassroots development brought together stolen lands, drug money, peasant associations and cooperatives, NGOs, private companies as well as national and international aid programs into a strategic ensemble (an apparatus).[26] The Curvaradó oil palm project is one of Colombia's most infamous cases of paramilitary-led dispossession; it clearly demonstrates the elaborate way the paras embraced grassroots development.

The mostly Afro-Colombian campesinos of the Curvaradó River basin, along with those of a neighboring basin, fled their family farms in 1997 when a joint operation by the army and the paras tore through the area.[27] In interviews, several survivors described that when the violence began, the paras came to their farms with the same chilling offer: "Sell us your land, or we'll negotiate with your widow." The campesinos took refuge in nearby towns, too afraid to even visit their farms. When some ventured back to have a look at their lands five years later, in 2002, they found a devastating sight. "All the work of my youth was gone," said an elderly campesino, recalling the day he first glimpsed his razed farm.[28] Reciting an inventory he had apparently repeated often, he added, "One hundred ten head of cattle, nine horses, my wife had tons of chickens, pigs . . . all of it gone." Tidy, seemingly endless rows of oil palm saplings had replaced the haphazard patchwork of fields, pastures, and forest that had previously shaped his farm.

A company called Urapalma had posted signs on the land with big block letters: Private Property. One of about a dozen other agribusiness firms, Urapalma led the development of Curvaradó's oil palm complex, which was slated to encompass some twenty-two thousand hectares of land. Although Urapalma and its allies planted only a fraction of their goal, they ultimately claimed ownership of more than thirty-five thousand hectares of land. The appropriated land was within the boundaries of a one-hundred-thousand-hectare collective property title that local Afro-Colombian communities had won under the ethnic rights provisions of the 1991 Constitution. The Constitution recognized rural Afro-Colombian communities as an "ethnic group," awarding them the same rights to collective territories once reserved for indigenous peoples. The inalienable collective titles for Afro-Colombians was another reason local elites had balked at the new Constitution; the titles effectively protected huge parts of Chocó from agribusiness development.[29] Yet the paras found ingenious ways around the supposedly inalienable nature of the collective title.

In an interview with a national news magazine in 2005 Vicente Castaño boastfully admitted, "In Urabá we [paramilitaries] have palm cultivations. I personally found the businessmen that invested in those projects." He described the project as a form of state building, a way of making the state, in his word, arrive. He said, "The idea is to take rich people to invest in those kinds of projects in different parts of the country. By taking the rich to these zones the institutions of the state also arrive. Unfortunately, the institutions of the state only support those things when the rich are there. So you have to take the rich to all those regions of the country, and that's a mission shared by all the [paramilitary] commanders."[30]

By 2000, when Urapalma launched the project, oil palm had become the darling crop of national government agencies, which gave generous tax breaks and subsidies to the industry. The agribusiness lobby had been banking on oil palm as a way of diversifying the country's agricultural portfolio.[31] Palm oil is not only used in countless consumer products—from packaged food to cosmetics—it is also an important source of animal feed and is increasingly used as a source of biofuel. As petroleum and food prices reached record highs in the late 2000s, global oil palm production boomed. In Colombia President Uribe was one of the oil palm sector's fiercest advocates. During his two terms in office (2002–10) the area of land in Colombia planted with oil palms more than doubled, turning the country into the world's fifth-largest producer of palm oil.[32] During these years the industry also gained a well-deserved reputation for conspiring with paramilitaries. The case of Curvaradó was the most egregious.[33] In addition to simply forcing people to leave or coercing them into selling at giveaway prices, the Castaños devised an intricate process for stealing land. The most notorious case involved Lino Antonio Díaz, a long-time campesino resident of Curvaradó who had an individual title to his land. The government had awarded Díaz his individual title for eighteen hectares of unclaimed land (*tierras baldías*) in 1990. The collective titles given to Afro-Colombian communities in subsequent years did not nullify these preexisting private properties, so some campesinos like Díaz retained their individual titles within the new territories.

On May 27, 2000, ten years after securing his title, Díaz supposedly filed paperwork at a public notary office increasing his property of 18 hectares to almost 6,000 hectares. This gigantic property gain, according to the documents, was owing to alluvial "natural accession," meaning supposedly that an adjacent river had changed course and thus enlarged his property by the improbable sum of 5,982 hectares.[34] On the very same day Díaz turned around and sold the newly enlarged property for a nominal price to a group calling itself the Association of Small-Scale Oil Palm Growers of Urabá. The problem is that Díaz had been dead since 1995, five years before the transactions, which contained his signature and fingerprint, took place.

The Association of Small-Scale Oil Palm Growers of Urabá was a paramilitary front. Land registration documents show that the association's director, an active member of the Casa Castaño, immediately divided Díaz's now-hefty six-thousand-hectare lot into four separate plots. Parceling out a property helps launder the land because each new parcel gets a new registry number (*matrícula inmobili-aria*), thereby wiping clean the detailed chain of transactions and ownership recorded in a property's registry documents.[35] The four parcels themselves were subdivided, and some plots a third time, further scrambling the paper trail. In

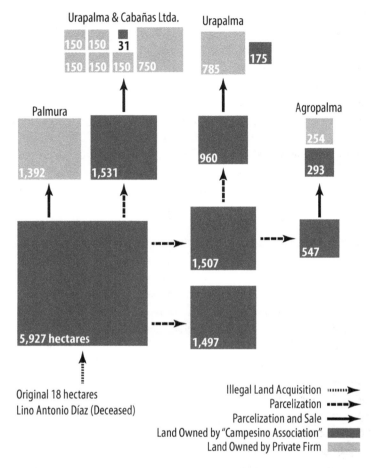

FIGURE 15. How the paramilitaries laundered a dead man's land.

(Credit: Author)

the end, through subdivisions and sales the association transferred more than 90 percent of the six-thousand-hectare spread to the private palm companies, including Urapalma.

The farm of another dead campesino, Sixto Pérez, met a similar fate. In this case, the dead man's land ballooned from thirty-three hectares to about forty-two hundred, again, thanks to the natural movements of a river and the same legal loophole as before. Since the Constitution protects Afro-Colombians' collective titles as indivisible and inalienable, the enlargement of a previously existing private title was the only way of legally encroaching on the communal lands. In this case, the buyers of the dead man's forty-two hundred hectares were two oil palm associations of self-proclaimed small-scale producers. After parceling out the property, these small-scale producers sold off most of the land to the private companies.

By far the most active alleged peasant organization involved in these shady land deals was the Association of Agricultural Producers of Belén de Bajirá (Aso-probeba). For several years the director of Asoprobeba was none other than Sor Teresa Gómez, Doña Tere, the unofficial treasurer of the Casa Castaño. One of her purchases was for eleven hundred hectares that local communities claimed a midlevel drug trafficker had stolen from them years before. After subdividing the property to again muddle the paper trail, Doña Tere ceded six-hectare plots to her organization's "affiliated members" through contracts that gave campesi-nos indefinite use-rights (usufruct) over their plots while Asoprobeba retained legal ownership of the lands.[36] The paras used the land leases managed by NGOs like Asoprobeba as a way of repopulating a portion of the stolen lands with beholden groups of client-campesinos. The association recruited its members from neighboring villages and from groups of peasants displaced from other parts of Urabá.[37] Ultimately, Doña Tere's NGO settled some six hundred families on the usurped lands. During my fieldwork, conducted a full decade after their initial arrival in 2003, Asoprobeba's campesinos were still there.[38]

The paras' frequent reliance on NGOs as their favored institutional façade served both ideological and practical purposes. On the ideological front, their use of NGOs coopted the primary institutional form of their harshest critics, the human rights community. It was also easy to present the NGOs as disinter-ested do-gooders fostering empowerment and participation. On a practical level, compared to corporations, NGOs in Colombia face much more lax rules about transparency and the information they must report to authorities, making them ideal instruments for the paras' illicit activities. Besides serving as a legal–insti-tutional structure for repopulating and controlling the stolen lands, the NGOs, as small-scale, local producer associations, helped the agribusiness ventures gain access to soft loans and grants through what the government, the private sector, and aid agencies call strategic alliances.[39] Strategic alliances are a form of corpo-rate–peasant contract farming subsidized through government-backed grants, loans, tax breaks, and foreign aid. Urapalma, for instance, secured US$2.1 million from the government's agrarian bank for what the loan's award letter described as the company's "system of associative strategic alliances."[40] The strategic alliance system involves a three-way deal between private agribusiness firms, campesino communities, and development agencies. The companies offer seed capital and infrastructure in exchange for exclusive purchase rights over future harvests, while the campesinos, usually organized into cooperatives, provide land and labor. Meanwhile, national and international development institutions, among them the U.S. Agency for International Development (USAID) and the UN, help subsidize the projects with grants and technical assistance.

Globally, USAID and the World Bank had been aggressively pushing this form of corporate–peasant contract farming for decades. The World Bank made these "dynamic partnerships" an integral part of its revamped agenda of "putting peasants first" and "targeting the rural poor."[41] In Colombia the strategic alliances gained particular force and proliferated in the 2000s thanks to the state-building initiatives backed by Plan Colombia, Washington's antidrug and counterinsurgency package. Originally named the Plan for Peace, Prosperity, and the Strengthening of the State, Plan Colombia, especially the nonmilitary side of its assistance, was all about state building.

Under Plan Colombia the strategic alliances were supposed to help wean farmers off of growing drug-related crops, but they were also seen as the cornerstone of what the aid program's original white paper described as a process of consolidating state power through "community and institution building."[42] The plan envisioned the strategic alliances as "sustainable, integrated, and participatory productive projects" that would especially target regions that combined "high levels of conflict with low levels of State presence, fragile social capital, and serious environmental degradation." As environmentally friendly, participatory projects and with community and institution building as additional goals, the alliances brought communities, NGOs, private companies, government agencies, and foreign aid into a strategically coordinated ensemble. Over Plan Colombia's life span (2000–2015) Washington supported strategic alliances all over the country by funneling almost US$1 billion toward USAID's "alternative development" portfolio.

One of the companies that applied for USAID's alternative development grants was Urapalma. In 2003 the paramilitary-backed company drafted a six-page grant proposal titled "The Afro-Colombian Oil Palm Cultivation and Development Project."[43] The proposal made it to the final stages of USAID's application process. Although Urapalma was on track to receive US$700,000 in grants and technical assistance, it left its application pending. (Paramilitary-linked oil palm companies in other parts of the country did receive USAID money.)[44] Still, Urapalma's six-page application reveals telling details about how the company deployed the grassroots development apparatus as a way of both legitimating and operationalizing its land grab.

The overall framework of the application described the proposed project as a "united effort by a group of farmers beginning in 1999"—somehow, at the height of the paramilitary terror and dispossession—"with the long-term goal of implementing a viable, environmentally, and economically sustainable business in the region of Urabá." The proposal continued, "[The] timing is ideal for establishing a sustainable social program. . . . It could become an exemplary model of development between business owners and communities sharing all decisions and responsibilities while working side by side." The application emphasized the absolute subsidiarity of the project by repeatedly referring to its beneficiaries as "small-scale producers" and "families." Amid deep-seated assumptions about women's role in the division of household labor and social reproduction, the gender-coded reference to families was a way of ticking off three boxes at once: it framed the project as small-scale, participatory, and gender-sensitive.

One of the many handwritten edits on the application, made by an unidentified company employee, recommended shoring up the project's green credentials. Next to a list of rationales behind the project the editor added an extra bullet point of justification: "Environmental: Reforestation in areas degraded due to lack of economic alternatives." Playing into USAID's counterinsurgency and antidrug mission under Plan Colombia, the application further noted, "This zone is susceptible to all kinds of influence by the illegal armed groups, who see in the region a corridor for trafficking drugs and arms, given the area's waterways and dense vegetation." In closing, the proposal stated the company would give "juridical form" to this "strategic alliance" by "working collectively hand in hand with the community." The ultimate goal, it concluded, was "to produce a glimpse of what we all long for: A peaceful and developed Colombia."

The paras' use of these grassroots discourses could easily be dismissed as just a rhetorical move or window dressing. But the discourses presupposed and enabled a whole set of concrete practices (the parceling out, laundering, and repopulation of the lands) along with a host of institutional relationships that included the NGOs, cooperatives, peasant associations, the companies, along with national and international development agencies. Urapalma's activities demonstrate it was precisely the local and participatory grassroots structure of the strategic alliances that made them such appealing and effective vehicles for seizing and laundering the lands.

Indeed, the strategic alliance structure afforded the paramilitaries a ready-made grassroots infrastructure that perfectly suited their needs. All Doña Tere, Vicente Castaño, and their agribusiness associates had to do was plug their own components into the model. While situating the oil palm project within some of development's most contentious terrain—the local, the environment, race, and gender—they turned the grassroots development apparatus into their very own antipolitics machine.[45] Although this elaborate use of grassroots development was first introduced into Urabá by the Castaños, El Alemán and his BEC took it to a whole new level.

Forests Make the State Arrive

Shortly into his first term President Uribe released an elaborate four-year plan for his administration. Titled "Towards a Communitarian State," the three-hundred-page manifesto laid out a path designed to make the state more participatory, austere, managerial, responsible, transparent, efficient, and decentralized—the first paragraph of the text contains all of these words. Besides making assurances about "recovering state authority," the document promised that the implementation of the plan would help Colombians "recover the feeling of the State's presence in *las regiones*."[46]

Uribe's manifesto for a "communitarian state" bears chilling resemblances to the book by the paramilitary ideologue Ernesto Báez about "achieving peace through the construction of regions." In fact, the written sentence of the court that convicted Báez pointed out these similarities, noting quite diplomatically that Uribe's manifesto "contains some concepts and narratives that share a certain likeness" to those in Báez's book.[47] The judge then devoted four pages of the sentence to illustrate the word-for-word similarities with side-by-side comparisons of the two texts. Indeed, the regionalist politics of paramilitary populism squared perfectly with Uribe's carefully crafted political persona as a hardworking *paisa* and a man of the people. Despite being born and raised in Medellín, his family's extensive rural landholdings in Antioquia and Córdoba allowed him to present himself as a straight-talking "man of the regions" with a soft spot for the countryside. Uribe's style of populism, a mix of authoritarian militarism and paternalistic pastoralism, was perfectly summed up in his campaign slogan: *Mano firme, corazón grande*, meaning an iron fist against the FARC but a big heart for the common folk, especially those in the regions.

Uribe put USAID's alternative development programs at the center of his plans for stirring up the "feeling of the State's presence in *las regiones*." His manifesto explained, "Our Development strategy in conflict zones draws on elements from Plan Colombia . . . but incorporates a novel aspect by articulating the concept of alternative development with an emphasis on regional development based on increased productivity and the strengthening of institutions and communities as well as the improvement of physical and social infrastructures."[48] Alternative development was thus conceived as an elaborate, multiscalar process of state formation and "regional development" that would not only foster "physical and social infrastructures" but also link nationally directed state policies and programs with newly formed local- and community-scale organizations in las regiones.

One concrete policy proposal for accomplishing this elaborate model of state building was an "illicit crop-substitution program through forestry development projects and environmental services supported by conditional [cash] subsidies."[49] The idea evolved into the still-active Programa Familias Guardabosques (the Family Forest Rangers Program). Guardabosques, as it is known for short, is a conditional cash-transfer initiative that tries to turn farmers away from growing drug-related crops. During the Uribe administration the program was run by the now-defunct social welfare agency called Acción Social (Social Action) with assistance and money from the UN's Office on Drugs and Crime (UNODC).

Campesinos joined Guardabosques by signing contracts with Acción Social in which they promised to keep their lands free of illicit crops while promoting the "reforestation and conservation of strategic ecosystems."[50] In exchange for protecting forests and forswearing coca cultivation, affiliated families received a cash award of about US$350 every two months for a period of up to three years. In 2003 Uribe's high commissioner for Plan Colombia, Sandra Suárez, began advertising the new Guardabosques program. As soon as El Alemán heard about the call for participants, he scheduled a meeting with all the presidents from the Juntas de Acción Comunal in Tulapas and a few neighboring areas. At the meeting, he announced, "I'm going to send you all to go see this lady in Bogotá," offering to pay their airfare. "Tell her you paid for the flights by selling pigs or something but make it clear that the communities want to eradicate all the coca."[51] In interviews with me, community leaders corroborated El Alemán's story, acknowledging he had paid for their trip and had encouraged them to join the program.[52]

El Alemán has always insisted that his bloc's only involvement in the drug trade was "taxing" traffickers' shipments as they moved through his territories, but his U.S.-based indictments suggest much deeper involvement. When I asked him why he backed Guardabosques, he claimed he had always tried to turn campesinos away from growing coca. However, since 2003 was also the year paramilitaries began their demobilization talks with the government, I suspect it was secondarily (if not primarily) a smart way of trying to establish his antidrug credentials in the hope of warding off his possible extradition to the United States on drug-trafficking charges. Yet it is also true, as I've noted earlier, that the paras' ability to broker these kinds of projects was a key aspect of their power and territorial hegemony.

The campesinos' meeting with Suárez in Bogotá was brokered by one of the senators El Alemán helped elect through Urabá Grande.[53] To keep tabs on the campesinos El Alemán also sent Cocinero, his most trusted PDS, who at the meeting posed as just another community leader from Tulapas. To further bolster their grassroots legitimacy the campesinos portrayed themselves as part of the Asociación Comunitaria de Urabá y Córdoba (Asocomún), the NGO founded by El Alemán's brother that styled itself an association of allied juntas. Cocinero said it took them only fifteen minutes to convince Suárez to make Tulapas a pilot project for the new Guardabosques program.[54] A few months later she traveled to the town of Necoclí, near Tulapas, where she was greeted by a throng of campesinos hoisting uprooted coca bushes into the air. Over the course of 2004 more than thirty-two hundred families in Tulapas and the immediate surroundings joined the Guardabosques program, uprooting around one thousand hectares of coca: coca EPL guerrillas had left behind many years earlier. Cocinero said that on some days the communities' coca eradication brigades were short staffed, so some of the BEC's soldiers lent a hand in pulling up the crops. Although Acción Social and UNODC oversaw the Guardabosques program, they contracted Asocomún and Urabá's regional development corporation, Corpourabá, as the on-site operators of the project. Since Asocomún was publicly registered as an association of juntas "promoting communities' integral and sustainable development," it was an ideal partner for Guardabosques's objectives as a local, green, and participatory form of alternative development. In a video of coca eradication shot by Asocomún and sponsored by Guardabosques the campesinos pulling up the plants can be heard yelling, "We got a project! The project arrived! [¡Llegó el proyecto!] We're done with coca in Urabá!"

The arrival of the project marked the long-sought-after "feeling of the state's presence" in Tulapas. This notion of arrival came up repeatedly in my conversations with people in Urabá, whether with ex-combatants, campesinos, politicians, or landowners. They often referred to the state by using various conjugations of the Spanish verb *llegar* (to arrive), which can also mean "to reach." In other words, the use of this verb had both temporal and spatial connotations. On countless occasions I heard people say some variant of "aún no ha llegado el estado" (the state hasn't yet arrived/reached here). In addition to bemoaning a historical and geographical absence, a place abandoned in both time and space, the phrase expresses an expectant spatio-temporal inevitability: the arrival of the state *here* is only a matter of *time*.

As one campesino described it, the feeling of the state's presence came only after the paras and Asocomún had helped bring the project: "Asocomún has been really good to us . . . because the state hadn't wanted to help us and in fact hadn't even arrived yet, so Asocomún arrived instead." One campesina even credited El Alemán with making Guardabosques not just a reality but also a success. "El Alemán would come around from time to time, especially during the Guardabosques program. Once Guardabosques began, he kept much closer tabs on us and brought us lots of projects," she said. "In the beginning the only beneficiaries were going to be the people growing coca. Or, you know, you would get included only if you were friends with so-and-so in the junta. But, no, he made sure everyone got the subsidies so there wouldn't be any jealousy between us."[55]

President Uribe consummated the symbolic and material arrival of the state with a personal visit to Tulapas in 2004. In an artful combination of stagecraft and statecraft he looked like a character out of a García Márquez novel: dressed all in white linen and sporting a long-sleeve guayabera and a folksy straw hat called a *sombrero vueltiao*—all iconic vestments of the Caribbean coast.[56] Standing on a stage in front of thousands of campesinos, Uribe handed out the symbolic first check of the Guardabosques program in Tulapas. In his speech Uribe described it as money well spent, saying he much preferred that "the bit of money the state has" (*la platica del estado*) end up in the hands of regular families rather than "being wasted on state bureaucracies."[57] He invited the Guardabosques families to help him "defeat terrorism, corruption, and laziness."

In practice, with Asocomún publicly at the helm of the project and El Alemán's PDSs in the shadows, the juntas became the core institutional hubs for Guardabosques. Every junta organized a Community Control and Social Verification Committee. The job of each junta's committee was to verify that the jurisdiction of a neighboring Junta was staying free of coca. That way, as one campesina, using a local aphorism, explained to me, "The verification would be more impartial because you weren't dealing with the chicken in your own yard."[58] Every two months agents from the local UNODC branch would make their own verification visits. Although some campesinos complained that Asocomún took a 10 percent cut from their Guardabosques bimonthly checks, most described the project as a godsend. In one village a barrio of homes built with money from the program still bears the name El Bosque in honor of the program.

In relation to the key discourses of the grassroots development apparatus—local, green, gendered, and multicultural—Guardabosques was an unequivocal success story, at least according to the joint reports filed by Acción Social and UNODC. They lauded the program for creating a nationwide symbiosis between antidrug efforts and environmental conservation. According to their reports, Guardabosques, besides keeping four million hectares of land free of coca, had helped conserve more than 270,000 hectares of primary forests, reforested another 53,000, and created "green incomes and jobs in socially and environmentally strategic areas."[59] On the multicultural front, indigenous and Afro-Colombian families eventually made up nearly a quarter of Guardabosques's beneficiaries. The gendered dimensions of the program were especially pronounced. A year into the program Acción Social began "privileging women as the signatories of the contracts, as a way of guaranteeing better use of the [cash] incentive."[60] Eventually, women made up as much as two-thirds of the program's participants.

Uribe had actually floated the idea of feminizing the program during his speech at the launch of the project in Tulapas. He advised the campesinos in the crowd to let "the women of the house handle this bit of money [*la platica*] so it doesn't end up going toward beer and liquor." Even more than the oil palm plantations of Curvaradó, Guardabosques rested on deeply gendered and patriarchal conceptions of family. Guardabosques positioned women as instruments for achieving its broader goals of state building, good governance, and the rule of law. Feminist scholars have argued that these kinds of initiatives are part of a broader turn in which aid organizations have increasingly channeled their assistance "through families as the unit of entitlement with women often required to conform to dominant stereotypes of 'good' wives and mothers."[61] Guardabosques enlisted women in the U.S.-backed war on drugs while at the same time citing them as a vulnerable population and using them to signal the absolute subsidiarity of the program through a focus on the scale of household. Official documents from the program almost always cast women as the responsible, child-rearing, money-saving, micro-enterprising drivers of what these reports obsessively referred to as a "culture of legality."

Ironically, despite taking credit for this blossoming culture of legality Guardabosques was serving a confluence of interests that mostly benefited drug-trafficking paramilitaries. As an internationally backed development program Guardabosques added another layer of legitimacy to the paras' stolen landholdings in Tulapas. By bringing the project, the BEC shored up its territorial hegemony among the area's campesinos, who, in turn, enjoyed the program's cash rewards. And in El Alemán's eyes it helped him beef up his case against possible extradition on drug-trafficking charges. The Uribe administration, meanwhile, boosted its coca-eradication numbers to help make its case for the billions of dollars in U.S. military aid that hung in the balance. Finally, Acción Social and UNODC claimed a success story for their grassroots alternative development programs, having fostered a culture of legality in a supposedly lawless frontier zone.

USAID used Plan Colombia's strategic alliances as a longer-term complement to the Guardabosques programs. The cash transfers from Guardabosques were supposed to help tide over the campesinos until the USAID-backed agricultural projects started generating income. By beginning the bilateral collaboration between the two programs in Tulapas, USAID hoped that "starting there will maximize the chances of delivering an early success and demonstration of the benefits," spurring similar joint efforts elsewhere in the country.[62] Together, Guardabosques and Plan Colombia's strategic alliances formed the backbone of the Uribe administration's reemboldened alternative development program for las regiones.

All the agencies involved in these programs, including Acción Social, UNODC, and USAID, claimed the projects created a culture of legality by promoting social capital, entrepreneurship, land tenure, environmental conservation, and local institution building—that is, many key components of grassroots development.

They saw a culture of legality as a crucial part of state formation. One USAID report said the programs would "ensure that [recipient] communities effectively transit into legality and reinforce the legitimacy of the State."[63] Similarly, Acción Social's audit of its projects in Tulapas claimed they had fostered a culture of legality by strengthening local institutions, specifically citing the juntas and Corpourabá as examples. Even more important, Acción Social added, the projects had "boosted the State's credibility and legitimated national, departmental, and municipal institutions among the communities."[64] By their own analysis they had broken through the "panorama of illegality" and succeeded in recovering what Uribe had called the "feeling of the state's presence" in the area.[65]

Acción Social credited itself with having helped reverse the "low levels of social capital (in some cases negative)" in places like Tulapas by fostering trust, solidarity, and community savings.[66] The creation of community organizations and cooperatives was especially important because they provided government agencies with localized institutional counterparts for establishing the social relations of statehood. As Acción Social put it, "Consolidating a culture of legality in these zones depends on the state's presence through the institutional articulations generated by [the programs]."[67] All over the country, through the joint workings of Guardabosques and Plan Colombia, grassroots development steered the work of government entities, international donors, NGOs, companies, and campesinos toward state formation. When El Alemán's paramilitary bloc began its demobilization process, they employed many of these same strategies, making grassroots development the foundation of how the BEC envisioned its postconflict future.

Demobilization: State Building from the Grassroots

When demobilization talks between the Uribe administration and paramilitary leaders began in early 2003 El Alemán left the negotiating table after the first meeting. A long-standing divide among the paramilitary leadership had become irreparable, and the demobilization talks made the rift even wider. The paramilitary movement was born with a congenital tension between the imperatives of drug trafficking and counterinsurgency. After years of rarely entering into conflict the two missions had progressively hardened into two polarized and in some cases violently opposed factions: commanders who prioritized drug trafficking versus those who, like El Alemán, placed at least equal emphasis on counterinsurgency. By 2003 the drug-trafficking wing of the movement had become the dominant faction, so El Alemán was already on the outs with the national leadership.

El Alemán's falling out with the narco-leaning faction, which was led by Vicente Castaño, became definitive when Vicente ordered the killing of his younger brother, Carlos—reportedly for exploring a plea deal with U.S. antidrug authorities. Since Carlos had recruited El Alemán into the movement, mentored him, and promoted him as the leader of his own bloc, his loyalty to Carlos within the paras' internecine struggles was well known. At the time, El Alemán feared he would be targeted next. After leaving the bargaining table the BEC began separate talks with the government and ultimately negotiated an independent demobilization agreement. El Alemán's civilian adviser and spokesperson during the negotiations was Juan García, a lawyer and the brother of the murdered paramilitary chief known as Doble Cero, whose death was another casualty of the narco faction's power grab.

In 2004 García and El Alemán presented an elaborate postdemobilization plan to the government. The Proyecto de Alternatividad Social (PASO, Project for a Social Alternative), as they named it, was a wide-ranging, ambitious, even utopian proposal. It envisioned displaced peasants, demobilized paramilitaries, landless campesinos, and private agribusinesses all working together on donated lands toward reconciliation and shared prosperity. Victims' groups immediately criticized the proposal, calling it an inversion of justice. They pointed out that the implementation of the PASO would effectively convert victims into hired help on lands that had been stolen from them and with their former victimizers as bosses. As things turned out they were not far off the mark.

When asked what made the BEC's proposals such as the PASO different from those of the other paramilitary blocs, García responded, "The BEC's process is aimed at the grassroots [... *tiene una proyección a la base social*]." Explaining what he meant by this, he described the basic outlines of the strategic alliance structure: "The idea is for productive projects to be developed for the communities and for lands to be acquired with the help of wealthy ranchers. With the land as capital, the labor will come from campesinos and reinserted [i.e., demobilized] paramilitaries. El Alemán's goal is for the communities to participate in the expansion of [oil] palm, banana, rubber, and teak cultivation."[68] The projects implemented under the auspices of the PASO folded in seamlessly with the elaborate institutional landscape created by the BEC's political work and the implementation of Guardabosques and Plan Colombia's strategic alliances. As an extension of these efforts, the PASO called for "peaceful and sustainable development through self-sustainable ecoforestry farms."[69]

In practice, the PASO not only materialized the grassroots development apparatus but also became the Uribe administration's de facto policy program for the entirety of Urabá after the paras' demobilization. In partnership with UNODC, the Uribe administration created the Gerencia Social de Urabá, a regional management and coordinating body for implementing many of the ideas first outlined by the PASO.[70] The head of the UNODC hailed the new initiative as "a model that could be ... replicated in other parts of the country facing the scourge of criminal organizations."[71] As El Alemán proudly noted, "The government incorporated our proposals, putting it at the head of a promising process . . . in which our disarmament and demobilization was not an end goal in itself but rather the starting point for a project promoting a genuine reconstruction of the social fabric."[72] Despite El Alemán's idealized description the PASO, as part of the grassroots development apparatus, it also served the much shadier purpose of laundering the paras' illicit landholdings.

The BEC had been preparing for the demobilization long before it happened, in late 2006. In 2002, when Uribe's election as president made the paras' disarmament all but assured, El Alemán sent his PDSs scrambling into action. According to the court testimony of one PDS, El Alemán ordered him to start "resolving the problem with those lands [in Tulapas]."[73] The paras had overseen agribusiness projects in Tulapas for almost a decade, but with their coming demobilization they needed to resolve "the problem with those lands" by legally ratifying, or laundering, what until then had been an illegal and de facto possession of the properties left behind by the campesinos who had fled in 1995.

In Tulapas alone paramilitary operatives and their allied agribusiness companies laundered over twenty thousand hectares of stolen properties by making them part of the PASO's strategic alliances. Although the rightful campesino owners of the lands had been displaced since 1995, the bulk of the transactions and bureaucratic machinations that "legally" ratified the land grab happened between 2002 and 2006, the exact period when the BEC was negotiating its exit from the war. The land laundering first required that the true owners, the displaced campesinos, relinquish their titles to the properties. To carry out this task the paras' main agent for setting up the shady land deals in Tulapas was Doña Tere, who had overseen the deals for the oil palm projects in Chocó. In her position as the director of Funpazcor, the NGO created by the Castaños, she developed an elaborate process for laundering the land seizures.

First, she enlisted a handful of intermediaries, one of whom was a well-known campesino resident of Tulapas. The paramilitaries' intermediaries tracked down the displaced campesinos and, with the complicity of corrupt public notaries, Doña Tere forced them into giving her power of attorney. As their proxy she then sold their properties to third-party individuals. Some of these people were supposedly members (on paper at least) of Funpazcor. The new owners then either immediately sold the properties to agribusiness companies linked to paras or joined cooperatives that then ceded the lands to the same companies via usufruct agreements—that is, long-term, no-cost land concessions.

By means of this process four companies became major landowners in Tulapas and its immediate surroundings: two rubber companies, Procaucho and Caucho San Pedro, and two forestry companies, La Gironda and El Indio. Covering almost four thousand hectares of land, the PASO's rubber and teak projects followed the strategic alliance model with orthodoxy. Between them, the four companies received a total of US$11 million in start-up capital from Incuagro, a mixed company bankrolled by the Inter-American Development Bank.[74] USAID negligently chipped in an extra U$445,000 in grants to the forestry companies.[75] The sham cooperatives gained a stake in the companies through the land their campesino members ceded in usufruct to the projects. The members of the cooperatives were mostly either campesinos who had reset-tled Tulapas with the paras' permission or the BEC's soon-to-be-demobilized combatants. In either case the only real benefits they gained from "participat-ing" in the projects were the wages they received as hired help and tiny plots of land for subsistence crops.

The companies' promotional materials and their agreements with funders described the rubber and teak plantations as environmentally friendly, bottom-up, cooperative-driven projects that would help stymie the spread of illicit crops. The BEC's NGO, Asocomún, lauded the projects as a model and claimed in breathless praise that Tulapas had "become a laboratory of peace and social inclusion where excluded groups had used the power of collective action for gen-erating peaceful spaces of coexistence through new sources of economic produc-tion that are both self-sustaining and environmentally friendly."[76]

By far the largest new landowner in Tulapas was the Fondo Ganadero de Córdoba, a mixed public–private company involved in the cattle trade that had once included the Castaño brothers on its board of directors.[77] With Doña Tere's help the company acquired thousands of hectares in Tulapas. In one case, for instance, she arranged the coerced sale of one of the larger campesino properties in Tulapas to one of her intermediaries. A year later the intermediary resold the property to the Fondo Ganadero for a hugely inflated price—usually a telltale sign of money laundering. The Fondo Ganadero incorporated the farm, appro-priately named El Engaño (The Scam), into a thirty-six-hundred-hectare spread. As a major agribusiness player in Tulapas, the company also became heavily invested in the PASO's strategic alliances, becoming a major shareholder in the two rubber companies.

After the initial establishment of the PASO's projects in 2005 the land-concession arrangement between the cooperatives and the companies gradually dissolved: bit by bit the members of the cooperatives sold their properties outright to the companies. On paper the strategic alliance had called for the campesino cooperatives to eventually buy out the private investors, but what ultimately happened was the opposite: the companies bought out the campesinos. The cooperatives had served their purpose: the paras had used them to keep the massive land seizure distributed across numerous front owners, thereby keeping the acreage of each individual transaction small enough to fly under authorities' radars—a practice called smurfing in money laundering. As they had done in Curvaradó, the paras had split, resold, ceded, fused, and resplit the properties to cover their tracks.

Once again the discourses, practices, and institutional formations of the grassroots development apparatus did not just help cover up the paramilitary land grab; they were its conditions of possibility. By the time I began visiting Tulapas in 2012, seven years after the start of the PASO, the teak trees were tall and thick, and the rubber trees already had latex oozing out of the spiral gashes running down the length of their trunks. Small wooden signs with the names of the companies announced the private ownership of the land, as did the barbed wire fences on either side of the area's access road.

At his trial El Alemán protested, with a palpable sense of resentment and betrayal, that the true beneficiaries of paramilitary violence were the "political and economic mafias of the country that, like every mafia, relied on an illegal coercive apparatus" to do their dirty work. He added, "Many accuse the autodefensas of having waged war and terror as a way of gaining ground for the political and economic mafias. That's the accusation made by many—and with good reason."[78] Indeed, while commanders like El Alemán landed in jail, the wealthy regional and national elites who directly or indirectly reaped the benefits of paramilitary violence have remained mostly in the shadows. El Alemán's reference to mafias was not a suggestion that all along there had been some kind of conspiratorial cabal of masterminds pulling the strings. Rather, his comment indicates a realization that paramilitaries had been the armed wing—the illegal coercive apparatus, as he called it—of powerful interests that were so pervasively and diffusely embedded within society that, with some exceptions, they practically remained nameless. To this day no one in Tulapas can say for sure who owns the rubber and teak plantations that continue rolling out their harvests.

The discourses, institutional forms, and practices of the grassroots development apparatus allowed the paramilitary-backed companies to secure and legally sanction an industrial-scale land grab. Even Plan Colombia's strategic alliances and government antidrug programs like Guardabosques, which were supposed to cultivate a culture of legality, became an integral part of the paras' illicit economies and networks of territorial control. As instances of the frontier effect, the grassroots development projects were frontier state formations insofar as they sought to build up the presence of the state in places where it had supposedly not yet arrived.

In reference to the PASO, El Alemán summed up his bloc's state-building efforts in the roseate terms of postconflict reparations. Raising his voice to emphasize certain words, he said, "Some people understand reparations as just money. Reparation is also that the state *arrives*. And not just with police and soldiers, but for *all the state to arrive* in those far-off regions of our national geography—with health, with education. So that our campesinos finally *know* the state—*know what the state actually is*."[79] By the time I met El Alemán in 2012, when he was still serving his jail sentence, the PASO, at least as a demobilization project, had long since fizzled out. By then it had been entirely cannibalized by the private companies. The only project from the PASO that was still receiving a shred of government support was the fishing cooperatives of the Guardians of the Gulf (Guardagolfos) program. "But even Guardagolfos is drowning," El Alemán told me. He asserted that the government and international aid agencies needed an entirely new approach to postconflict development, adding, "I'm going to throw out a term that maybe you've heard lately . . . *resilience*."

"Resilience?" I asked, surprised. "Resilience," he confirmed. I nodded, trying to contain my surprise at his use of the latest development buzzword, which has come to be associated with everything from national security to climate change. He continued, "Resilience is like someone who has suffered a lot, who's had a hard time in their life, and then decides to stop being the victim. Resilience, because the person stops and says, 'What has happened, happened, so I'm going to get on with my life and liberate myself—liberate myself from being the victim.'"[80]

El Alemán was not only absolving himself as a victimizer and denying his survivors the higher moral ground of victimhood, but also resituating the post-conflict environment within the latest discourse of the development apparatus. Indeed, resilience, with its connotations of flexible adaptation, socioecological complexity, and self-help is the next logical evolution of grassroots development. As our conversation began winding down, El Alemán said, "You should go meet my lawyer friend and a few demobilized friends of mine." He gave me their contact information, and the next day I took him up on his suggestion and visited them. They were all former members of the BEC, and almost all were ex-PDSs. Now they composed the staff of El Alemán's latest brainchild: an NGO named the Fundación Pro-Resiliencia. The organization had a series of projects it was shopping around in the context of Colombia's emergent postconflict transition. One, euphemistically called the Diaspora of the Atrato, was about helping displaced Afro-Colombians from the Atrato River basin rebuild their lives. Another proposed that the NGO would train campesino leaders in Urabá to make them more resilient to the challenges of the postconflict. What had been the BEC's Promoters of Social Development were now recast as Promoters of Resilience and Reconciliation.

As in the case of "civil society" in the 1990s, nowadays the only question to be asked of "resilience" seems to be, How can we get more of it?[81] Resilience has turned into a pliable, all-purpose bonding agent capable of configuring strategic ensembles for addressing a seemingly infinite menu of threats and crises, everything from financial or environmental catastrophes to personal mindfulness and self-help. Grassroots development and building resilience have become practically synonymous.[82] The similarities between the two are all the more apparent in policy circles focused on the links between conflict, development, and human security.

A case in point is the World Bank's 2011 "World Development Report on Conflict, Security, and Development." The report's main conclusion is that the only way for "fragile or conflict-affected states," including those with high levels of criminal violence, to break away from recidivist cycles of violence is by building more resilient institutions (broadly understood). In this iteration grassroots development translates into hyperlocalized, "best-fit" approaches that create quick-impact economic opportunities and help restore public confidence in state institutions. Foremost among the bank's prescriptions are "programs that support bottom-up state-society relations" as a way of "forging and re-forging trust in state institutions and in state-society relations."[83] From this perspective, building resilience against conflict requires a combination of government-led programs and local grassroots' initiative. In other words, almost all of the bank's recommendations mirror the precise forms through which Urabá's paramilitaries worked the grassroots development apparatus to arrive at their own predatory ends. All three cases discussed here—the Afro-Colombian oil palm project, Familias Guardabosques, and the PASO—are perfect examples of the kind of two-way (top-down and bottom-up) programming endorsed by the bank.

The discourses of grassroots development I analyze here could be easily interpreted as just a case of corporate players and their armed accomplices trying to whitewash their malfeasance with the development-speak du jour. But the problem is deeper and more serious. Grassroots development was a practical, discursive, strategic, and institutional articulation—an apparatus—that made paramilitaries' economies of violence and liberal state formation into mutually reinforcing processes. Paramilitary plunder and land laundering worked alongside and actually through government-led projects aimed at boosting institutions, good governance, the rule of law, and capitalist rural development. In short, Urabá shows how the grassroots strategies being endorsed by the World Bank in the name of resilience are not immune to mass dispossession, illicit economies, and violent political projects. And yet the frontier state formations constructed by the paras as a way of resolving the absence of the state in Urabá became the terrain upon which the region's postconflict future would now have to be built.

THE POSTCONFLICT INTERREGNUM

The crisis consists precisely in the fact that the old is dying and the new cannot be born; in this interregnum a great variety of morbid symptoms appear.

—Antonio Gramsci, *Prison Notebooks* (1930)

On the morning of January 5, 2012, a Thursday, nobody in Urabá went to work. The banana plantations and roadways in the countryside were desolate. In the towns not a single store raised its shutters; the streets, normally swarming with motorcycles, were empty. Everywhere an eerie silence replaced the usual early-morning hustle and bustle. An armed group known as Los Urabeños had declared a two-day *paro armado*, an armed general strike or lockdown: in effect, a forty-eight-hour curfew. The Urabeños had become Colombia's largest, most powerful drug-trafficking organization, so its armed strike paralyzed about a third of the country, including most of the Caribbean coast and parts of Medellín. In a communiqué the Urabeños, a group founded by midlevel paramilitary commanders who never demobilized or who slipped back into the war, announced that the paro armado was "in retaliation for recent events."[1]

The recent events had occurred just a few days earlier. As the sun rose on New Year's Day the national antidrug police raided a lavish party taking place just a few miles from the turtle nesting grounds of Playona. During the raid police shot and killed Juan de Dios Úsuga, better known as Giovanni, the Urabeños' second-in-command. The group's communiqué announcing the lockdown alleged that police had captured Giovanni alive and then executed him in front of his family, calling it a "vile assassination" that exposed the true nature "of the state and its rule of law." The Urabeños concluded the missive with a warning: "Everything is suspended. . . . [W]e don't want to see anyone working or traveling around."

In Urabá public compliance with the two-day lockdown was absolute; the only exception to the chilling calm was Giovanni's funeral, an event attended en masse in Necoclí, the Urabeños' hometown. A foot soldier of theirs who was enforcing the curfew at an impromptu roadblock said the point of the armed general strike was to "make clear to the authorities who really calls the shots in the region [*quién manda en la región*]."[2] As a contorted version of Walter Benjamin's argument that the "general strike sets itself the sole task of destroying state power," the Urabeños' paro armado made a very public show of exposing the pretense of state sovereignty for what it is: a brittle and contested claim.[3] The government's response came a month later.

On February 11, 2012, President Juan Manuel Santos visited Necoclí to publicly launch one the most important bills passed during his two terms (2010–18) in office: a law on victims' reparations and land restitution. President Santos had served as Uribe's minister of defense and was his handpicked successor, but once in office Santos began distancing himself from the hardline policies of his former boss. The law on reparations and land restitution, which created a program for returning stolen lands to their rightful owners, was a way of marking out that distance (it also helped set the stage for peace talks with the FARC that began in secret later that year).

Since Urabá had become a national symbol of paramilitary violence and dispossession, the region provided a powerfully symbolic site for the stage-managed introduction of the new land restitution program. Necoclí was also the Urabeños' unofficial headquarters, so Santos was sending the emboldened group a defiant message by staging the ceremony on their home turf. The Urabeños had single-handedly turned their namesake region into the most dangerous place in the country for land-rights activists. In a single move the president's visit challenged the Urabeños' local authority and helped cast a national spotlight on land-related violence in the region.

As in the past, the presidential visit to Urabá was equal parts stagecraft and statecraft. In his speech Santos said, "All the violent groups have been here: the FARC, the EPL, all the guerrilla movements, paramilitaries, and now the criminal bands."[4] The new label "criminal bands" was the government's generic name for the Urabeños and the other successor groups of the paramilitary movement that had taken control of the drug trade. Santos described the land restitution law as a major break with Colombia's violent past. He also tried to calm the fears of landed elites who had fiercely opposed the law. "This is not a struggle between rich and poor or a conflict between campesinos and landowners; this is not a class struggle," he said. "Plain and simple, this is a crusade of the legal against the illegal. . . . We have to go back to a fundamental respect for the rule of law."

Santos emphasized that land restitution would amount to more than simply returning a property to its true owner: "More than just giving back a plot of land, we're going to come in with all the help the state can bring: with technical

FIGURE 16.   President Juan Manuel Santos introducing the land restitution law from a stage in Necoclí.

(Credit: SIG/Felipe Ariza)

assistance, strategic alliances, and infrastructure." He pointed to the public officials seated in the rows behind him on the stage, saying, "This is why all of the state is represented here at this event." From their seats the cabinet ministers, judges, senators, congressional representatives, military officers, local mayors, and Antioquia's governor looked on approvingly. They personified the promise that land restitution would, as Santos said, bring the state to the country's war-torn frontier zones.

The new land restitution program was a more concerted continuation of the postconflict initiatives that had begun with the transitional justice provisions of the paras' demobilization. During Santos's presidency postconflict policy making gained another boost with the start of peace negotiations with the FARC and further intensified with the successful resolution of the talks in 2016. However, even with the paras out of the picture and with the FARC's demobilization, postconflict Colombia remains a country very much at war: the military is still fighting a few holdout rebel groups, including remnants of the FARC, and drug-trafficking armies like the Urabeños still control large swaths of the nation. Indeed, in Necoclí the juxtaposition of the paro armado and the rollout of land restitution reflected the dramatic contradictions of Colombia's new postconflict environment.

The postconflict conjuncture has become the latest springboard for Colombia's frontier state formations. Throughout the country's purportedly stateless frontiers, which continue to be major sites of organized violence and a still-raging war on drugs, the forces of law and order have not so much trumped the power of violent outlaw groups as become fused with them. In what follows, I explore these antinomies of postconflict statecraft through an ethnographic account of land restitution in Tulapas. This small region demonstrates how the contradictions of postconflict state formation have materialized sharply around the politics of community.[5] It is at the scale of community that the postconflict's intense yet often hushed renegotiations of rule are taking place. From the perspective of war-torn communities like Tulapas, the postconflict moment in Colombia is less a transition from war to peace than an indefinite interregnum in which, as Antonio Gramsci put it, "the old is dying and the new cannot be born."[6]

From the stage in Necoclí President Santos predicted that land restitution would be a "crusade of the legal against the illegal" and would help bring the state to Colombia's unruly frontier zones. The scholarship on these issues suggests this was a reasonable expectation. Researchers have shown how the administration of property rights and its accompanying grids of legibility can be forceful modalities for the territorialization or reterritorialization of state power.[7] But the ethnographic portrait of the state that comes into view here is not that of a preformed entity descending from on high and imposing its will through an all-powerful set of legal, calculative, cartographic, and classificatory techniques. Land restitution in Tulapas was a messy, largely improvised process through which rule was not so much imposed as negotiated. The reconfiguration of postconflict rule was a multiparty affair that included a disparate set of actors: from the drug-trafficking Urabeños and all kinds of government entities to aid organizations and the campesino communities themselves.

In early 2013 Urabá's regional branch office of the national government's land restitution agency did not yet have a full staff or even a full set of office furniture, but it had already officially designated Tulapas as a priority case. The choice of Tulapas was partly due to the fact that the transitional justice component of the paras' demobilization had already laid some of the legal groundwork for adjudicating the ownership of the lands; it was also one of the largest single cases of mass dispossession in all of Antioquia. As land restitution officials soon discovered, Tulapas had also become a major territorial stronghold—a veritable headquarters—of the Urabeños.

The Urabeños had emerged when some of El Alemán's lieutenants abandoned the disarmament process in the wake of his demobilization in 2006. They regrouped under the command of El Alemán's brother Daniel Rendón, better known as Don Mario. Don Mario joined forces with Vicente Castaño, who had never fully demobilized, and together they began reactivating the drug-trafficking wing of the disbanding paramilitary movement. Their new army began filling the power vacuum left by their demobilized comrades, and as it violently swallowed up weaker drug-trafficking outfits across the country its rivals named the new army Los Urabeños, meaning "the people from Urabá."

When the Urabeños publicly announced their existence via a communiqué in 2008 they did so by naming themselves the Autodefensas Gaitanistas de Colombia after Jorge Eliécer Gaitán, the martyred left-leaning populist leader whose assassination sparked La Violencia. But Urabeños was the name that stuck.[8] In that first communiqué the Urabeños adopted the key discourses of paramilitary populism, saying they had grown out of a need to "defend the interests of the most vulnerable communities who remain *abandoned by the state* and victimized by its *politico-administrative corruption*."[9] From its inception the group has employed familiar and lofty rhetoric like this in an attempt to shed its reputation as an apolitical drug-trafficking syndicate and reposition itself as an ideologically motivated combatant group on the side of the poor and marginalized. It has been helped in these efforts by the large proportion of former members of the EPL and the Bloque Elmer Cárdenas in its ranks.

In fact, several of the Urabeños' main leaders were born and raised in Tulapas. They have been warring in the area since they were teenagers, first with the EPL and then with the paras. After Vicente Castaño disappeared, reportedly at the hands of rival traffickers, and after the authorities captured Don Mario in 2009, these native sons of Tulapas became the top commanders of the Urabeños. Drawing on their wealth of experience in the armed groups, they have repeatedly tried to emphasize the Urabeños' populist credentials. In doing so they have redeployed many of the same practices and discourses—sometimes word for word—honed by El Alemán. Despite the group's considerable symbolic and material investment in these populist tactics, Colombia's security establishment has insistently classified them as an entirely depoliticized *banda criminal*.

However, the Urabeños did in fact have a political streak, both through the relationships they forged with the campesino communities in their territories and in the way they protected the interests of landowners. The Urabeños, for instance, became the land restitution program's most violent opponents, killing dozens of land rights activists all over the country and particularly in Urabá. Indeed, the regional land restitution office had set itself an incredibly difficult task by choosing Tulapas, the heart of the Urabeños' home turf, as its local test case for the program. With a map of Urabá spread across his desk, the director of the local land restitution office acknowledged it was a tall order. "But if we can do it here," he said, his finger pointing to Tulapas on the map, "we can do it anywhere."[10]

The Politics of Land Restitution

Tulapas not only was a microcosm of the threat posed by the Urabeños but also encapsulated one of the most complicated questions surrounding land restitution: if the original peasant-owners reclaimed their lands, what would happen to the thousands of campesinos who had resettled portions of those lands under paramilitary rule? Lawmakers had not seriously considered this question. Apparently since paramilitaries had a well-deserved reputation as armies of dispossession, the authors of the land restitution law had overlooked the way the paras had resettled portions of their stolen lands with campesinos whose support they actually needed and actively cultivated. As one lawmaker regretted, they had assumed displacement had been a "black and white" process with "victims on one side and victimizers on the other."[11] If things had been that straightforward, land restitution would have been a much simpler process; instead, it led to almost as many problems as it set out to resolve.

The displaced campesinos now seeking the return of their farms in Tulapas had spent the past fifteen years living in towns scattered across Urabá and beyond. During this period their lands had become not only the site of depopulated, paramilitary-backed plantations but also home to hundreds of campesino families who, with the paras' consent, took up residence on the lands. Most of these incoming families farmed the portions of land that had not been consumed by the rubber, teak, and cattle operations belonging to the paramilitary-linked companies. By the time the land restitution process was set to begin in 2012 these campesino squatters had been living in Tulapas for almost a generation. Restitution thus pitted the *reclamantes* (reclaimers)—that is, the true peasant-owners of Tulapas seeking the return of their lands—against the equally poor and marginalized campesino squatters.[12]

On the surface the relationship between these two groups of campesinos, the reclamantes and the squatters, was surprisingly amicable. Elsy Galván, whose family lost its farm to the paras in the mid-1990s, was a leader of the dispossessed reclamantes. She assured me that they harbored no ill will against the squatters occupying their farms. "They have never opposed our return," she said. "They just want the government to respond with some kind of relocation program so that they don't suffer the same displacement and abandonment that we've had to face during all this time."[13] Elsy was right: the squatters assumed it was only a matter of time before they would have to vacate the lands, but they held out hope that the government would provide for their relocation, ideally within Tulapas.

Elsy said she and her fellow reclamantes had no problem with the idea of the squatters staying on in the area. "There's enough land for everyone," she said. "But when we return, we're not going to just give away parcels for free." Elsy hoped that Incoder, the national government's rural development agency, would purchase small parcels of land from returning campesinos like her and use them to relocate the squatters. For this reason the squatters had to be careful not to alienate Elsy and the other reclamantes: the chances of a relocation program for the squatters improved if it counted on support from the rightful owners of the land.

The main leader of the squatters, Elsy's counterpart, was the campesino named Víctor Martínez whom I mentioned earlier (see chapter 3). Víctor had arrived in Tulapas in 2002, that is, seven years after Elsy and her neighbors had been forced to flee. Along with many other campesinos he went there after hearing that the local plantations were looking for workers. Since then he had built a decent life for his family by farming the land and working with the other squatters in a cooperative they founded called Uprurac.

Víctor had an impressive background as a community organizer. His leadership experience came from the years he had spent working with the banana unions in Apartadó. He said it was through the unions that he had "learned about the law and about how to build social relationships with communities." The long, winding path he took to Tulapas began in 1994, when he fled from Apartadó after the FARC massacred thirty-five people in his neighborhood. After years of moving from place to place chasing jobs he finally settled in Tulapas, becoming a respected leader of the squatters and the president of their cooperative. With land restitution looming, the squatters were now counting on Víctor to represent their interests and secure a decent deal for them.

I met Elsy and Víctor for the first time the same day I was introduced to Carmen Palencia. Carmen had been one of the people sitting behind President Santos onstage when he introduced the land restitution law with all the fanfare in Necoclí. She was the national director of an activist NGO called Tierra y Vida that was aiding Elsy and the other reclamantes in the land restitution process. Carmen is a tireless, combative organizer who got her start working within the civilian ranks of the EPL. She began as a militant of its legal party and then worked with a few Juntas de Acción Comunal that grew out of the EPL's land occupations. Her left-wing activism made her a target of the paras. When they came for her in the late 1980s they killed her husband. In 1995 she survived another attack on her life by paras, but this time she ended up with five gunshot wounds and spent two months in a coma. Unfortunately, this would not be the last attempt on her life. Just nine days after she appeared onstage with President Santos in Necoclí a pipe bomb exploded on the doorstep of her home. Away on a trip, she was unharmed.

My introduction to Carmen, Elsy, and Víctor took place one morning outside the mayor's office in Turbo. I had arrived with Carlos Páez, the head of Tierra y Vida's founding chapter in Urabá. They were all there at the request of Turbo's mayor, who had scheduled a meeting with them to talk about the land restitution process in Tulapas. As those with the most at stake in the meeting, Elsy was representing the reclamantes and Víctor was representing the squatters. After several hours the mayor's assistant finally waved us in, and Carlos invited me to come along. As we filed into the office Urabá's overbearing heat gave way to the frigid chill of an air conditioner in the corner of the room. Beneath the pale glow of fluorescent lights, the mayor, William Palacio, sat at the head of a long table. He was annoyed, claiming the meeting was not on his schedule.

Not hiding his irritation, he opened the floor: "Well, here I am, go for it [*hágale*]." Carmen and Carlos from Tierra y Vida took the lead and gave an overview of the situation in Tulapas. Elsy and Víctor occasionally chimed in with some details. The gist was that, with the land restitution process likely moving ahead, they wanted the mayor's office to support the process. Elsy and Víctor mentioned the need for a school and a clinic, but they placed special emphasis on the need for a road into the area. Víctor turned on his considerable charm, saying that the municipality's assistance was in everyone's best interests. He said *el retorno*, meaning the return of reclamantes like Elsy, would be pointless without "municipal accompaniment." Víctor also repeatedly made sure to emphasize that the two groups of campesinos, both the squatters and the reclamantes, were working in harmony to realize the successful return of the latter.

After hearing the pitch, the mayor began his response by reminding everyone that Turbo was an officially bankrupt municipality. He pointed out that during his last visit to Tulapas he had reached an agreement at a community assembly with a few dozen campesino leaders from the area. He had promised them the municipality would build a school and a clinic in the village of Paraíso at the far northern edge of Tulapas near Turbo's border with the neighboring municipality of Necoclí. As soon as the mayor mentioned the community assembly in Paraíso with the local leaders, Carmen scoffed loudly and interrupted, "But those leaders don't represent the *true* owners of the land." She was pointing out that the mayor's meeting had been with the squatters currently living in Tulapas, not with the reclamantes still waiting on the restitution of their farms.

Carmen and the mayor got into a heated exchange. She added that Paraíso made no sense for the promised school and clinic because the village was miles away from where most of the people in Tulapas lived. The mayor took her objection as an appeal for special treatment. "I'm not just the mayor of Tulapas," he said. "I'm the mayor for *all* of Turbo."

"I thought the whole point of this meeting was to plan *el retorno* to Tulapas," said Carmen, raising her voice.

"This meeting wasn't even on the books!" he yelled, losing his patience. "I accepted it as a show of good will."

"Look, Mister Mayor, you're not doing us any favors here. This is your *obligation* under the land restitution law." Carmen waving the law in his face was the final straw.

He slammed his palms on the table and sprang out of his seat: "No one comes into my house imposing anything on me!" Carmen also stood up. At well over six feet tall, the mayor towered over the diminutive, five-foot Carmen, but she held her ground as they debated the finer points of administrative responsibility spelled out by the law. Fed up, the mayor cut her off: "I'm not getting into any more of your byzantine conversations." He demanded Tierra y Vida leave the meeting so he could speak to the campesino representatives (Elsy and Víctor) without the NGO's interference. I followed Carmen and Carlos back out into the midday heat.

Full of nervous energy from the confrontation with the mayor, Carmen rehashed what had happened. She believed the reason the health and education facilities were going to Paraíso was because the Urabeños controlled the village. "That's part of their territory, and they want to strengthen it," she argued. Her theory was that the Urabeños had manipulated the community leaders behind the scenes to make sure the projects went to Paraíso as a way of building support for the group in the village. She supported her argument by pointing out that Paraíso was right next to one of the rubber plantations owned by the companies that had participated in El Alemán's demobilization project. Carmen made no distinction between the Urabeños and their predecessors: "Paramilitaries, neo-paramilitaries, bandas criminales, it's all the same thing. They're the exact same people." She grabbed her bicep where combatants don their group's identifying armbands and quipped, "Same dog, different collar."

Carmen's read on the situation was entirely plausible, but I suspect the mayor's choice of Paraíso had another motivation. Paraíso is located near Turbo's disputed municipal border with Necoclí, meaning the small village is caught between overlapping municipal–territorial claims. Twice during the meeting the mayor made the point that "Turbo is the largest municipality in all of Antioquia," making it especially difficult for it to "maintain an effective presence across its entire territory." With the municipality's territorial integrity in jeopardy, the mayor may have been using the proposed school and the clinic in Paraíso as a form of flag planting, a way of creating what he had described as "an effective presence" of the state, while also ensuring local loyalty to his municipality.

The meeting in the mayor's office that day was a personification of the frontier effect. Local government officials and civil society leaders—that is, representatives of the communities and the NGO—literally sat around a negotiating table haggling over where and in what form the state would attain an effective presence. It was frontier state formation in real time. Elsy and Víctor were making claims on the state's responsibility to provide for the basic well-being of local communities. Meanwhile, as Carmen marshaled the letter of the law to pressure the mayor, he cited the power and political authority of his office ("no one tells me what to do in my house"). The mayor was also at pains to reinforce Turbo's territorial claim against the geopolitical encroachments of a neighboring municipality. From his perspective the planned projects for Paraíso already addressed demands for a state presence in Tulapas through the deal he had made with the other community leaders from the area. Carmen questioned the legitimacy of these leaders, suggesting their status as squatters made them unlawful interlocutors. After about fifteen minutes Elsy and Víctor came out of the municipal building. They excitedly told us that the mayor had agreed to their most pressing and long-standing demand: the construction of a road from Turbo's municipal seat into Tulapas. The reclamantes had been demanding a road into the area since before their displacement in the 1990s. Once the squatters took up residence in Tulapas, they too had pleaded for an access road and actually made some headway in getting it done. During the Guardabosques negotiations with Uribe's Plan Colombia czar the squatters secured a promise for the road as part of the coca-eradication deal. Unfortunately, the government abandoned the project after building only a single bridge and a few miles of dirt road that dead-ended into rutted footpaths. Turbo's mayor had now made a commitment to finish the job.

Elsy and Víctor reported that they had gone straight to the point after the mayor threw us out of the meeting by making clear that the construction of the road was their top priority. The mayor called the commander of Urabá's local army base, the only institution in the region with its own set of heavy machinery, and cut a deal: the military agreed to provide its engineering team and the machinery if Turbo covered all their expenses. Elsy and Víctor relished the fact that they had cajoled the mayor by turning his arguments against him. What better way to ensure that the far reaches of Tulapas stayed within Turbo's territorial fold, they argued, than with a direct road from its municipal seat? As it stood now, getting to Tulapas from Turbo's urban center required a circuitous three- to five-hour drive through the rival municipal seat of Necoclí; the road would make it a quick twenty-five-minute drive without going outside Turbo's borders.

Elsy began daydreaming about what the road would mean for the reclamantes. "Can you imagine?" she said. "We could even work our farms while still living here in town [in Turbo's municipal seat], which we've become so attached to [amañados]." Since it had been almost twenty years since their displacement from Tulapas, many reclamantes had made permanent homes in the urban areas of Urabá. By now their children and in some cases their children's children had spent their entire lives living in the towns. Most of the younger generation had no interest in permanently relocating to the countryside. For Elsy, the road meant she could continue living in town while keeping up with her farm, thus keeping a foot in both places. Despite the squatters' uncertain future, Víctor also emerged from the mayor's office imagining the possibilities. As the president of Uprurac, the peasant cooperative he founded with the other squatters, his mind was on what the road could do for his organization's agricultural products. He mentioned improved market access, reduced transportation costs, and cutting out greedy intermediaries; plus, he said, it would make Tulapas a more viable site for national and international aid programs. "Once we get the road, all kinds of projects will start arriving," he predicted.

Víctor mentioned another detail about how they made their case with the mayor. Víctor said he told him that the municipality's assistance could help turn Tulapas into a national success story of restitution and grassroots reconciliation. Víctor claimed Tulapas could prove that reclamantes and squatters could work together in "repairing the social fabric."[14] The problem of squatters being pitted against reclamantes had become a major, nationwide snag in the land restitution program, so Víctor's attempt to get the road by selling Tulapas as a potential place of harmonious coexistence between squatters and reclamantes was a shrewd political move. But Elsy and Víctor knew better than to count on the mayor's promises alone, so they kept clamoring for the road in every other institutional opening created by the postconflict conjuncture. Víctor, for instance, said, "We've also been knocking on the doors of a project from the departmental government for collective reparations. And what are we asking for? The road."[15]

The meeting with the mayor in Turbo is another testament to campesinos' skillful tactical manipulation of the state. Within the broader framework of the national land restitution program they secured a promise for the road by tapping into the mayor's geopolitical anxieties about the intermunicipal border dispute between Turbo and Necoclí. But leaving nothing to chance they also continued working their demands at every other political scale and institutional channel made available to them through the postconflict. In everyday conversation the campesinos may have casually referred to the state in reified terms as a homogenous entity with functional desires that "does this" and "does that." But in practice they displayed a keen awareness of and fully exploited the state's disaggregated complexity and internal contradictions.

The run-in with the mayor also shows how Elsy and Víctor navigated their political relationships with government agents and institutions through a careful combination of hardnosed negotiation and lowly supplication. Carmen from Tierra y Vida had led the confrontational approach with the mayor. As a good-cop, bad-cop routine, Carmen's belligerence made the campesinos' demands and approach seem all the more reasonable. As one campesino from Tulapas confided in me, "Doña Carmen doesn't know how to ask for things, but she's good at opening doors."[16] Elsy and Víctor, meanwhile, smartly relied on a strategically essentialized presentation of reclamantes and squatters as a unified collective subject capable of mending the nation's war-torn social fabric. Yet the public narrative of a harmonious alliance between reclamantes and squatters papered over the deep tensions between the two groups.

Subaltern Land Struggles

The relationship between reclamantes and squatters may have appeared to be convivial, but many reclamantes displaced in the 1990s saw the squatters as paramilitary proxies, people almost as guilty of the dispossession as the paras themselves. An elderly campesina who told me she was too old to go back to Tulapas and start over said, "Of course they collaborated with the paras! How else could they have lived there for all those years without a care [*tranquilos*]?"[17] When I mentioned to her that the squatters had arrived in Tulapas after the war displaced them from their own homes, she interrupted me with what she said was "a small correction." "They *say* they were displaced," she insisted. "That's what they *say*. If they were really displaced, why haven't they gone back where they came from to reclaim their own lands, like we're doing in Tulapas?"

When I presented squatters with a more diplomatic version of this question, the responses varied. Some said they never had any land of their own to begin with, while others said they simply did not want to leave a place they now called home. A few told me they were too afraid of the dangers they would face if they returned. Some squatters evaded the question altogether or pointed out that the restitution process was too long and tedious. The reclamantes, after all, had been fighting for the return of their lands for almost a decade, ever since the paras' demobilization in the mid-2000s. Even now, with the land restitution law on the books, their cases were still wending their way through the courts at a snail's pace.

The elderly campesina's rebuke of the people on her land is an example of how the reclamantes sometimes lashed out against the squatters for their collaboration with the paramilitaries. More often, however, they recognized that the squatters had mixed reasons for their actions: some had arrived as landless or displaced campesinos looking for opportunities; others had come at the express invitation of the paras; still others may have had shadier dealings with the paramilitaries. Most reclamantes knew from their personal experience of living with the guerrillas that "complicity" was too strong a word. They knew that blanket accusations of complicity with the armed groups were a gross oversimplification of the complicated, fluid relationships forged between civilian communities and combatant groups.

Nonetheless, Víctor was evasive whenever I asked him about how the squatters had managed daily life in Tulapas under paramilitary rule. The closest he came to giving me a direct answer was wrapped in a metaphor: "You have to learn how to live wherever it is that you are," he began. "But if you swim against the current of a river, you drown. If the river runs that way and you swim this way, the current wears you down, you get tired, and then you drown. But if you calmly go with the current, then nothing happens to you, and that's how it is with these things."[18] Víctor knew a thing or two about going with the flow: he had been part of the campesino delegation that El Alemán had sent to Bogotá for the Guardabosques negotiations with President Uribe's Plan Colombia czar. Víctor ended up being one of the main community leaders of the coca-eradication process and worked closely with Asocomún, the NGO run by El Alemán's brother that helped manage the project.

Víctor drew on these organizational experiences when he helped found the squatters' agricultural cooperative Uprurac. The cooperative actually evolved from the organizations created through the Guardabosques program. Uprurac now had almost eight hundred members, most of them squatter families that had settled in Tulapas when it was under the paramilitaries' control. Víctor and the other squatters never disputed the reclamantes' claim on the lands, but they understandably harbored some resentment toward them for upending their lives through the restitution process. Although land restitution was a polarizing force, it was also sometimes the source of common ground and situational unity between reclamantes and squatters. On several occasions the two groups overcame their mutual distrust through pragmatic alliances like the one that secured the promise of a roadway into Tulapas from the mayor of Turbo.

The president of a Junta de Acción Comunal for one of the largest communities of squatters in Tulapas recalled that "when the reclamantes started to want to come back, they treated us like paramilitaries."[19] But as the restitution process gained momentum he noticed a shift toward increased collaboration, thanks in part to a complementary division of political labor at different levels:

> There's been a lot of collaboration because internally we [the squatters] had already been seeking support and organizing projects [*gestionando proyectos*] through our community organizations, not with the national government but with the local municipal level. Whereas the people displaced from Tulapas brought another level of organizing work [*otro nivel de gestión*], but they were doing it with the national government. . . . We settled these lands, but, like the reclamantes, we're also *desplazados* [displaced people], so we're in the same situation. At first there was a lot of mistrust, but we started linking up, working together

to find resources, to push the area forward, to develop. And our hope is that the reclamantes will keep this in mind in the future, so that we'll eventually get some land of our own.

The junta president's comment reiterates my point that the old and new residents of Tulapas worked on multiple political-administrative scales in nuanced, strategic ways. As he notes, most instances of collaboration between reclamantes and squatters emerged out of efforts to secure, in his words, projects, resources, and development from all levels of government and from international agencies whose programs were increasingly aimed at promoting the country's postconflict transition.

The remarks of the junta president also pointed to the complex politics of victimhood introduced by the postconflict. He deliberately positioned himself and the squatters in saying, "we're also *desplazados*," which was a way of situating his community as deserving moral subjects within the postconflict politics of transitional justice, reparations, and land restitution. Although some of the reclamantes questioned the squatters' victimhood ("they *say* they were displaced"), his comments demonstrate how *desplazado* and *víctima* had gained powerful symbolic currency and significant material stakes. In claiming this constellation of categories, he marked out the squatters' innocence within the moral universe of postconflict Colombia. The politics of victimhood and its assumed hierarchies of suffering between reclamantes and squatters were voiced even more strongly in a complaint I heard from another displaced reclamante from Tulapas. She criticized the squatters as undeserving opportunists: "They are just waiting for us to get some benefits from the government, so that they too can benefit, and that's the kind of behavior we don't like. I'm representing my family and my community and fighting for our lands, and they are just there waiting for their relocation to fall out of the sky.... Those are the kinds of things one sees and doesn't like—it doesn't seem very honest or fair to me."

The reclamante found it especially objectionable that the squatters, whom she criticized for having collaborated with the paras, were reaping most of the rewards from reparations programs, which she claimed should instead be going to "the *true* victims of the conflict." She added, "The state has a moral debt with Tulapas, but not even 10 percent of the people living there right now are actually from the area. If the state is going to give out benefits, then they should go to the people that have actually lived and suffered through the conflict."[20] As another example she cited Pueblo Bello, the town where Fidel Castaño killed forty-two people in retaliation for the theft of that many head of cattle. "They got collective reparations, but only 10 percent, at most, of the families now living in Pueblo Bello were actually there when the massacre happened," she noted.

I heard some version of this complaint several times from the reclamantes displaced from Tulapas: whereas they were left wallowing for years and scraping by as refugees in their own country, the squatters who had resettled Tulapas with the paras' help had enjoyed multiple government-backed development projects like Guardabosques and the strategic alliances. The reclamantes complained that the postconflict was now reproducing the same inversion of justice, rewarding those "least deserving" of reparations and government assistance. Reclamantes pointed to the Uprurac cooperative led by Víctor. He admitted that about three-quarters of Uprurac's eight hundred members were farming lands that belonged to the reclamantes.[21] And yet by positioning Uprurac as an organization made up of *desplazados* and *víctimas*, the cooperative was receiving multiple streams of support from local, departmental, national, and international aid programs.

One of Uprurac's agricultural projects, billed as "a source of employment and livelihood for victims of the conflict," was backed by funding from a collaboration between the departmental government of Antioquia, the municipality of Turbo, and the UN Development Program (UNDP). In 2012 Turbo's municipal government made a deal with the national Agrarian Bank that gave seventy-eight squatter families in Tulapas soft loans in the amount of $850 per hectare of land for a maize-growing project. Another Uprurac initiative, a plantain-growing scheme for one hundred families, received US$80,000 in grants from a "Good Governance" program managed by the Administrative Unit for Territorial Consolidation, a national government agency tasked with "guaranteeing the governance, legitimacy, and presence of the state" in the country's most conflictive areas.[22]

Unlike the aid projects in Tulapas from a decade earlier, these new initiatives took place amid a rich, diversified institutional ecology. During the days of Guardabosques and El Alemán's demobilization in the mid-2000s, reports from national and international development agencies described Tulapas as a barren institutional wasteland completely bereft of civil society organizations. By contrast, field dispatches from these new projects described a flourishing institutional landscape. "All kinds of institutions have a presence in the territory, offering a menu of programs and projects," said the UNDP in a celebratory report. "On top of this, most of the projects, especially those focused on the victims of the conflict, come from the national level and are operated through local municipal ministries and other decentralized entities."[23]

The reason these development-focused reparations projects found such an amenable institutional environment in Tulapas is thanks largely to the meticulous state-building practices by El Alemán and his troops. The projects operated through all the methodically constructed social-institutional infrastructures put into place by the paras: the juntas, the NGOs, the cooperatives, and all their multiply-scaled linkages with governmental and international institutions. Paramilitary statecraft was an extraordinary success insofar as it helped established these strong, productive, and long-lasting political articulations. But these same social-institutional formations and linkages also served the Urabeños and help explain why the group was able to gain control over Urabá so quickly and so thoroughly. The Urabeños repurposed the established political landscape in ways that helped consolidate their rule. Paradoxically, the Urabeños' near-total territorial control ended up actually helping rather than hindering the land restitution process in Tulapas—albeit after a rather rocky start.

Land Restitution and the Urabeños

Two years into its existence in 2013 the national government's Unidad de Restitución de Tierras (Land Restitution Unit) had already amassed a caseload of 2.4 million hectares' worth of land reclamation requests. The Unidad de Tierras, or the Unidad, as I will call it, has more than two dozen branch offices located in various areas of the country where dispossessions were widespread. For the most part the Unidad's local offices began their efforts by focusing on the largest and most emblematic cases of dispossession in their jurisdictions. For the Unidad's office in Urabá, as I mentioned above, one of its first cases was Tulapas.

In April 2013 the Unidad sent a team of its staff along with a handful of reclamantes into Tulapas to collect information on-site. They traveled under heavy police and military escort. When the convoy rumbled into the tiny village of San Pablo in Tulapas the situation immediately grew tense. As soon as police disembarked from their trucks, they began frisking villagers and cross-checking their ID numbers against a criminal database. The police officers ignored the complaints of the Unidad staff that the visit was taking on the appearance of an intelligence-gathering operation. Within minutes radio traffic and chatter from the Urabeños began crackling on the radios. "It gave us the feeling that we were surrounded," an official from the Unidad told me. "You have no idea how close or how far away the people on the radio might be." Afraid they were about to be attacked, the Unidad staff called off the visit and beat a hasty retreat.

The implications of the Unidad's botched visit to Tulapas became especially serious because of another incident that occurred just a few days later: a commando unit from the antidrug police raided a ranch in the heart of Tulapas, killing Francisco Morela, better known as El Negro Sarley. He had become the Urabeños second-in-command after police killed his predecessor, Giovanni, in the New Year's Day raid near Playona. Sarley's main job had been moving cocaine out of Urabá and into Central America, at which point local cartels took custody of it. One of the things that made Sarley such a good smuggler was his strong ties to Tulapas: he had served in the area with the both the EPL and the Casa Castaño.

One local resident, a demobilized paramilitary, said, "Sarley and his people [the Urabeños] were practically part of the community. He moved around the area as if he were in his own house. With his experience in the armed groups, he still had that characteristic—a natural ability, I'd say—of winning over the communities."[24] Giving examples of the Urabeños' ability to win over locals' loyalties, the former paramilitary cited many of the paras' practices from the past: paying for medical treatments or agricultural supplies, providing transportation, and sponsoring community events. "Sarley and his people didn't need to threaten anyone, they didn't kill anyone," he continued. "It's been years since a dead body has turned up—there are no displacements, no disappeared. What I mean is that the community is very relaxed with those guys."[25] Police discovered Sarley's hideout in Tulapas only after stumbling on one of his shipments near a beach in Turbo: three tons of cocaine with an approximate street value of $75 million.

César Acosta, the director of the Unidad de Tierras in Urabá, worried that the deadly raid against Sarley was going to have violent repercussions in relation to the restitution process in Tulapas. Since it occurred just days after and only miles from his staff's aborted visit to Tulapas, César feared the Urabeños would think the two events were related; the mission's actions during the visit had certainly given them good reason to think so. César thought the Urabeños' control over Tulapas now posed a real danger to his staff and the reclamantes.

About a week later he received a letter from a group of reclamantes trying to assuage his fears. The campesinos began the letter by mentioning that they had recently visited their old farms. "Some of the lands are just abandoned," they noted. "Others are planted in rubber and teak."[26] Then came the main point of the letter: "The people currently living in the area [the squatters] have expressed their support for *el retorno* of the displaced communities, guaranteeing favorable conditions. They have assured us there are no threats of reprisals and that current conditions in the area present no dangers of any kind for the returning communities."

The reclamantes knew César was still alarmed by the recent events. They feared the Unidad was going to suspend the restitution process in Tulapas because it was legally prohibited from sponsoring the return of displaced communities in places where they faced imminent threats. More than reiterating that the squatters supported the reclamantes' return, the letter was suggesting, between the lines, that the Urabeños had greenlighted the restitution process. By saying locals had "assured" the reclamantes that they faced no "threats of reprisals" or "dangers of any kind," the letter was implying that the squatters had consulted the Urabeños. The Unidad's staff clearly understood the message; they were surprised less by the direct lines of communication the campesinos had with the Urabeños than by the fact that the armed group had given the restitution process its blessing.

I had been hearing the same thing. Several reclamantes told me they had gotten "permission" from the Urabeños to go ahead with the restitution process. When I asked how they went about securing such permission, one campesina was matter of fact: "You go to a *político*—one of their people that's always out there hanging around."[27] The políticos were the Urabeños' version of El Alemán's PDSs, but their name had reverted to the simpler one used by guerrillas for these community liaisons. For confirmation, I asked, "A político is someone from the [armed] group?" "Right, a político is one of their people who lives in the village; that knows who such-and-such is, about who comes and goes; that knows everything about what is going on. So, I asked the guy [about reclaiming my land], and he said, 'You have nothing to worry about, we know you have good intentions. And if there's anything we can do to help, all you have to do is ask. Those lands are yours. If there's someone there on your land, it's only because they needed a place to work. We have nothing to do with that.'"

When another displaced campesino sought permission to reclaim his land, he said the político told him, "You're welcome to come back, just don't make too much noise about it."[28] A campesina got the same message: "They told me there was no problem with reclaiming my land as long as I didn't bring *la institucionalidad*," meaning government institutions. "Especially, the police and the army," she clarified. In short, the reclamantes had permission to proceed with the land restitution, as long as they did so quietly and without la institucionalidad in tow.

The letter from the reclamantes to the Unidad had made all this sufficiently clear. A member of the Unidad staff put it this way: "One way of looking at the letter is that the real author behind it [*el autor intelectual*] was the armed group, and it was obviously addressed to the Unidad."[29]

"So, the Urabeños were also giving *you* permission for the restitution?" I asked.

"Basically, yes."

Not long after receiving the letter the Unidad began preparing a second visit to Tulapas. This time it was sending a team of surveyors to map the properties subject to restitution. A rumor going around again raised security concerns. The story was that Guido Vargas, a longtime resident of Tulapas who had been Doña Tere's main intermediary for the land laundering she coordinated back in the early 2000s, had been going around telling locals that the Urabeños had changed their mind. Vargas, it was said, claimed they were now against the Unidad's visit. But Urabá's regional police chief reassured the Unidad, saying it had nothing to worry about. Apparently, the police had intercepted communications in which the Urabeños' commanders had ordered their minions to steer clear of any land controversies in the area.

Nonetheless, the rumor about Vargas and fear of retaliation from the Urabeños cast a dark cloud over the Unidad's preparations. When the survey team finally arrived in Tulapas, however, Vargas ended up assisting the Unidad's representatives every step of the way, even helping them track down some of the campesinos they were looking for. I asked César Acosta, the Unidad's local director, what he made of Vargas's dramatic about-face. He speculated, "My suspicion is that the Urabeños kept him in check so that the restitution wouldn't cause them any problems with the authorities."[30]

"Do you think that allowing the land restitution was also a way for them [the Urabeños] to build support among the returning campesinos?"

"Without a doubt, because the land restitution is happening one way or another," he reasoned. "The process has already gained too much force at every level [of government], so they are accommodating themselves to the process."

The rest of the visit went smoothly. This time the security detail kept to itself and mostly stayed huddled beneath the shade of a tin roof. Two humanitarian observers from the Organization of American States (OAS) accompanied the visit. One of the OAS observers later recalled her surprise at all the help the squatters gave to the Unidad team, which was essentially taking measurements for their eviction. She also noted that the presence of the Urabeños was palpable, claiming they kept a close watch over the proceedings through their eyes and ears in the community. Wherever she went in the village in her official capacity as a humanitarian observer a member of the local Junta de Acción Comunal would suddenly pop up. "It was like something out of Macondo," she joked. "The people from the junta were everywhere. We could actually see them running from place to place as we went around trying to talk to people about their situation."[31] When I asked Marta, one of the reclamantes, if the Urabeños ever harassed her or other peasants for reclaiming their lands in Tulapas, she said, "No, all they ask is that we not cause any problems for the people living there [the squatters]."[32] Marta explained why: "Because the people living there now are [the Urabeños'] point of support. If I put you somewhere so that I can hide behind you, then I'm going to take good care of you, right? That's the way it works." In other words, the Urabeños did not want the reclamantes disrupting the social relations of their territorial control, which they had long since established with the squatters.

The squatters had to be careful not to antagonize those returning to their lands lest they jeopardize the chances of a government-sponsored relocation inside Tulapas; the reclamantes likewise had to tread carefully to avoid upsetting the squatters, who had become the Urabeños' "point of support." The Urabeños had the power to be the spoilers of the restitution process. Instead, they made it clear that if the reclamantes wanted their land back they would have to make room for the squatters. As Marta explained, "For example, if one of their políticos comes and says, 'Look, why don't you give this little old lady a small parcel of land for a little house.' You have to be flexible." She described the process of the reclamantes' return to Tulapas as a careful balancing act between demanding what was rightfully theirs while not being confrontational or intransigent: "We can't go back into Tulapas leaning one way or another—neither friend nor enemy, neither here nor there. Knowing how things really are, you have to just be like that: neutral."

Cued by her openness, I asked about a rumor I had heard: "Do you think the squatters get economic support from the [Urabeños]?" I had heard that the Urabeños helped bankroll some of the squatters' agricultural projects, the same ones that had received government and foreign aid.

"*Ave María!* Do they receive economic support! I'd be lying if I said they didn't," Marta affirmed. Impersonating the supposed characters, she said, "'Oh, you need something? Come, *m'hijo*, why don't you go talk to the *político*?' And the *político* comes up with the money. 'Oh, you need this? Come, *m'hijo*, let me help you. . . . '"

When I asked members of the Unidad and campesino reclamantes why the Urabeños had acceded to the land restitution process in Tulapas, they all had the same hypothesis: the Urabeños' main concern was keeping things quiet enough for them to keep moving drugs through the area. As a drug-trafficking organization, the Urabeños' ultimate goal seemed to be preserving Tulapas as a strategic corridor and a key home base of their operations.

The Urabeños had not always been this accommodating to campesinos' land claims in the area. In fact, in the years preceding the Santos administration's land restitution law, they had lashed out violently against the reclamantes of Tulapas. For example, David Góez, an outspoken reclamante and one of the founders of the NGO Tierra y Vida, fled to Medellín in 2010 after receiving death threats for his organizing efforts. A year after Góez arrived in the city an old neighbor of his from Tulapas lured him to a place where gunmen drove up in a motorcycle and killed him with five gunshots fired at close range. The Urabeños had paid off Góez's neighbor for the betrayal. Indeed, the reclamantes have paid dearly for trying to reclaim their lands.

Once Santos passed the land restitution law and when Tulapas became Unidad's showcase for the program in Urabá, the Urabeños had few choices beyond reluctantly resigning themselves to the process. Violent opposition had become futile: land restitution, as César Acosta from the Unidad had put it, had "gained too much force at every level." In addition, given the national government's commitment to the process in Urabá, retaliation against the reclamantes would have been counterproductive, prompting police and military action and potentially destroying a prized territorial stronghold. By allowing and even welcoming the reclamantes, as long as they made some room for the squatters and did not make too much fuss or rouse la institucionalidad, the Urabeños would maintain their territorial hegemony.

The strategic value of Tulapas for the Urabeños and perhaps, too, their personal connections to the area, apparently saved it from the broad pattern of systematic violence against land rights activists in postconflict Colombia. Much of this violence has been concentrated in Urabá, and much of it has been perpetrated by the Urabeños. Tierra y Vida has been hit especially hard. Since the organization began its work in 2008, hit men have killed nine of its members. During my fieldwork fliers from the Urabeños threatening the NGO ended with the same refrain: "You sons of bitches want land? You'll have it: six feet of it on top of your head." One morning when Tierra y Vida's staff opened their office they realized someone had slipped a letter under the door. It was a death threat from the Urabeños signed in blood.

The Urabeños' attacks on land rights activists is one reason the group's populist claims of being an army fighting for the poor and marginalized ring so hollow. Nonetheless, they continue trying to change their image through elaborate rebranding efforts as the Autodefensas Gaitanistas de Colombia. They have become savvy producers of social media and even published a single-edition printed newspaper (*El Gaitanista*). On their website they post editorials and book reviews along with YouTube videos they share via Twitter (@gaitanistascol). One video shows a platoon of their troops armed to the teeth in full camouflage creeping through the jungle with the caption: "Patrolling the deepest parts of Colombia, those that don't exist for the central powers, always on the side of our forgotten communities."[33] A blog post that accompanied the video claimed they were out to defend the common folk in "areas in which *the state has shone for its absence*"—El Alemán's trademark phrase.[34]

Most observers dismiss the Urabeños' political posturing as empty rhetoric aimed at prying open the door for negotiations with the government. If the Urabeños gained official recognition as genuine combatants—or belligerents in the parlance of international humanitarian law—they could negotiate their demobilization and enjoy the legal benefits of the transitional justice process alongside the FARC. Most important, this could protect their leaders from being extradited to the United States as drug traffickers. To fit the bill of traditional combatants, they tailor their media outputs to emphasize all the key hallmarks of a traditional politico-military organization: their troops always appear in full uniform, wearing arm patches with the group's insignias and holding assault rifles and lightweight artillery; the videos also feature their troops practicing military rifle drills and singing the "Gaitanista Anthem." The group has also taken to mimicking the kind of social work once conducted by the paras. They have built roads and parks, sponsored roaming health brigades, and financed local sports teams for rural communities. All of this too ends up on their social media accounts.[35]

Over the years the Urabeños have also lent their support to more traditional forms of political activity. In one of the more bizarre twists of the postconflict they publicly backed the 2014 plantain growers' strike in Urabá when farmers protested against the export monopoly controlled by the banana companies. Made up of Urabá's smallholding underclass, the plantain sector is the poor and neglected sibling of the powerful banana industry. According to government intelligence agencies, the Urabeños helped the strikers by providing transportation and logistical support to the protests, which brought the entire region to a standstill for several days. If in previous years paramilitary politics had driven the formation of statehood, postconflict statecraft was now producing paramilitary politics. The Urabeños' combination of crime and politics is a premonition of Colombia's postconflict future in which the war has not so much ended as evolved.

The Urabeños' political practices are self-interested insofar as they help buttress their territorial hegemony and reinforce their self-presentation as an ideologically motivated combatant group. But it is also true that the territorial imperatives of the Urabeños, like those of the guerrillas and paramilitaries before them, have a way of drawing the group into political relationships with civilian communities by the force of their own logic. Territorial control requires building relationships of reciprocal, if deeply imbalanced, ties of mutual support with civilians. For the Urabeños, as for any other combatant group, the production of territory is made not only through coercion but also through their ability to address the needs of actual communities made up of real people with real problems. For instance, territorial control over the strategic area of Tulapas required the Urabeños to resign themselves to and, in many ways, manage the land restitution process.

Land restitution in Tulapas was not the territorialization of an all-seeing state, nor was it the orderly restoration of legality envisioned by President Santos onstage in Necoclí. The Urabeños practically became the midwives of land restitution's messy trial run in the region. The drug-trafficking group even helped mediate the problems arising from the fact that land restitution implied the remaking not just of property but also of community. Land restitution both tightened and tore the fabric of community. The land dispute created deep, sometimes vicious underlying tensions, including, in the case of David Góez's murder, a fatal betrayal. Although scholars and activists often depict community as a warm and idyllic social formation, a safe space for all that is good and wholesome, Tulapas shows the sinister, even vicious political life of community.[36]

Indeed, land restitution churned up the meaning and politics of community in particularly contentious ways. Yet as they navigated between the Urabeños and the Unidad reclamantes and squatters also sometimes found common ground and forged practical alliances.

In the process the implementation of land restitution turned into a quiet reconfiguration of rule, a hushed negotiation of postconflict statecraft; it involved the Urabeños, the Unidad, the reclamantes, the squatters, government institutions at all levels, and multiple development projects. The Santos administration may have designed the land restitution policy and the Unidad's local office may have implemented the program, but it was the Urabeños who decided the scope and scale of the process, and it was the campesinos who had to live with it. Far from supplanting the Urabeños' territorial hegemony, land restitution actually worked through it and probably even enhanced it by improving the group's image among campesinos. In the meantime the campesinos navigated the antinomies of the postconflict interregnum as best they could.

Most accounts of Colombia's armed conflict position paramilitaries as all-powerful victimizers and campesinos as their hapless and helpless victims. It is absolutely undeniable that campesinos suffered the brunt of paramilitary violence, but binaries of victims and victimizers or the powerful and powerless are oversimplifications that impoverish our understanding of the conflict. The war and its legacies have created impossible situations for campesino communities. The simple fact that they made do as best they could is in itself a heroic act.

URABÁ

A Sea of Opportunities?

> The tradition of all dead generations weighs like a nightmare on the brains of the living. And just as they seem to be occupied with revolutionizing themselves and things, creating something that did not exist before, . . . they anxiously conjure up the spirits of the past to their service, borrowing from them names, battle slogans, and costumes in order to present this new scene in world history in time-honored disguise and borrowed language.
>
> —Karl Marx, *The Eighteenth Brumaire of Louis Bonaparte* (1852)

In 2004 Colombia's Congress passed a bill celebrating the upcoming one-hundredth anniversary of Urabá's reincorporation into Antioquia. Introduced by one of the "quadruplets" elected with El Alemán's help, the bill was a mostly symbolic measure, except for a single clause: "With this law, the National Government through its respective ministries will craft a 'Strategic Plan' for Urabá that will promote the region's integral development."[1] Gradually, this single sentence—a couple of dozen words buried in an obscure piece of legislation—snowballed into a massive regional planning apparatus called the Plan Estratégico Urabá–Darién (Urabá–Darién Strategic Plan, or PEUD).[2] Laid out in a series of reports, spreadsheets, slideshow presentations, and concession contracts, the PEUD was a coordinated and multiply scaled effort to, as a local official described it, "finally bring the presence of the state to Urabá *once and for all*."[3]

As yet another outgrowth of the postconflict interregnum, the PEUD's proponents explicitly called it a Marshall Plan that would help turn the region into *la mejor esquina de América* (the best corner of the Americas). The plan included everything from microcredit loans for campesino families to huge infrastructural mega-projects built through public–private partnership contracts worth hundreds of millions of dollars. The crowning achievement of this new push for what the plan repeatedly described as Urabá's modernization was to be a gleaming new port system. As was true of the regional modernization projects of the past, the main force behind the PEUD was the city of Medellín: specifically, its municipal government, its economic elites, and the governor's office of Antioquia.

The PEUD was in many ways a revival of the high-modernist fixations and frontier imaginaries that drove the Highway to the Sea, a continuity suggested by the PEUD's main tagline: "Urabá: A Sea of Opportunities." Although the plan's advocates were at pains to distance it from the history of neocolonial exploitation by paisa elites and the United Fruit Company, the PEUD still rested on similar assumptions about Urabá as a space, a frontier, that had yet to be fully shaped by the forces of progress. Unlike these past ventures, however, the PEUD had a strong humanitarian bent, and it even celebrated the region's racial and cultural diversity. One of the PEUD's officials, for instance, claimed the plan would tap Urabá's "tremendous potential not only because of its strategic position and its place on the sea, but also because of its productive lands and its cultural mix of indigenous peoples, blacks, mestizos, and whites."[4] Despite these notable differences, however, the main thrust of the Strategic Plan for Urabá was fundamentally geared toward Medellín's own prosperity.

Once lauded by *Life* magazine as a "South American showplace" and a "capitalist paradise," Medellín had spent much of the 1980s and 1990s as ground zero for the global war on drugs, racking up the highest murder rate in the world. But by the time the PEUD began in 2005 the city had gained international notoriety for an altogether different reason: in the words of the World Bank, Medellín had become a global "model of urban transformation and social resilience." Or, as a far less wonkish newspaper headline put it, the city had gone "from murder capital to hipster holiday destination."[5] Medellín's revitalization was spurred by a series of urban planning initiatives associated with what came to be known as social urbanism. Through major public investment in the poorest slums, social urbanism transformed the city: murders reached an all-time low, artistic initiatives blossomed, tourism took off, and the economy boomed. The Medellín Miracle, as some called it, became the blueprint for Urabá's new strategic plan.

As an extension of Medellín's dramatic makeover, the PEUD was part of a broader effort aimed at promoting the city's internationalization.[6] City boosters hoped to capitalize on its newfound fame as a hot spot of urban innovation. At one meeting Medellín's city council resolved, "We want the entire world to pass through Antioquia. Internationalization is a necessary tool for our development within the context of globalization."[7] A representative from the governor's office agreed, saying, "A key part of this [internationalization] has to be for 'the Antioquia of the mountains' to meet 'the Antioquia of the sea.' The entire zone of Urabá gives us an opportunity to connect with the world by developing projects like the ports and the fully planned city that some have started calling 'Ciudad del Mar.'"

Ciudad del Mar was a throwback to plans from a century before (see chapter 1), when paisa elites imagined a seaside metropolis rising from the terminus of the Highway to the Sea. Back then they had named it Ciudad Reyes in honor of the president who had just helped Antioquia regain territorial dominion over Urabá. They, too, had couched it as the "spirit of the mountains" gracing the wallowing lowlands by the sea. One hundred years later the PEUD was borrowing the plans and time-honored slogans of the past, an echo of Marx's famous dictum that "all great world-historic facts and personages appear, so to speak, twice. . . . The first time as tragedy, the second time as farce."[8]

The PEUD was the culmination, which is not to say the end, of the long history of frontier making discussed in previous chapters. As a scaled-up version of Medellín's social urbanism, the PEUD was supposed to "finally bring the presence of the state to Urabá *once and for all*." It was the latest and one of the more elaborate iterations of the frontier effect. Although the state-building efforts of the PEUD—at least under this official name—started fizzling out in 2016, their effects are written into Urabá's social and physical landscape, becoming yet another layer of the sedimented histories that continue shaping the political life of this frontier zone.

The Social Urbanism Blueprint

In a reassertion of the frontier relationship, Medellín's position at the helm of the PEUD was institutionally enshrined in the Tripartite Commission, a planning entity made up of officials jointly appointed by the governor of Antioquia (who is based in Medellín), the mayor of Medellín, and the board members of the Aburrá Metropolitan Area (i.e., Greater Medellín). Founded in 2008, the commission had as its sole purpose ensuring the city's and, by extension, Antioquia's "global competitiveness." From the beginning the commission seized on Urabá as the geopolitical cornerstone of its strategy for the metropolitan region's continued success in the world economy. Although the PEUD worked in consultation with local municipal governments in Urabá and with other organizations based in the region, the Tripartite Commission's technocratic planners were the main architects of the strategic plan. Since many of the planners had been directly involved in Medellín's transformation, they explicitly made social urbanism their model for the new regional planning effort in Urabá.

Social urbanism generally refers to a series of civic-minded reforms in Medellín stretching back to the mid-1990s, when its municipal government began introducing a string of policies aimed at reducing violence, poverty, inequality, and social marginalization in the city.[9] In the 2000s one of the most transformative and highly visible aspects of social urbanism was the huge investment made in the construction of socially oriented infrastructure projects in the most impoverished parts of the city. The municipal government built a network of cable cars and outdoor escalators that connected the hillside slums to a world-class metro system. The slums became the site of public Library Parks, massive high-tech, community-oriented libraries and cultural centers. The city also engaged in a major expansion and renovation of public spaces and built several new sports and recreational facilities.

Although some of these projects preceded his time in office, social urbanism is most closely associated with the administration of Sergio Fajardo, who served as the mayor of Medellín from 2004 to 2007. Under Fajardo the city earned global praise for how its socially conscious forms of urban planning had helped turn around the city's abysmal security situation. International funders and media gushed over the city's metamorphosis from "the murder capital of the world" to a world-renowned model of urban revitalization. Fajardo's award-winning brand of social urbanism—it has indeed become something of *a brand*—is now firmly institutionalized in the city, with multilateral development agencies considering it a "replicable model" and "international example" of urban rebirth.[10]

FIGURE 17.   The cable cars and the Library Park (*top left*) of the Comuna 13 district in Medellín have become icons of social urbanism.

(Credit: Ben Bowes/CCPL 2.0)

Social urbanism's investment in the slums was aided by the fact that Fajardo's term came in the middle of a major economic boom in the city: from 2000 to 2011 Medellín's economy grew at an average rate of 10 percent a year.[11] The city also counted on the extraordinary financial muscle of its public services conglomerate, Empresas Públicas de Medellín (EPM). Although a municipally owned entity, EPM functions as an independent company and has operations across Colombia (including in Urabá) and, increasingly, Central America. In 2014 alone the firm brought in a record US$900 million in net profits, a mandatory 30 percent of which goes into municipal coffers.[12] Fajardo made education another major component of social urbanism. His administration allocated 40 percent of the city budget to education and built ten new schools in the poorest parts of the city.[13] He also expanded its participatory budgeting system and stepped up support for small businesses and micro-enterprises.

When Fajardo's administration ended in 2007, the city had one of the lowest murder rates ever recorded there. In 1991, at the height of Pablo Escobar's war against the government, murders had reached an all-time high of 381 per 100,000 inhabitants. (In New York City the same rate today would amount to 32,000 murders in a single year—it had fewer than 300 in 2017.) By the end of Fajardo's tenure homicides had dropped to 34 per 100,000, a rate lower than that of several U.S. cities.[14] Although social urbanism deserves some credit for these statistics, they were also attributable to darker forces underlying the reforms. Fajardo's term coincided with a Pax Mafiosa in the city's criminal underworld thanks to the rise and uncontested rule of a drug capo turned paramilitary commander nicknamed Don Berna.

In the early 2000s Don Berna, with the help of the Castaño brothers, began seizing control of the city's guerrilla-controlled slums. His takeover was coordinated with a series of military offensives led by the state security forces. The most infamous, Operation Orion, claimed the lives of around three hundred civilians in a single slum. After securing ironclad control over the hillside slums and lacking any serious contenders, Don Berna's criminal reign coincided with the precipitous drop in homicides. At the time, Fajardo's critics said the city's unprecedented *gobernabilidad* (governability) could more honestly be described as *donbernabilidad*. Despite the high body count that made it possible, social urbanism won the city multiple international prizes for its "urban innovations."[15] According to one analysis, social urbanism's most consequential overarching effect was that it had successfully reversed the "generalized *absence of the State*" in the city's violent slums.[16] From this perspective, the redeployment of social urbanism to the regional scale of Urabá made perfect sense. Fajardo used his success and popularity as mayor of Medellín to get himself elected governor of Antioquia in 2012. Being a former university professor and citing his track record in Medellín, he won office by campaigning as a technocratic political outsider and reformer free of the political commitments and horse trading that compromised a machine politician. But since Fajardo's family owned one of Medellín's largest construction firms, he also had strong ties to the city's moneyed elite. Under his leadership as governor the PEUD's implementation became more intensive and increasingly took on the features of a scaled-up version of social urbanism. Fajardo had the luck of counting on the support of Medellín's new mayor, Aníbal Gaviria, the heir of an elite local family that pioneered and was still heavily invested in Urabá's banana industry. Holding control of two-thirds of the Tripartite Commission, Fajardo and Gaviria made the transformation of Urabá along the lines of the Medellín Miracle a top priority.

Fajardo appointed a longtime collaborator named Federico Restrepo to lead the gargantuan planning effort. Restrepo, a suave businessman with a heavy antioqueño drawl, is a well-known fixture in Medellín's elite circles. An engineer by training, he spent much of his career working for a construction firm specializing in huge hydroelectric projects, most of them contracted by EPM, the city's public utilities powerhouse. When Fajardo launched his mayoral bid Restrepo became a major campaigner for him, especially among Medellín's high-end business class. Once in the mayor's office, Fajardo named him director of city planning, so Restrepo played a major role in the development of social urbanism. After this stint in government he spent four years as the head of EPM. It was on his watch that the company reaped record profits by, among other things, expanding into Central America and buying up public utilities in Urabá. Restrepo's firsthand knowledge of social urbanism, his engineering background, and his experience as the head of EPM made him a perfect fit for leading the Strategic Plan for Urabá.

In 2013, at his office in Medellín, Federico Restrepo pored over a map of Urabá as he laid out for me the PEUD's key moving parts—most of which hinged on the repair and expansion of the Highway to the Sea.[17] In the jargon of social urbanism the new and improved highway was a *proyecto detonante* (detonating project), which refers to how a major strategic intervention, like the libraries and the cable cars in Medellín, are supposed to detonate a chain reaction of wider collateral improvements. When Restrepo and his colleagues worked in Medellín they referred to the same idea as "urban acupuncture"—that is, pinpointed interventions that can have system-wide effects.[18]

In language that divulged his engineering background Restrepo explained, "The road is a detonator, a structuring axis, a detonator of development. A goodquality connection to the rest of Colombia will necessarily induce more industry and more commerce in the region." As it stood, the drive from Medellín to Urabá was a twisting roller-coaster ride descending 5,000 feet across 210 miles. Depending on road conditions, the trip took at least eight hours, and sometimes landslides made the road impassable. The PEUD's plans to construct new tunnels through the mountains and a second lane in both directions would cut travel time in half. Without the plan's revamped highway, said Restrepo, "everything else falls apart."

Restrepo personified the PEUD's combination of technocratic planning and elaborate flights of imagination. At one point, for instance, he mused, "Once the road is done, just imagine, why not move the Antioquia governor's office to Urabá? A kind of Brasília for the twenty-first century!" When I asked if he was serious he dialed back his excitement: "My point is that turning the political and administrative attention of the center toward an area that's not the capital of the department is a way of inducing the development of the region. It opens up a sea of opportunities." With all the talk about Ciudad del Mar as a reincarnation of the never-built Ciudad Reyes perhaps his suggestion of a fully planned modernist metropolis in the mold of Brasília was not so far-fetched.

The PEUD was far from the first macro-planning initiative with starry-eyed proposals for Urabá. One of its reports devotes some thirty pages of text to reviewing every other major regional planning scheme that came before it. Averaged out over time, a new strategic plan of some kind for the region has materialized about every two years since 1978, beginning with the internationally backed integrated rural development programs (see chapter 5). Restrepo described these previous plans as a long list of serial failures. "So why do you think it's going to be different this time?" I asked.

"Urabá is the most overdiagnosed region of Colombia," he began, "so there have been many other top-down, macro-level visions, but they have all conceived the development of the region as something that's supposed to be at the service of Medellín." Despite his assurances to the contrary and as much as Restrepo and his colleagues tried to distinguish the PEUD from earlier patterns of internal colonialism, the strategic plan was just as much, if not more, about what it could do for the city as what it could do for Urabá. Like Antioquia's previous designs on the region, the PEUD was steeped in the ideology of modernization and related assumptions about "bringing progress" to a backward frontier zone. A banal yet stark example of this was the message printed on all the billboards erected wherever the Highway to the Sea was undergoing reconstruction: "We're building a modern country!" The novelty with the PEUD was that these discourses of modernization were accompanied with the humanitarian features of social urbanism.

Rescaling the Medellín Miracle

Restrepo described Urabá as being caught between its history as an agricultural export enclave and its potential as an international commercial and industrial hub. He said his team's top priority for correcting the mistakes of the past was ensuring that Urabá attracted more "endogenous and value-added" industries capable of offering more "socially responsible forms of development." The expansion of basic public services beyond the region's largest urban centers, especially water and electricity, was a crucial part of their commitment. In this respect the PEUD was building on some of the foundations first laid by Urabá's guerrilla movements. The EPL and the FARC had backed the popular protests that brought these basic services to the region.

Restrepo envisioned the expansion of public services as part of an unapologetically capitalist and export-oriented model of development. He said that Urabá's "self-sustained development"—its takeoff in the lingo of modernization theory—would be possible only in conjunction with an improvement in people's actual living conditions. Otherwise, he argued, the plan would simply recreate the conditions for its own undoing by antagonizing popular sectors and, worse, perhaps swelling the ranks of the insurgencies. The PEUD aimed to avoid these problems by taking what social urbanism had accomplished at the scale of the neighborhood in Medellín and extrapolating it to the scale of the municipality in Urabá. "If in [Medellín], the main structuring axes were the Library Parks, the cable cars, or other modes of transportation," explained Restrepo, "then for Urabá's municipalities the main axis is going to be the educational parks."

Built in a striking modernist style, the educational parks are smaller versions of the huge library complexes that, thanks to social urbanism, now dot the slums of Medellín. The first of six educational parks built in Urabá by the governor's office was in the municipality of Vigía del Fuerte. Far to the south of the gulf

FIGURE 18.   The Ancestral Knowledges Educational Park in Vigía del Fuerte was the first of six of these facilities built by the governor's office in Urabá.

(Credit: Taller Síntesis Architects)

on the eastern bank of the Atrato River, Vigía del Fuerte is reachable only by air or by boat, and its mostly Afro-Colombian and indigenous Emberá residents are among Urabá's most impoverished communities. The choice of Vigía del Fuerte mirrored social urbanism's tactic of directing its most conspicuous *proyectos detonantes* to places with the most dire human development indicators. The educational parks formed the centerpiece, or "structuring axis" in Restrepo's words, of each municipality's locally designed integral development plan. Vigía del Fuerte's Integral Municipal Plan was backed by an additional US$13 million in joint funding from the governor's office, private foundations, and international donors such as USAID.[19]

Vigía del Fuerte's educational park opened in 2014. The two-million-dollar complex, named the Ancestral Knowledges Educational Park by local residents, includes classrooms, computers, and a sports complex with a full-size running track. Multiple times in interviews government planners both in Medellín and Urabá highlighted the PEUD's sports component, telling me the region's multiracial population made for "exceptional athletes." As one of the PEUD's local officials assured me, "We're such a mix—blacks with mestizos and paisas with mestizos— that it's generated a human biotype with tremendous athletic abilities." The essentialism and racism surrounding the region's multiracial demographic composition lives on in new ways.

As in Medellín's experience with social urbanism, the PEUD's educational parks and its other community-oriented projects were developed through consultative processes with local residents that included extensive meetings, forums, and workshops. Besides fostering ownership over the projects the point of these exercises was to turn the implementation process itself into a means of community building and of strengthening ties between municipal governments and their local constituents. Since they operated at the municipal scale the PEUD's community projects took root by working through the same decentralized structures and institutions that the paramilitary movement had helped consolidate just a few years earlier.

The PEUD was, in its own words, a program of "territorial reordering and development" geared toward "deepening the process of decentralization" in Urabá.[20] The educational parks, for example, brought together the Juntas de Acción Comunal and municipal administrations in the design and implementation of its highly localized interventions. The parks also received a third of their funding from municipal budgets. In other words the PEUD operated through the same decentralized fiscal, administrative, and political structures that the paras had enlisted in waging their war of position; in fact, as I have argued, the paras had not only mobilized these decentralized structures, they had actually created them (see chapter 3). Besides making Urabá safe and available for a mega-project like the PEUD, paramilitary counterinsurgency also constructed the social and institutional infrastructure through which the plan's implementation, as a process of postconflict statecraft, was now taking place.

The guerrillas may have coined the phrase "the combination of all forms of struggle," but, as I have shown repeatedly, it was the paramilitaries who perfected the idea in practice: they formed and "gave juridical life," as they liked to say, to countless Juntas de Acción Comunal; they elected politicians at all levels through a powerful electoral coalition built around a sophisticated set of populist politics; they created all kinds of peasant associations, campesino cooperatives, and NGOs. All of this social and institutional work of the paramilitary war of position was the political-ideological front of an otherwise scorched-earth campaign of violent counterinsurgency.

Indeed, as was true of Medellín's social urbanism during Don Berna's iron rule, the PEUD was built on the mass graves of countless innocent victims. But at the same time—again, much like its urban counterpart—the plan brought some badly needed and long-sought-after improvements to the region. At the university level alone the governor's office spent US$30 million on three new satellite campuses of the top-ranked Universidad de Antioquia. Colombia's national trade school network and polytechnic institute similarly increased their presence in the region. Another major boost on the human development front was the Clínica Panamericana, a US$30 million hospital that opened its doors in 2014. Fajardo also expanded a rural electrification project across the region and built water and sewage treatment facilities in two towns. It was the lack of such basic amenities that had enabled the paras to position themselves so effectively as the saviors and defenders of this forgotten region. The PEUD was implicitly—some might say explicitly—a response to the grievances channeled by the paramilitaries in their populist appeals for regional affirmation and integration. Although the PEUD made some laudable socially oriented interventions, it was overwhelmingly a plan for capitalist development and accumulation. Unsurprisingly, it bore a strong resemblance to the neoliberal portrait of regional integration once envisioned by the paramilitary-backed politicians of Urabá Grande (see chapter 4). After all, it was one of El Alemán's handpicked *parapolíticos* who wrote the legislation introducing the PEUD. While the plan made some notable progress toward improving people's everyday well-being, the vast majority of its efforts and resources went to massive export-oriented infrastructural projects, especially highways and seaports.

Plans for the building of a major port on the Gulf of Urabá date back to at least the 1920s, when Antioquia, just as construction on the Highway to the Sea began, commissioned a viability study from the German engineering firm Siemens. The cover letter to the governor of Antioquia presenting the study's findings, which approvingly recommended a port, was written by Gonzalo Mejía, the "dream maker" behind the highway project. In the letter Mejía wrote, "The port will be the gateway to Antioquia—that grandiose pueblo of the future—whose great destiny is now guaranteed by the Highway to the Sea."[21] It would be decades before the highway was completed, while the port, like so many of the overly ambitious plans of that era, never materialized.

Almost a century later, Restrepo assured me that the PEUD would "finally achieve that dream of a world-class port in Urabá [*un puerto de talla mundial*]." At last count, the PEUD had contracted not just one port project on the gulf's shores but three. The plan's managers justified the port-building spree by citing the raft of free trade agreements Colombia had signed with the United States and others in recent years as well as the gulf's proximity to the widened Panama Canal. They also relished and frequently repeated the statistic that a revamped highway would turn Urabá into the nearest seacoast for a swath of Colombia that comprised 70 percent of its GDP.

The architects of the strategic plan predicted that the improved highway would boost the fortunes of Urabá's duty-free Special Economic Zone, which had been languishing for years with the new Clínica Panamericana as its only tenant. The free trade zone was supposed to become a thriving cluster of export-processing factories (*maquiladoras*). One of the strategic plan's PowerPoint slide-shows predicted that "the area will attract national and international industries that want to take advantage of the region's coastal location and its competitive supply of public services and infrastructure."[22] Planners expected the new indus-trial complex, once linked to the new ports and the highway, would be another detonating project and that it would "induce the consolidation of a midsized Regional Urban Pole" along the gulf's eastern shore.[23] With an architectural rendering that I discovered came from an urban redevelopment project in Bra-zil, the PEUD slideshow presentation illustrated what the idyllic and futuristic Ciudad del Mar would look like. In 2017 Fajardo's successor in the governor's office began scouting Urabá for a potential site for this city-made-from-scratch, explaining matter-of-factly, "It's easier to build a whole new city than to fix the ones we already have."[24]

The strategic plan imagined the new city by the sea surrounded by sustain-able agribusinesses, including cacao, pineapple, oil palm, and teak plantations. Through strategic alliances (see chapter 5) the broad menu of crops would help reduce the region's overdependence on its two main exports, bananas and cocaine. As Restrepo noted, "The banana industry is a necessary but insufficient driver of development. And the gap between 'necessary' and 'insufficient' is being filled by the criminal economy." The expansion of grassroots-oriented agricultural ven-tures was aimed at turning locals away from Urabá's thriving illicit economy.

"Above all," Restrepo said, "we want a region committed to legality, a region that bets against the criminal economy and promotes a culture of legality."

Even as Restrepo and I were speaking at his office in Medellín, Colombian security forces in Urabá were engaged in Operation Agamemnon, the largest manhunt for a drug trafficker since they had killed Pablo Escobar. The new U.S.-backed military operation was aimed at bringing down Dairo Úsuga, or Otoniel, the Urabeños' top leader. Like many of the group's commanders, Otoniel was born in Tulapas and had cycled through all the armed groups in the area, meaning he had extensive ties with local communities. A government intelligence report recognized that this made the operation particularly difficult because the area constituted "a support network for [the Urabeños'] criminal operations, a comfort zone, and a long-standing refuge for the leaders of the group."[25]

In a dispatch from 2012 Alfredo Molano, a veteran war correspondent and sociologist, detailed the micro-mechanics through which the Urabeños exercised and maintained their territorial hegemony. "Some of the Urabeños don uniforms and weapons; others, the majority, are informants and collaborators," wrote Molano. "They have three branches: the military wing patrols with pistols and machine guns; the political wing controls votes and, by extension, elected officials; the social wing is in charge of community-oriented work through the Juntas de Acción Comunal, sports groups, and other civic organizations. They recruit youths through these same means and have also devised a new one: student loans."[26]

The activities described by Molano reveal the extent to which the territory-making practices of Colombia's various armed groups have become practically institutionalized, forming a well-established repertoire of accumulated tactics received and passed down by each generation of fighters. Molano's report also indicates how quickly the Urabeños have accommodated and countered some of the PEUD's hallmark initiatives, like its support for sports and education. The Urabeños' so-called scholarships were financing students who were taking advantage of the PEUD's expansion of higher education in the region. Presumably, once these students moved into their professional careers, as, say, IT specialists or nurses, they would become part of the drug-trafficking group's resilient civilian networks of social and logistical support.

The institutional practices crafted by El Alemán and the personnel he groomed proved especially useful to the Urabeños. In 2013, for instance, authorities arrested the ex-paramilitary nicknamed Slimy for coordinating the Urabeños' alliances with local politicians. Under El Alemán's command Slimy had been the irritable ("Shut up, toothy!") PDS who did extensive groundwork for Urabá Grande's political alliances in the early 2000s. Alarmed by the Urabeños' growing political influence, a government investigator in 2015 claimed that no other group had "the corrupting power of the Urabeños inside the institutions of the state."[27]

The PEUD's massive investments and its conspicuous interventions notwithstanding, the power of the Urabeños remained stubbornly intact. As in the case of the grassroots development projects (see chapter 5) or the land restitution program (see chapter 6), the PEUD, as a state-building project, did not supplant or even diminish the localized hegemony of Colombia's outlaw combatant groups. The Urabeños quickly adapted, incorporated, and even repurposed the PEUD's interventions in ways that suited and reinforced their power.

Similar to previous government-led efforts aimed at subduing this frontier zone through state building, the plan came up against and at times even worked through the existing social-spatial sedimentations of all the frontier state formations that came before it: the juntas, the grassroots projects, the community organizing, and more. Far from bulldozing everything in its path and producing a clean slate, the Strategic Plan for Urabá was just one more frontier state formation among many others: another of the unruly, sometimes fleeting, sometimes more durable political assemblages produced at the imagined limits of the state. As a project of state formation in Urabá, the PEUD, at least in the minds of its architects, should have been the last.

The Frontier Effect's State Formations

The strategic plan is a final illustration of this book's argument that Urabá has never been a simple Hobbesian tale of violent political disorder caused by the so-called absence of the state. Every step of the way, in every chapter, the state, as an instrument and an effect of political strategies and power relations, has never been absent. It has been everywhere: not only in the direct physical presence of the military, national agencies, municipal entities, elected officials, development projects, and all their attendant practices but also in the ways in which the state, even amid its presumed absence, has shaped—at a distance, as it were—the content and conduct of political relationships in the region. In Urabá, as in many other parts of Colombia, statelessness has been and is still a powerful material and ideological force, pushing nearly everyone, from guerrillas to paramilitaries, from technocratic planners to local politicians, into the business of state formation; that is the power of the frontier effect.

In this book, I could have simply critiqued the claim of state absence by documenting all the different ways in which formal governmental structures have actually always had a presence in Urabá. Instead, rather than dismissing commonsense notions of state absence as examples of misguided mystification and fetishism, I have demonstrated how "statelessness" has played a formative role in the imaginaries, practices, institutions, and relationships that make up the political life of this frontier zone. In short, I have provided a critical, yet non-dismissive, historical and ethnographic account of how the limits of the state are imagined and acted upon in a space, a frontier, in which it supposedly does not exist. Urabá is not an isolated case of the frontier effect. The Colombian anthropologist Margarita Serje has pointed out the powerful "myth of state absence," as she calls it, in many other parts of the country. As a constitutive feature of frontier spaces, these discourses of statelessness externalize and compartmentalize violence as something that only happens "out there" beyond the pale, in the Other Colombia; they gloss over the role of government institutions in the organization of violence in these supposedly abandoned spaces; and they obscure the workings of state-sponsored terror.[28] Similar discourses of statelessness with comparable consequences can be found in many of the world's violent places, including countries as far afield as Afghanistan, Burma, Democratic Republic of Congo, Guatemala, Iraq, and Somalia.[29]

In Colombia, paramilitaries' violent state project was particularly well served by this discourse of absence, but, as I have shown, it has also underwritten the political claims of subaltern groups. Statelessness, for instance, formed the basis of campesinos' demands for more meaningful forms of political representation, for the legal redress of violated rights, and for more tangible improvements to the quality of their daily lives. In one way or another campesinos' grievances were embraced by all the armed groups; guerrillas, paramilitaries, and Los Urabeños all built their respective territorial hegemonies by denouncing and counteracting Urabá's supposed abandonment by the state.

Through its powerful effect on local political subjectivities, state absence paradoxically enabled and coexisted with recursive efforts aimed at the consolidation of formal governmental structures and practices. Indeed, the long-standing invocation of statelessness is a major reason why Urabá has been such an intense, persistent site of state-building projects. Again, such is the power of the frontier effect. Even the communist guerrilla movements were conducive to localized state formation. For the paramilitaries in particular state making was an essential part of the unrivaled power they amassed in the region; they both positioned themselves and were positioned by campesino communities as state builders. All of which is to say that Urabá has suffered from a surplus of state projects, not a lack of them. Although combatants often talk about their armed struggle as a contest *over* the state, Urabá is a reminder that armed conflicts also *produce* the state as an always-emergent effect and instrument of these pitched political battles.

Although cast by dominant geopolitical imaginaries as aberrant spatial exceptions—in a word, the outsides—of state rule, frontiers are spaces where the constitution of liberal government and capitalist development as actually existing systems of violence can be seen in real time. The lived experience of this putative outside is characterized by a condition where, to repeat Benjamin's words, the "state of emergency" is "not the exception but the rule."[30] The permanence of the exception, however, stems not from the frontier being stateless or somehow existing completely outside the law, but from the fact that it is a space in which the insides and outsides of the juridical order are utterly blurred and indecipherable. This extralegal terrain is the fertile soil of the frontier effect's mushrooming state formations.

"Frontier state formations" has been my term for the rival political ensembles constantly being made and unmade by an array of different actors to address the assumed absence of the state. Conceptually, frontier state formations emphasize the plural, contingent, and provisional nature of the political assemblages produced amid the absence of the state without any suggestion of a definitive accomplishment or teleological endpoint. Though irreducibly local, the political formations discussed throughout this book have been shaped by processes and forces operating at multiple spatial and temporal scales: from the local to the global, from the event to the *longue durée*.[31]

The frontier imaginaries that have so deeply marked Urabá's turbulent history date back to the earliest colonial encounters in the region, but they became even more consequential at the start of the twentieth century as Colombia faced a compounding set of national crises. After a severe economic downturn and a devastating civil war, the loss of Panama left lingering geopolitical anxieties about U.S. imperialism in the country that helped bolster Antioquia's territorial claim over Urabá (see chapter 1). With statelessness expressed through idioms of civilization and barbarism, the reincorporation of the gulf into Antioquia's jurisdiction allowed paisa elites based in Medellín to realize their long-held colonial designs on the region.

Medellín's civilizing mission, which had political, racial, cultural, and economic dimensions, culminated in the construction of the Highway to the Sea and the United Fruit Company enclave. In tracing this history, I used Henri Lefebvre's theories on the "social production of space" to conceptualize how Urabá became a real-and-imagined frontier. Relying on Lefebvre's understanding of space as a product of ideological, material, and social processes, I showed how the cultural politics of race and region were just as formative in the production of this frontier zone as foreign interventions and the concrete fluctuations of uneven capitalist development. Today, as then, the politics of race and racism and their material implications are central to the construction of Urabá's frontier status.

With the racialized labor exploitation and land dispossession unleashed by the highway and the banana industry in the background, the global geopolitics of the Cold War took center stage in Urabá as it became the site of an escalating cycle of violence between insurgency and counterinsurgency. As the armed groups, including rival rebel factions, battled for control of the region, they socially produced—again, in Lefebvre's elaborate sense—a fractious spatiality of violently clashing territories. Combatant groups produced their territories, as political technologies of social-spatial control, through deliberate choreographies of both coercion and consent. It was this process of building "territorial hegemony," as I called it, drawing on Lefebvre's conception of spatiality and Gramscian understandings of hegemony, that pushed both paramilitaries and guerrillas into the role of would-be state builders.

The frontier state formations of both armed groups were as much an intentional outcome of political conviction and deliberate practices as they were the inherent by-product of their attempts to build up their social bases of support. The paras made state making an explicit goal of their political program. The guerrillas, on the other hand, did not intend or frame their political work as state building. But the rebels helped bring public services to the region by backing popular protests; once elected, their politicians strengthened municipal administrations; and the guerrillas boosted political representation and participation on multiple fronts via their political parties, the juntas, labor unions, peasant cooperatives, and other kinds of community organizations. Intentional or not, these various activities would certainly qualify as state formation by almost any definition.[32] As the EPL's Gerardo Vega assured me, "In Urabá, we were the ones who built the state!" In fact, the guerrillas' success in building a rebel state, as El Alemán would later call it, was what led Urabá to being designated the red corner of Colombia, consolidating its reputation as a lawless frontier zone.

The other reason Urabá earned its ignominious nickname as the red corner was the unprecedented bloodshed that came with the counterinsurgent blowback against the rebels' powerful territorial hegemony. Although the paramilitary takeover of Urabá was a brutal campaign of counterinsurgency, it also involved a subtler ideological front in which the paras retooled and redeployed the full repertoire of political–territorial practices pioneered by the guerrillas. State building was at the core of the paras' revanchist political, economic, and military project against the insurgencies (see chapter 3). Applying Gramsci's concept of the war of position, I analyzed the paras' painstaking political work and organizing efforts as a struggle for hegemony pressed into the service of a particular vision of statehood, a vision that was as dynamic and elaborate as it was contradictory. The paramilitary war of position sought to reconcile the brutality of primitive accumulation and counterinsurgency with the practices, discourses, and institutional formations of Colombia's constitutionally enshrined liberal-democratic order.

The paras' electoral scheming was another part of their state-oriented war of position (see chapter 4). My dissection of the paramilitary-backed electoral coalition known as Urabá Grande revealed how the paras and their allied candidates refashioned the racialized politics of Colombian regionalism and professed state abandonment into a dominant populist project of regional affirmation and integration. Urabá Grande conflated the construction of regionhood and statehood, making it a single endeavor. Across the country right-wing politicians positioned *las regiones* as aggrieved and forgotten victims whose redress required their integration "into the body politic of the nation" through the "arrival or return of the state," as one paramilitary ideologue put it. Even though Urabá Grande operated through the same electoral networks of patronage and clientelism as the status quo, paramilitary populism put anticorruption at the forefront of its politics. The paras' brand of authoritarian populism thus doubled as a performative critique of the state: as they denounced institutionalized corruption and bureaucracy, paramilitaries delivered basic public services and helped forge closer ties between municipal administrations and subaltern communities.

Yet the paras were not selfless, good Samaritans engaged in state building as a disinterested patriotic service (see chapter 5). They used grassroots development to both build up a state presence in their territories and launder the massive amount of land they stole from campesino farmers. In putting the grassroots development apparatus to work, the paras went beyond a simple rhetorical whitewashing of their economic ventures by describing them as green, gendered, local, and multicultural. These discourses came with and enabled a whole set of practices and institutions that helped execute and legally ratify their land grab. While neutralizing some of the development industry's most politically contentious issues, these projects won praise from international funders and government agencies for promoting local institution building, good governance, and the rule of law. In this way grassroots development made the paras' economies of violence conducive to and compatible with formal projects of liberal state building.

With the paramilitaries' demobilization in 2006 and with even greater intensity once the FARC began peace talks with the government in 2012, Colombia's postconflict political horizon became the latest crucible of Urabá's frontier state formations. The postconflict along with the state-building projects it has enabled, can be seen, as I argued, not as a transition from war to peace but as an indefinite interregnum (see chapter 6). Land restitution, as a symptomatic manifestation of this interregnum, was not the orderly restoration of state authority that lawmakers hoped it would be but a hushed renegotiation of rule closely managed by a new breed of outlaw combatants, the Urabeños. Similarly, the regional planning initiative, the Strategic Plan for Urabá, is another example of how the attempted projection of state power has worked alongside and even through the region's illicit networks. Land restitution and the strategic plan both reflect how decades upon decades of conflict and violence in Colombia have produced astoundingly resilient extralegal regimes of accumulation and rule.

Space, Territory, and Land

My analysis of Urabá stands in sharp contrast to Lefebvre's thesis—echoed by the work of several scholars—that capitalism and modern statecraft always thrive on the production of what he called "abstract space."[33] In its ultimate, idealized form abstract space would be something like a frictionless blank slate allowing the smooth, unencumbered operation of capitalism and state power. But as this book has shown, powerful political and economic forces in Urabá have actually operated through the region's contested spatialities and their historical sedimentations, not in spite of them. The hypercomplexity of the frontier's multiple overlapping and interpenetrated territorial arrangements have been both a medium and the result of ultraviolent forms of capitalist extraction and state formation in the region. State building has never quite succeeded in ending the region's violent political disorder.

The commonplace view that state building always results in peace building assumes there are no real substantive political or material stakes involved in the question of the state itself; the "build it and they will come" mentality assumes that political opponents are broadly in agreement about the meaning, purpose, and organization of rule. Many mainstream accounts of contemporary mass violence make the same depoliticizing move by drawing a sharp distinction between the political and economic dimensions of violent conflict. In this analysis today's so-called New Wars are driven more by combatants' greed and other economistic dynamics like the resource curse than by political grievance or ideological differences.[34] This book's emphasis on land and territory has demonstrated why sharp binaries of greed and grievance or economics and politics are inadequate for analyzing the social complexities of armed conflict.

Even if the political convictions or intentions of armed groups can be questioned as disingenuous, self-interested, or even completely lacking, the fact that combatants must socially produce and constantly reproduce their territories means they inevitably find themselves in a position of power that is inherently or, more often, overtly political. The reason for this is that communities are not passive subjects devoid of political agency; once a territory stabilizes, civilians make demands and have expectations that must be reasonably met by the armed groups as a way of upholding territorial control. The relationships between civilians and combatants are not forged in the absence of the state; combatants usually address civilians' material and political claims by drawing on and sometimes even creating established state structures, routines, and practices. Despite their blustery rhetoric, in practice, combatants rarely renounce official governmental structures altogether (the EPL made this mistake in its early days). Within the territorial struggles that define irregular warfare, state formation is as much a deliberate practice and outcome as it is a structural effect of combatants' territorial imperative. One reason state building in Urabá has never resulted in the orderly restoration of law and order expected by its proponents is that land remains the unresolved violent meeting point of the political and economic conflicts there. Land and, more specifically, property have been an integral part of Urabá's territorial struggles. The region has faced an endless cycle of territorialization, deterritorialization, and reterritorialization in which the constant making and breaking of social relations around land have played a fundamental role. It began with Antioquia's repossession of the gulf, triggering the primitive accumulation unleashed by the Highway to the Sea and the United Fruit Company. Next, amid the human fallout of this dispossession, the guerrillas terraformed their territorial hegemony through mass land occupations of public and private properties; they also sponsored the colonization of unclaimed lands beyond the property frontier. It was the intimate social bonds between land and territory, which formed the foundation of rebel hegemony, that were so violently crushed by paramilitary zone breaking.

For their part, paramilitaries built their territories not only by carrying out wholesale massacres and the political–ideological battles of the war of position but also by brutally seizing huge tracts of land and legally consolidating their plunder through land laundering. The paras' combination of mass dispossession and counterinsurgency is a perfect example of how greed and grievance operate as inseparable, reciprocal forces in the Colombian conflict. For the paras, land was as much a part of breaking territories as it was of building them back up. As a way of shoring up the social bases (or hegemony) of their territorial conquests, the paras doled out land to subaltern campesinos and in the process gained tight control of a newly loyal political clientele.

El Alemán even made these stolen lands the basis of his troops' demobilization program, which extended their territorial control over Tulapas into the postconflict. The social–spatial control produced by his token agrarian reforms was strong enough that even years later the government's land restitution efforts were still contending with its legacies. In fact, as the heirs of the paramilitary movement the Urabeños ensured their own hegemony over the area by quietly overseeing the delicate complexities of land restitution and the postconflict renegotiation of rule it required at the intimate scale of community.

Paradoxically, although locals and outsiders alike have pointed to Urabá's notorious land conflicts as indicators of the state's absence and thus of the region's frontier status, struggles over land have constantly invoked the state's presence by eliciting, in however perverse a form, the exercise of state power through the law, rights, and its juridical authority. Although scholars have pointed to the administration of property rights as a means of establishing and exercising state authority, Urabá is a case in which things worked out quite differently.[35] Despite claims to the contrary, neither paramilitary-backed agribusiness plantations nor the implementation of the land restitution law resulted in the consolidation of an all-seeing state capable of disciplining this unruly space. Nonetheless, formal governmental institutions, laws, policies, and practices, far from being absent, have played integral roles in these land struggles. Urabá's violent conflicts over land may be unresolved, but they are not proof of state weakness or failure: they are the conditions in which state rule becomes possible.

In an article titled "The Imperative of State-Building" the prominent political scientist Francis Fukuyama, who famously proclaimed that liberal democracy and free-market capitalism as universal ideals had irreversibly ushered in "the end of history," bemoaned, "The modernity of the liberal West is difficult to achieve for many societies around the world. While some countries in East Asia have made this transition successfully over the past two generations, others in the developing world have either been stuck or have actually regressed over the same period." He further offered that "many of the world's most serious problems, from poverty and AIDS to drug trafficking and terrorism," could be solved by state building, which he defined as "the creation of new governmental institutions and the strengthening of existing ones."[36]

Fukuyama and other scholars who espouse similar views about the imperative of state building often assume a Weberian litmus test of statehood. According to Max Weber, "The state is the form of human community that (successfully) lays claim to the *monopoly of legitimate physical violence* within a particular territory—and this idea of 'territory' is an essential defining feature."[37] Weber intended this ideal-type definition of the state as a heuristic analytical device, but Fukuyama and others have run with it as if it were an attainable empirical reality. Colombia's paramilitaries made this idea a central part of their mission, claiming that their ultimate goal was "reestablishing the monopoly of force in the hands of the State."[38] Indeed, the question of statelessness is not some irrelevant, esoteric academic debate; in Colombia it has had life and death consequences.

Colombia's many frontier zones, those spaces of presumed statelessness, are often described in popular discourse as the country's forgotten regions. Since Gabriel García Márquez hailed from one of these regions, it makes sense that he turned forgetting and remembering into a dialectical force of his stories.[39] Urabá is an object lesson in the geographical marginalization and exploitation—the solitude as he called it—that García Márquez so eloquently explored in his novels. As the story of one of these places, this book has tried to expose all the discomforting histories that have been covered up, silenced, and willfully forgotten in the production of Urabá's solitude. Beginning with the loss of Panama in 1903, this book has peeled back the complex layers accumulated over more than one hundred years that have resulted in Urabá's geographies of solitude.

This book represents what I am able to offer to the obviously much more consequential efforts of the region's residents, who continue struggling against all odds to avoid meeting the same fate as the villagers of Macondo. When Colonel Buendía's nephew returns to Macondo as the sole survivor of the banana company's massacre, a biblical deluge has swamped the village for years, and it remains under martial law, but no one besides him remembers why the state of emergency was declared in the first place. He desperately tries to remind everyone about the massacre, but the fog of amnesia is impenetrable. "You must have been dreaming," insists a police officer. "Nothing has happened in Macondo, nothing has ever happened, and nothing ever will happen."[40] Against the erasures of dominant histories, remembering, said García Márquez when accepting his Nobel Prize, is the first step toward ensuring that "the races condemned to one hundred years of solitude will have, at last and forever, a second opportunity on earth."[41] But Urabá's second opportunity—not the "sea of opportunities" of technocratic planners but the opportunity for a better life that it so deserves—will remain out of reach if its entrenched social, political, and economic struggles continue to be misattributed to the absence of the state.

The idea that state building can end political violence in conflict zones or frontier spaces by pulling them out of the Hobbesian netherworld in which they are supposedly stuck, as Fukuyama put it, persists across popular, policy, and scholarly circles. Indeed, the myth that the state saved humanity from a short and brutish existence is one of modernity's most enduring conceits. Although no group has ever held a monopoly on violence in Urabá, the region has never been a complete vacuum of formal state practices and institutions; these may have been patchy and uneven, but they have never been absent. Legally recognized projects of liberal state building and capitalist development have been an integral part of the region's violent regimes of accumulation and rule. Illicit networks of power and profit have been intricately connected to their formal counterparts; the two have operated through and drawn strength from each other. Far from a zero-sum opposition, the legal and the illegal have melded together as the core alloy of frontier rule in Urabá. El Alemán was an expert of this legal alchemy. As one of his lieutenants told me, "In Urabá, we constantly legalized the illegal."

Though subject to these extralegal regimes of governance, frontiers produce the state as a structural effect by spatially marking out the insides and outsides of its rule. As a result of this frontier effect, all kinds of actors make a headlong rush into the business of state formation, all the while conceiving of their actions as operating outside of the formal political order. That is the generative power of the frontier effect. While Urabá might seem like a provincial case of one state's inability to maintain a monopoly on violence, it actually reflects a deeper, more universal condition: perhaps the more consequential monopoly of the state is the one it has on our political imaginations.

Notes

INTRODUCTION

1. The state-sponsored historical commission, the Centro Nacional de Memoria Histórica (CNMH), found paramilitaries responsible for 94,754 of the 215,005 civilians killed in the conflict.

2. The CNMH says the conflict forcibly displaced 6,459,501 people from 1985 to 2014.

3. Glemis Mogollón Vergara, "El Alemán contradijo versión de Mancuso," *El Colombiano*, June 6, 2007.

4. "No más festejos en la versión libre de ex Auc," *El Colombiano*, June 8, 2007.

5. Faulkner 2011, 69.

6. Freddy Rendón, Versión Libre, Fiscalía General de la Nación, Unidad de Justicia y Paz, June 5, 2007.

7. For an authoritative account of La Violencia in Antioquia, see Roldán 2002.

8. Letter on "Orden Público," February 3, 1953; Archivo Histórico de Antioquia (AHA), Ministerio de Gobierno, 1945/1953, D.G. 079, 553.

9. Although the FARC officially disbanded in 2017, Colombia still faces widespread low-intensity conflict as well as some pockets of extreme violence between a smattering of armed groups, including some dissident remnants of the FARC.

10. Rendón, Versión Libre, June 5, 2007.

11. Over the course of two years, from the beginning of 2012 until the end of 2013, I split my time between Bogotá, Medellín, and Urabá conducting interviews, ethnographic-style fieldwork, and archival and public records research. The ethnographic portions of my fieldwork involved monthly one-week or two-week stints in Urabá accompanying either campesinos from an area called Tulapas or demobilized members of El Alemán's paramilitary group. For a fuller discussion of my methods, positionality, and epistemological approach for this project, see Ballvé 2019.

12. The question of statelessness was one of the more interesting debates raised in the eight-hundred-page study commissioned by the peace process between the government and the FARC. Published under the title "Contribución al entendimiento del conflicto armado en Colombia" (Toward an understanding of the armed conflict in Colombia), the report contains twelve chapters, each individually written by prominent experts with contrasting views on the main roots of the conflict.

13. A passing footnote by Gupta (2012, 300n3) in which he's discussing an article by Nielsen (2007) helped me refine the wording of this question.

14. I use "state formation," "state building," "state making," and "statecraft" as interchangeable, synonymous terms to avoid repetition in the narrative. Berman and Lonsdale (1992) offer a much-cited distinction I find empirically and methodologically untenable. They define state building as "a conscious effort of creating an apparatus of control," while state formation is a "historical process whose outcome is a largely unconscious and contradictory process of conflicts, negotiations, and compromises" (Berman and Lonsdale 1992, 5). Besides the problem of deciphering intent, the two processes they describe are intimately interrelated and difficult if not impossible to disaggregate.

15. Collier et al. 2003.

16. The New Wars framework, though often misinterpreted as an empirical category, was proposed by Kaldor (1999, 2013) and is frequently used in tandem with dichotomous understandings of greed and grievance (Collier and Hoeffler 2000; Berdal 2005). For more on these debates, see Mundy 2011.

17. Rangel's work (2000) is an example, but even Duncan's (2006) pathbreaking account of paramilitaries can be overly dismissive of armed groups' political motivations, which, as I show, are inseparable from their economies of violence.

18. I especially have in mind the scholars associated with the Centro de Investigación y Educación Popular (CINEP), such as González, Bolívar, and Vásquez (González, Bolívar, and Vásquez 2003; González 2014), who are part of a wider tradition of scholarship on state formation in Colombia (Oquist 1978; Rubio 1999; Pecaut 2001; M. T. Uribe 2001; Richani 2002; Serje 2005, 2012; M. C. Ramírez 2011; Grajales 2017; among others). Julio Arias (2016) provides a very helpful review of this body of literature in relation to Gupta's *Red Tape* (2012).

19. Margarita Serje (2005, 2012), in particular, has critically analyzed this discourse.

20. González, Bolívar, and Vásquez (2003) provide an exhaustive survey of the vast body of literature on statehood, violence, and conflict in Colombia.

21. The special issue of *Third World Quarterly* introduced by Marquette and Beswick (2011) examines the state-building "renaissance," while Gutiérrez (2010) and Dugas (2014) lay out the use and abuse of the whole "failed state" and "ungoverned spaces" paradigm in the Colombian context.

22. The best example of this trend is the World Bank's surprisingly insightful *World Development Report* titled "Conflict, Security, and Development" (World Bank 2011). For more on the security–development nexus, see the special issue of *Security Dialogue* 41, no. 1 (2010).

23. Lefebvre 1991.

24. Elden 2010.

25. A richer conceptualization of territory gives theoretical corroboration to the insights provided by Kalyvas (2006) and Arjona (2016); territory is also, in my view, an essential piece of the puzzle for understanding the dynamics of what Arjona and others have called the micropolitics of civil wars and the forms of "rebel governance" that often accompany them (Mampilly 2011; Arjona, Kasfir, and Mampilly 2015).

26. Although my understanding of Gramsci's concepts is based on close readings of the English translations of his *Prison Notebooks* (Gramsci 2011), for ease and consistency my citations are from *Selections from the Prison Notebooks,* translated and edited by Quintin Hoare and Geoffrey Nowell Smith (Gramsci 1971). My use of Gramsci's concepts is also informed by recent reinterpretations of his work by Thomas (2009) and by the authors represented in the collection edited by Ekers et al. (2012). My understanding of Lefebvre's work draws from a related body of work by several geographers (Elden 2004; Goonewardena et al. 2008; Brenner and Elden 2009a, 2009b).

27. This was the crucial insight of the anthropologist William Roseberry (1994, 360).

28. Williams 1977, 112. My understanding of hegemony also draws on Stuart Hall's work (1977).

29. Kalyvas 2006, 16.

30. Arguably the question of the state was most provocatively posed by Abrams (1988), but there are now other classic takes on the matter (Corrigan and Sayer 1985; Mitchell 1991; Taussig 1992; Joseph and Nugent 1994; Hansen and Stepputat 2001; Aretxaga 2003; Das and Poole 2004). Much of the literature on the anthropology of the state is summarized and compiled in an edited volume (Sharma and Gupta 2006). Too often, though, in much of the subsequent writing that draws on this critical work authors warn against reifying the state and cite this literature but then analytically proceed with business as usual. *Red Tape* (Gupta 2012) is a notable counterexample.

31. The few exceptions include Radcliffe 2001 as well as Ferguson and Gupta 2002. Goswami 2004 is a more historical and nation-oriented project than mine, but it remains a conceptual inspiration with clear relevance for ethnographic approaches to the state.

32. Diana Bocarejo, "An Ordinary Peace in a Disparate Landscape of Longings," *Cultural Anthropology* (online), April 30, 2015: https://culanth.org/fieldsights/676-an-ordinary-peace-in-a-disparate-landscape-of-longings. María Clemencia Ramírez (2011) and Simón Uribe (2017) have also done critical work on the popular sense of abandonment by the state in Colombia.

33. My formulation of the state here draws on several sources (Jessop 1990, 2015; Mitchell 1991; Lemke 2007). Following Lemke's (2007), my approach poses a challenge to both positivists for taking the state for granted and strict constructivists for dismissing its existence altogether. In Marxist terms, the state is a "concrete abstraction" or a "realized abstraction" (Lefebvre 2009; Stanek 2008). The relationship between the abstract and concrete with relation to the state is dialectical, not a temporal sequence—one does not precede or follow the other.

34. Aretxaga 2003, 395.

35. The frontier effect is a social–spatial corollary to Timothy Mitchell's point about the state as a "structural effect" produced by a series of discursive practices that "create the appearance of a world fundamentally divided into state and society" (1991, 95); in the case of frontiers, however, the bifurcation is fundamentally expressed in spatial form—that is, between state space and a stateless (or nonstate) space. On a more philosophical level, Žižek (2004, 35) makes this point about the generative power of absence and negativity.

36. Jessop 1990, 9.

37. Blomley 2010, 2016; Lund 2018; Peluso and Lund 2011; D. Hall, Hirsch, and Li 2011.

38. Urabá thus stands as a counterpoint to many important accounts of frontiers that examine the relationships among land, property, and statehood (Blomley 2003; Banner 2005; Li 2007; Peluso and Vandergeest 2011; J. W. Moore 2015), bearing out Scott's arguments about why high-modernist schemes are doomed to fail (1998).

39. Hobbes 1987, 186.

40. From Juanita León's *País de plomo* (2006, 16–17), which, despite these occasional misfires, is an engaging chronicle of the war.

41. The first chapter of Colombia's 1991 Constitution has a section that begins as follows: "The authorities of the Republic have been constituted to protect all the resident peoples of Colombia, their life, honor, property."

42. In Schmitt's framework (1985, 2003), guerrillas would certainly classify as "unjust enemies" since they pose an existential threat to the established juridical–spatial order, or *nomos*, of the state system. For Schmitt, unjust enemies are so far beyond the pale of political recognition or inclusion that the only responsible law-preserving response is indiscriminate annihilation. Paramilitary commanders held a similar position vis-à-vis the guerrillas.

43. Author interview with Freddy Rendón (alias El Alemán), paramilitary chief, in Itagüí, Antioquia, September 17, 2012.

44. Author interview with Gerardo Vega, labor lawyer and former EPL operative, in Medellín, Antioquia, March 13, 2012.

1. PRODUCING THE FRONTIER

1. The 350-page untitled manuscript was submitted to the courts as part of El Alemán's testimony: Freddy Rendón, Versión Libre, Fiscalía General de la Nación, Justicia y Paz, Medellín, November 23 to December 4, 2009.

2. In Spanish, *el fabricante de sueños*. See "Gonzalo Mejía Trujillo," ficha biográfica, Banco de la República, Bogotá, Colombia: http://enciclopedia.banrepcultural.org/index.php/Gonzalo_Mejía.

3. *Álbum de la carretera al mar*, Fray Máximo de San José, ed. (1930), 43.

4. "¡Hacia Urabá!" was the headline of an op-ed in Medellín's paper of record, *El Colombiano*, November 13, 1913.

5. Quoted in Steiner 2000, 9.

6. Benjamin's remarks (1968, 257–58) are a meditation on Paul Klee's painting *Angelus Novus*.

7. Besides my theoretical framework derived from Lefebvre's ideas (1991), my understanding of frontiers draws from a literature so extensive that I limit myself to citing works that have been particularly influential in my thinking: Hecht and Cockburn 1989; Watts 1992, 2017; Alonso 1995; Blomley 2003; Brown 2004; Banner 2005; Goodhand 2005; Tsing 2005; Baretta and Markoff 2006; Coronil and Skurski 2006; Markoff 2006; Redclift 2006; Pratt 2008; Peluso and Lund 2011; Peluso and Vandergeest 2011; Eilenberg 2012; Li 2014; Rasmussen and Lund 2018.

8. Penelope Harvey, who has written extensively on the anthropology of roads, notes, "Roads can invoke both the presence and the absence of the state" (2005, 131). Simón Uribe (2017) provides a striking political history and ethnography of a road in southern Colombia with, not surprisingly, striking parallels to the Highway to the Sea.

9. This is my riff on a line by Marx (1990, 799).

10. My arguments in this chapter combine insights on uneven development from both Latin American *dependistas* (González Casanova 1965; Stavenhagen 1965; Frank 1967) and Anglophone Marxist geographers (D. Harvey 2006; Smith 2008).

11. "Informe de Comisión Región Urabá," Ejército Nacional, IV Brigada, October 16, 1950, in AHA, Comando Ejército, 1950/1951, D.G. 029, 314.

12. For a broader survey of frontiers in Latin American history, see Weber and Rausch 1994.

13. The term "imagined communities" is Anderson's (1991). To keep the scope of this book manageable, I have admittedly cast aside the complicated questions of Colombian nationalism and nation building, which have been covered elsewhere (Steiner 2000; Appelbaum 2003, 2016; Múnera 2005; Serje 2005; J. Arias 2007; Pratt 2008).

14. Serje's brilliant book *El revés de la nación* (*The Opposite of the Nation*, 2005) traces the enduring legacies and contemporary manifestations of these frontier ideologies. She shows how Colombia's so-called peripheral spaces and their discursive construction as savage no-man's-lands have, in fact, been central to the formation of nationhood and capitalist development in the country.

15. For a deeper analysis of mestizo nationalism in Colombia, see P. Wade 1995; J. Arias 2007.

16. Michael Taussig has written on the brutality of the rubber boom (1984, 1987), while Jane Rausch has surveyed the cattle frontiers of Colombia's *llanos orientales* (eastern plains), which stretch into Venezuela (Rausch 1984, 1993; see also Baretta and Markoff 2006; Markoff 2006; Coronil and Skurski 2006).

17. Sauer 1966, 266.

18. Though equally elite at the echelons of leadership and mixed in their class composition at the base, the Liberal and Conservative Parties have, for the most part, been on opposing sides of some key issues. Compared to Conservatives, Liberals have generally been more secular, more accommodating of decentralized government, and more inclined toward free trade. Conservatives, by contrast, have been fiercely pro-Church, suspicious of decentralized government, and inward looking in their economic policies (Bergquist 1978; Hylton 2006).

19. The comment was made by Miguel Abadía Méndez in Panama while on his way to Chile as Colombia's ambassador; quoted in Bergquist 1978, 214.

20. Quoted in Parsons 1967, 28.

21. Claudia Steiner's foundational book (2000) fleshes out the view of paisas' colonization of Urabá as a civilizing mission, while Nancy Appelbaum (2003) helps put paisa colonization and identity in a broader national perspective.

22. Prefect's letter to Antioquia's Secretario de Gobierno, June 12, 1911. AHA, Gobierno Municipios, Turbo, Tomo 143, Carpeta 1, 241.

23. Quoted in Steiner 2000, 9.

24. Prefect's letter to Antioquia's Secretario de Gobierno, June 12, 1911, 243–44. In her exhaustive history of Urabá, María Teresa Uribe specifically couches *antioqueño* colonization as a cultural–ethical political project (M. T. Uribe 1992, 22; Steiner 2000).

25. *Album de la carretera al mar*, 43.

26. Ipecac is a medicinal plant. Ivory palm, or *tagua* as it's called in Colombia, was a major bonanza in the region. The palm tree produces a nut almost identical to ivory that was a favorite raw material for button manufacturers in North America and Europe until they turned to plastic after World War I.

27. In Urabá, as elsewhere, all racial categories (white, indigenous, Afro-Colombian or black, mestizo, etc.) are fluid social–historical constructions with an ambiguous, inconsistent correspondence to the complexity and intersubjectivity of social identities. Several compelling historical accounts give more detail on race and the early settlement of the region than I present here (M. T. Uribe 1992; García 1996; W. Ramírez 1997; Ortíz 1999, 2007; Steiner 2000).

28. Emilio Restrepo, "Carretera al mar: La salvación de antioquia," Imprenta Oficial, Medellín, December 1929, 9. Moore, Kosek, and Pandian (2003) trace the workings of these conjoined essentialisms. In Colombia the racist associations between nature, climate, and elevation have been well established (Appelbaum 2003; Pratt 2008; Koopman 2015).

29. Quoted in Steiner 2000, 9.

30. The speech was by Tomás María Silva; quoted in Steiner 2000, 12.

31. "Ordenanza No. 49—April 29, 1913," Asamblea Departamental de Antioquia, 101–4.

32. "¡Al Mar!" *Progreso*, Issue No. 9, February 8, 1927, 1.

33. *Album de la carretera al mar*, 2, 18.

34. *Album de la carretera al mar*, 90.

35. "¡Al Mar!" 137.

36. My analysis here draws on Hylton 2007.

37. "Medellín: South American Showplace Hailed as a 'Capitalist Paradise,'" *Life* magazine, September 29, 1947, 109–15.

38. David Harvey lays out the spatial fix and its relation to uneven development in several publications (2001, 2006); Neil Smith, meanwhile, theorized uneven development more deeply (2008).

39. Hylton 2006, 28–33.

40. Cable to the Secretary of State from Jefferson Caffery, Legation of the United States of America, Bogotá, December 8, 1928.

41. The assassination and the riots that followed are often referred to as "*El Bogotazo*," but the geographic implication of the name as something circumscribed to the capital is misleading. Many Colombians remember the event "*el 9 de abril.*"

42. Letter from Personería Municipal de Turbo to Governor's office, January 29, 1949, in AHA, Gobernación de Antioquia, Secretaría de Gobierno, Gobierno Municipios, Turbo, Tomo 549, Carpeta 1. Mary Roldán's (2002) authoritative history of La Violencia

in Antioquia includes an exhaustive chapter focused on Urabá and western Antioquia that I draw on extensively later in this chapter. Most scholars would point to the two-volume *La Violencia en Colombia* (Gúzman, Fals Borda, and Umaña 1980) as a foundational account of the wider conflict.

43. "Estación de Radio Turbo," April 11, 1948, in AHA, Gobernación de Antioquia, Secretaría de Gobierno, Gobierno Municipios, Turbo, Tomo 539, Carpeta 3, 189.

44. Letter from Antioquia's Ministerio de Gobierno to Bogotá, August 25, 1950, in AHA, Ministerio de Gobierno, 1945/1953, D.G. 079, 201. 1949. "Oficio No. 423: Turbo," August 14, 1948, in AHA, Gobernación de Antioquia, Secretaría de Gobierno, Gobierno Municipios, Turbo, Tomo 549, Carpeta 1, 194.

45. Luis M. Gaviria, *Urabá y la carretera al mar* (Medellín: Tipografía Industrial, 1930), 108, 45.

46. My analysis of La Violencia's racial-regional dynamics draws on Roldán 2002, 176–78.

47. Letter from Luis Millán Vargas to the Governor, March 28, 1952, in AHA, Comando Policía, 1951/1952, D.G. 014, 641.

48. Letter to the Governor from Major Arturo González, December 5, 1950, in AHA, Orden Público, 1949/1952, D.G. 039, Tomo I, 226.

49. *Ingenieros militares en Colombia: 200 años de historia, 1810–2010* (Bogotá: Planeta), 19.

50. Report from the Fuerzas Militares de Colombia, Ejército Nacional, IV Brigada, December 30, 1950, in AHA, Gobernación de Antioquia, Secretaría de Gobierno, Gobierno Municipios, Turbo, Tomo 556, Carpeta 3, 141.

51. Archival folders in the AHA from this era are full of these blacklists. For instance, Oficio 23, Visitaduría Administrativa, August 31, 1951, in AHA, Gobernación de Antioquia, Secretaría de Gobierno, Gobierno Municipios, Turbo, Tomo 567, Carpeta 2, 181.

52. Oficio 103, Alcalde de Chigorodó, April 23, 1950, in AHA, Gobernación de Antioquia, Secretaría de Gobierno, Gobierno Municipios, Chigorodó, Tomo 552, Carpeta 1, 109.

53. Report from the Fuerzas Militares de Colombia, December 30, 1950, 140.

54. Quoted in Roldán 2002, 198.

55. Roldán 2002.

56. Quoted in Roldán 2002, 195.

57. Roldán 2002, 226.

58. LeGrand 1986, xvi.

59. "Gran zona banaera se localizará en Urabá," *El Colombiano*, September 4, 1962.

60. Latham 2000, 98.

61. Parsons (1967, 79–80) describes this division of labor, while García (1996, 39) corroborates his findings, noting that informants described these workers generically as *chocoanos*. Peter Wade (1995) offers much more detail on the complex racial–political and economic relationships among Antioquia, Urabá, and Chocó.

62. "Acaparamiento de tierras en Urabá," *El Colombiano*, September 14, 1962. Primitive accumulation is the subject of the final chapters of *Capital* (Marx 1990).

63. In several interviews with me, workers, unionists, and former guerrillas described these working conditions.

64. "Tierras para vivienda comprará la Caja de Crédito en Apartadó," *El Colombiano*, October 18, 1962; see also Parsons 1967, 80.

65. "Invasión de tierras se registra en Chigorodó," *El Colombiano*, September 22, 1962. García discusses companies posing as campesinos (1996, 40).

66. Parsons 1967, 97.

67. García Márquez 1970, 232–33.

68. In more theoretical terms, they are moments of a dialectical totality; for the framing of this "unitary theory," see Lefebvre 1991, 11–20.

69. Lefebvre 1991, 357.

70. "Informe de Comisión Región Urabá," Ejército Nacional, October 16, 1950, 319.

2. TURF WARS IN COLOMBIA'S RED CORNER

1. "Urabá, ahogada en sangre," *El Tiempo*, August 30, 1995.

2. "Ola de violencia solo busca la intimidación," *El Colombiano*, August 27, 1992. Barbarism was a recurring trope in articles about Urabá during this period; see, for example, "Sólo la barbarie pudo cometer el crimen: Gaviria," *El Tiempo*, October 28, 1992.

3. "Urabá: El gobierno manejará la situación de orden público," *El Tiempo*, April 10, 1992. "La subversión ahoga Urabá," *El Mundo*, March 21, 1992.

4. The ELN and one of its dissident factions did have a presence in Urabá, but they were far outnumbered by the EPL and FARC. Since the story of Colombia's armed conflict is so complex, especially in Urabá, I have tried wherever possible to spare the reader from a potentially endless barrage of names, acronyms, and organizations. This is why, as readers more familiar with the conflict might note, I do not explicitly name organizations like Muerte a Sequestradores (MAS), Los Pepes, Comandos Populares, Corriente de Renovación Socialista, Partido Revolucionario de Trabajadores, M-19, Esperanza, Paz y Libertad, Partido Comunista–Marxista Leninista (PC–ML), and many others.

5. She cited several reasons for turning herself in to the authorities: battle fatigue, poor troop morale, and, most important, the desire to see her daughter and grandchildren. Author interview with Elda Neyis Mosquera, former FARC commander (alias Karina), in Carepa, Antioquia, December 10, 2013.

6. While heavily informed by the literature on territory (Gottmann 1973; Peluso and Vandergeest 1995; M. Anderson 1996; Storey 2001; Delaney 2005; Brenner and Elden 2009a), especially Stuart Elden's pathbreaking work (2010, 2013), I reject the terminological-conceptual equivalence of "state space" and "territory" that is often either suggested or implied by most of this scholarship. Nonetheless, my application of Lefebvre's ideas to territory draws from Brenner and Elden 2009a. For more, see the debate between Elden (2010) and Antonsich (2011) and the forum in *Geopolitics* (Agnew 2010) revisiting Agnew's influential article, "The Territorial Trap" (1994).

7. Elden 2010.

8. The narrator here is Mario Agudelo; quoted in Andrés Suárez's book (2007, 110).

9. This section draws on several extended oral histories I conducted with some key figures of the EPL and its allies in Urabá's unions, peasant organizations, and neighborhood groups. Unfortunately, since the FARC was still actively in combat at the time of my research I was not able to collect an equally rich archive from its allies, not only because their fighters were still in *el monte* (the bush) but also because civilians' associations with them were still potentially criminal. On the history of the EPL, see Villarraga and Plazas 1994; Calvo 1987; on Córdoba's agrarian dynamics, see Escobedo 2009.

10. Author interview with Mario Agudelo, former EPL commander, in Medellín, Antioquia, April 10, 2012.

11. "*. . . nos calló como anillo al dedo*."

12. Author interview with Mario Agudelo, former EPL commander, in Medellín, Antioquia, May 23, 2013. For more details on Gutiérrez's break with the FARC, see Suárez 2007, 102–4.

13. The aptly titled *Identidades políticas y exterminio recíproco* gives the fullest account of the EPL–FARC rivalry (Suárez 2007).

14. Botero 1990, 55–69.

15. "Policarpa: Construyendo sueños solidarios," a 1992 report copublished by the UNDP and the national government's "Plan for National Rehabilitation," quoted in García 1996, 97.

16. Author interview with Guillermo Correa, former EPL member, in Apartadó, Antioquia, May 28, 2013.

17. Lefebvre's (1991, 88) suggestions on hypercomplexity means my view of Urabá's territorial conflicts differs from those of Ramírez (1997), who conceives of territory in a much more discrete, zero-sum way.

18. This is a point on which I disagree with Ávila's (2010) analysis of Colombia's armed actors.

19. García 1996; Suárez 2007, 107–8.

20. Suárez (2007) points out the paradoxical division of labor between the two groups: the formerly Maoist EPL held strong sway over the urban proletariat, while the pro-Soviet FARC had a stronger following among the peasantry and dominated the electoral field.

21. Author interview with Gerardo Vega, labor lawyer and former EPL operative, in Medellín, Antioquia, March 13, 2012.

22. Emphasis added. Author interview with Gloria Cuartas, former mayor of Apartadó, in Bogotá, DC, May 14, 2013. In a moment of violent polarization, Gloria was tapped by the archbishop of Urabá, who proposed her as a consensus candidate. The UP supported her candidacy, but she was technically an independent.

23. Dudley 2004, 79; Ronderos 2014, 175.

24. While many observers mark the turn toward cocaine-related financing as the beginning of the FARC's "political involution," Hough (2011) finds a more convincing explanation for the FARC's increasingly predatory activities in the 1990s: the territorial pressures and competitions caused by the expansion of paramilitaries and the U.S.-backed military offensive; see also Felbab-Brown 2005.

25. Dudley (2004) provides an incisive, in-depth account of the rise and fall of the party. These numbers are from "Renace la Unión Patriótica," *El Tiempo*, July 11, 2013.

26. Reyes 1997, 307; Ortíz 2007, 33–40.

27. Ballvé 2012, 608; cf. Gill 2016, 87–88.

28. Urrutia 1994, 286.

29. Ocampo 1994, 115.

30. Author interview with Carlos Alberto Mejía, plantation owner, in Medellín, Antioquia, May 11, 2012. Romero (2000) provides an eye-opening analysis of rural elites' dwindling fortunes and the cultural politics underlying the shift.

31. Quoted in Romero 2000, 59.

32. Thompson 1975, 108.

33. Williams 1973, 61.

34. The party's name was Esperanza, Paz y Libertad.

35. Many ex-EPL formed self-defense militias also known as Comandos Populares to fight back against the FARC, which they did by attacking the FARC's civilian social base, namely, members of the UP. The FARC responded by killing members of the EPL's own political party. The resulting tit-for-tat massacres over the next five years (1991–96) made this one of the bloodiest periods of Urabá's history.

36. "Quién financió el comienzo de las Accu?" *Verdad Abierta*, July 3, 2014.

37. Gramsci 1971, 210.

38. "Los tiempos de Pablo Escobar, Parte II," Caracol TV (Colombia), aired July 1, 2012.

39. For a fuller account of the territorial implications of the decentralization, see Asher and Ojeda 2009; Ballvé 2012.

40. Castro 1998, 15.

41. Author interview with retired banana company executive (anonymous) in Bogotá, DC, October 25, 2013.

42. Translation: Peasant Self-Defense Forces of Córdoba and Urabá. Although paramilitary leaders were usually agrarian elites, the rank-and-file soldiers were indeed mostly peasants;

still, the use of *autodefensas* and *campesinas* is a populist stab at legitimacy. The full name of El Alemán's BEC, for instance, was Bloque Elmer Cárdenas–Autodefensas Campesinas.

43. Carlos reportedly killed Fidel for making drug-trafficking deals with the FARC. A decade later, in 2004, Vicente ordered Carlos's execution for allegedly seeking a plea deal with U.S. authorities. Vicente, too, is believed to have met a violent death at the hands of rival traffickers, although he is rumored to be alive.

44. "[Redacted] Colombian Prosecutor Comments on Paramilitaries in Uraba [*sic*]," U.S. Defense Intelligence Agency, Intelligence Information Report, December 7, 1996.

45. "Subject: Paramilitaries in Colombia," Embassy Cable, U.S. Department of State, Bogotá, Colombia, November 1996. The declassified U.S. government documents cited in this chapter were obtained through Freedom of Information Act requests by Michael Evans of the National Security Archives, a nonprofit research institute in Washington, DC. He kindly shared them with me.

46. HRW 2001.

47. *Cooperativas de Vigilancia y Seguridad Privada*, Decreto No. 356 de 1994.

48. "Subject: Botero Human Rights Letter to A/S Shattuck," Embassy Cable, U.S. Department of State, Bogotá, Colombia, December 9, 1994.

49. "MoD Alleged to have Authorized Illegal Arms Sales to Convivirs and Narcotraffickers," Embassy Cable, U.S. Department of State, Bogotá, Colombia, April 9, 1997.

50. Tribunal Superior del Distrito Judicial de Bogotá, Sala de Justicia y Paz, Proceso No. 2007 82701, Sentence against Freddy Rendón, December 16, 2011, 181.

51. "Destape de un jefe 'para,'" *Semana*, April 8, 2007.

52. Toby Muse, "Colombian Prosecutor Probing U.S. Firms," *Washington Post*, April 30, 2007.

53. For contrasting analyses of the banana unions, see Romero 2005 and Chomsky 2008.

54. Known as the Justice and Peace Law (Ley de Justicia y Paz), officially: Ley 975 de 2005.

55. For revealing ethnographies on the experience of DDR for these low-level fighters, see Theidon 2009a, 2009b; Fattal 2018.

56. Freddy Rendón, Versión Libre, Fiscalía General de la Nación, Justicia y Paz, June 6, 2007.

57. "Hobbesian trinity" is from Nuñez 2001; the quote about Balkanization is by the former senator from Ohio Mike DeWine, "Future Challenges to Secure Democracy in Latin America," Heritage Foundation, May 3, 1999. These discourses and the key role of the "absent state" narrative in the making of Plan Colombia are analyzed by Tate 2015.

58. "Álvaro Uribe responde a críticas sobre las Convivir," *El Tiempo*, February 8, 1997.

59. Álvaro Uribe, "¿Por qué soy paramilitar?" Press Release, September 8, 2013: http://www.alvarouribevelez.com.co/es/content/por-que-soy-paramilitar.

60. Benjamin 1968, 257.

61. Agamben 2005, 87.

62. Author interview with Elkin Castañeda (alias Hermógenes Masa), paramilitary commander, Itagüí, Antioquia, September 17, 2012.

3. THE PARAMILITARY WAR OF POSITION

1. Raúl Hasbún and Freddy Rendón, Versión Libre Conjunta, Fiscalía General de la Nación, Justicia y Paz, Medellín, June 3, 2010.

2. Gramsci 1971, 239; Thomas 2009, 190–95.

3. Most scholars dismiss these practices as a foil for their criminal economies (Soto 2007; Duncan 2006; López 2010), while others chalk them up to the egos and the delusions of grandeur of a few charismatic commanders (Ronderos 2014).

4. The nonelite support received by paramilitaries is often downplayed or entirely discounted in many accounts of paramilitarism in Colombia (Hristov 2009; Romero 2011). While other scholars have acknowledged this popular support, they have done so by mainly attributing it to the changing cultural politics of class relations (Romero 2000, 2003) or to the symbolic capital introduced by the drug trade (Duncan 2006).

5. For more, see the ruling by the Inter-American Court of Human Rights on "Case of Pueblo Bello Massacre vs. Colombia," January 31, 2006.

6. "Pueblo Bello Massacre vs. Colombia,"

7. Taussig 1984, 494.

8. Author interview with anonymous peasant in Turbo, Antioquia, February 22, 2013.

9. Salvatore Mancuso, Versión Libre, Fiscalía General de la Nación, Justicia y Paz, November 11, 2011.

10. The paras described an area as being *saneada* or *limpiada*. Taussig (2003) provides a chilling account of a paramilitary-led *limpieza* (cleansing). Author interview with displaced peasant in Carmen del Darién, Chocó, November 29, 2007.

11. Some scholars claim that the scant amount of direct combat between paramilitaries and guerrillas shows that the paras were an ineffective counterinsurgent force not motivated by political conviction (Duncan 2006; López 2010). I would say that paramilitary violence against civilians, which was obviously widespread and systematic, is a much more relevant measure of paramilitary counterinsurgency than combat operations.

12. Author interview with Cocinero (pseudonym), demobilized paramilitary and former PDS, in Necoclí, Antioquia, September 23, 2013.

13. Freddy Rendón, Versión Libre, Fiscalía General de la Nación, Justicia y Paz, June 5, 2007.

14. Author interview with Víctor Martínez, campesino leader, in Turbo, Antioquia, May 9, 2013.

15. Author interview with displaced campesino (anonymous) in Turbo, Antioquia, June 19, 2013.

16. Rendón, Versión Libre, November 23 to December 4, 2009.

17. Rendón, Versión Libre, June 16, 2009.

18. Specifically, Law 80 of 1993 on municipal contracting; Law 136 of 1994 on the role, function, and organization of municipal government; and Law 743 of 2002, which further institutionalized and regulated the Juntas de Acción Comunal.

19. This assertion is according to prosecutors, who also mentioned thirty-seven out of sixty-nine in Arboletes and thirty-nine out of fifty in San Juan, alongside fifteen juntas in Córdoba and thirteen in Chocó, all under the control of the BEC.

20. Author interview with displaced campesino (anonymous) in Cartagena, Bolívar, October 2, 2013.

21. Author interview with displaced campesina (anonymous) in Turbo, Antioquia, July 16, 2012.

22. Although "make the state function" might be a more direct translation, I rendered it as "make the state *work*" to retain the rich double-meaning of her phrase.

23. ". . . *como frentándonos*." Author interview with displaced campesino (anonymous) in Necoclí, Antioquia, September 23, 2013.

24. Author interview with a group of campesinos in Turbo, Antioquia, February 22, 2013.

25. Author interview with Secretario (pseudonym), paramilitary leader of the PDSs, in Medellín, Antioquia, September 18, 2013.

26. Rendón, Versión Libre, November 23 to December 4, 2009. The metaphor of the state as pyramid is a perfect example of how, according to Ferguson and Gupta (2002), states are "spatialized" through metaphors of "vertical encompassment."

27. Document titled, "Propuesta capacitación política social: Promotores de desarrollo social," Bloque Elmer Cárdenas (BEC), October 28, 2002.

28. Deposition of anonymous paramilitary operative, Montería, Córdoba, Fiscalía General de la Nación, Fiscalía Especializada Estructura de Apoyo, April 7, 2010.

29. P. Harvey 2005; S. Uribe 2017.

30. "*...pa' que todo quedara bien organizadito*." Author interview with Cocinero (pseudonym), September 23, 2013. In Colombian Spanish *carretera* can mean both highway and road, even the unimproved kind.

31. Raúl Hasbún, Versión Libre, Fiscalía General de la Nación, Justicia y Paz, Medellín, August 8, 2008.

32. "*Pues, está buena la muchachita*." Author interview with Cocinero (pseudonym), December 6, 2013.

33. Author interview with Cocinero (pseudonym), November 11, 2013.

34. In my reconstruction of the two conversations in this section I have used direct, translated quotes, but the order has been rearranged to form a clearer, more linear narrative.

35. Author interview with Reina (pseudonym) in Turbo, Antioquia, December 7, 2013.

36. "*... entraron a punta de sangre y fuego*."

37. "At least there is hope for a tree: If it is cut down, it will sprout again" (Job 14:7).

38. Rendón, Versión Libre, June 11, 2010.

39. Author interview with Secretario (pseudonym), September 18, 2013.

40. Author interview with Roberto (pseudonym) in Los Córdobas, Córdoba, December 8, 2013.

41. The kidnapping and murder of the U.S. Drug Enforcement Administration (DEA) agent Enrique "Kiki" Camarena was dramatized in the hit Netflix series "Narcos: Mexico."

42. "*... háganle a eso [las tierras]. Tranquilos, no hay problema*."

43. See note 18 above describing these laws.

44. What he mentioned was "*acción de tutela, derecho de petición y una acción de cumplimiento, veeduría ciudadana*," which are all legal resources for the citizen-driven protection of rights enshrined in the 1991 Constitution. My English translations are close yet imprecise renderings of these legal motions.

45. Monsalve, whose real name is Jairo Rendón, turned himself in to the DEA in the late 2000s and served two years in jail for money laundering. Asocomún was registered in 2002. I have written about its wheeling and dealing in both scholarly and journalistic outlets (Ballvé 2012, 2011, respectively).

46. Hasbún and Rendón, Versión Libre Conjunta, June 3, 2010.

47. Col. John Waghelstein in a 1985 speech at the American Enterprise Institute (quoted in Schwarz 1991, 22).

48. Hasbún and Rendón, Versión Libre Conjunta, June 3, 2010.

49. For more on counterinsurgency as a form of conservative political restoration via state building, see Grandin and Joseph 2010.

50. Kilcullen 2010, 155–56.

51. Grandin 2010, 2–3.

52. "Declaración," Fiscalía No. 305 Estructura de Apoyo, Montería, April 7, 2010.

4. PARAMILITARY POPULISM: IN DEFENSE OF THE REGION

1. This is from the infamous 2001 Pacto de Ralito (not to be confused with the demobilization agreement the paras signed with the government in the same town, Santa Fe de Ralito, Córdoba).

2. Claudia López, "Votaciones atípicas en las elecciones de congreso del 2002," *Semana*, September 11, 2005. Investigators found 400 elected officials and 109 nonelected officials with links to the paras (López 2010, 29–30; 2007).

3. In 2000 Urabá Grande went by the name Poder Popular Campesino, which was modeled after the Castaños' Clamor Campesino Caribe. All of these were electoral alliances in which candidates pledged allegiance to the paramilitaries in exchange for their material support.

4. I mean "populism" in the basic colloquial sense of a political position capable of winning passionate, broad-based popular support. For more, see Hart's work for an incisive take on recent debates around populism (Hart 2014).

5. Autodefensas Campesinas Bloque Central Bolívar. 2004. *Escenarios para la paz a partir de la construcción de regiones*. Cuartel General de San Lucas, Sur de Bolívar. Although the book has no listed author, Báez later confirmed he wrote it. Ernesto Báez was his nom de guerre; his real name is Iván Duque Gaviria (no relation to Iván Duque Márquez, who was elected president of Colombia in 2018).

6. Emphasis added. Freddy Rendón, Versión Libre, Fiscalía General de la Nación, Justicia y Paz, Medellín, June 16, 2009.

7. ". . . *con el que pueden contar para construir región*." Bloque Elmer Cárdenas— Autodefensas Campesinas, Acta Reunión, Proyecto Regional Político: Urabá Grande Unido y en Paz, November 15, 2005.

8. M. T. Uribe 1992, 9.

9. Serje 2005; Arias 2007.

10. "*Unos degenerados . . . unos desarraigados sin ningún sentido de pertenencia*." Author interview with Gen. Rito Alejo del Río, excommander of the army's 17th Brigade, at the Batallón de Policía Militar No. 13 in Bogotá, D.C., October 17, 2013.

11. Emphasis added. Rendón, Versión Libre, November 23 to December 4, 2009.

12. "Bloque Elmer Cárdenas—Autodefensas Campesinas: Nuestro Credo Político," 12 pages, undated document.

13. See chapters 1 and 7, respectively.

14. In 1982, acting as the governor of Antioquia before the popular election of subnational executives, Villegas appointed Uribe mayor of Medellín.

15. El Alemán's comments here are all from the same source: Rendón, Versión Libre, June 6, 2007.

16. Declaración Oficio UNAT—F-22 2080, Unidad de Fiscalías Delegadas Ante los Jueces Penales del Circuito Especializados de Medellín y Antioquia, March 10, 2010.

17. "Declaración," Fiscalía, No. 305 Estructura de Apoyo, Arboletes, April 7, 2010.

18. Catalino Segura, Versión Libre, Fiscalía General de la Nación, Justicia y Paz, Medellín, March 8, 2012.

19. El Alemán's comments here are all from the same source: Rendón, Versión Libre, June 6, 2007.

20. ". . . *la misma politiquería de siempre*." Author interview with displaced campesino (anonymous) in Necoclí, Antioquia, September 25, 2013. The previous quote in the paragraph is from an affidavit submitted to prosecutors titled "Periódo 2001–2003: Años del terror administrativo en Acandí," undated document.

21. ". . . *embolatando a las personas*." Author interview with displaced campesina (anonymous), September 25, 2013.

22. "Período 2001–2003: Años del terror administrativo en Acandí," undated document.

23. Carlos Castaño is quoted in Aranguren 2002, 345, and Fidel Castaño in Reyes 2009, 94.

24. Tate 2018. In a comparable case, Nancy Ries (2002) describes how the systematic corruption and economic fallout of the post-Soviet transition in Russia positioned mafiosi—and mafiosi positioned themselves—as "honest bandits."

25. Rendón, Versión Libre, June 5, 2007.

26. ". . .*amiguitos contratistas*." Rendón, Versión Libre, June 16, 2009.

27. Quoted in Tate 2018, 13.

28. The details of this "Declaration of Programmatic Agreements" and of the event are from a video shot in October 2003 and obtained from an anonymous source by the author. The same incident was discussed in court: Bloque Elmer Cárdenas, Audencia de Control de Legalidad de Cargos, Sala Justicia y Paz del Tribunal Superior de Medellín, August 28, 2012.

29. One NGO, for instance, was Corporación Nacer Comunitario (Cornacom), registered in 2005 with Urabá's Chamber of Commerce. The government investigation is a field report to the attorney general: "Denuncia nexos de políticos con AUC en Arboletes Antioquia (07857–02993)," April 21, 2008.

30. Consejo Nacional Electoral, Resolution No. 0981 from 2011. Multiple testimonies by ex-paras corroborate the charges against the Unguía mayor Cayetano "El Ratón" Tapias.

31. Proyecto de Ley Estatutaria 117 de 2002 Senado, *Gaceta del Congreso*, 447/02, October 28, 2002.

32. Proyecto de Ley Estatutaria 72 de 2004 Senado, *Gaceta del Congreso*, 427/04, August 8, 2004.

33. Proyecto de Ley 048 de 2005 Cámara, *Gaceta del Congreso*, 494/05, August 5, 2005.

34. Proyecto de Ley 164 de 2005 Cámara, *Gaceta del Congreso*, 701/05, October 7, 2005.

35. Proyecto de Ley 029 de 2005 Cámara, *Gaceta del Congreso*, 478/05, August 3, 2005.

36. "Congreso concedió orden de la democracia a Asocomún," *Urabá Hoy*, August 1–15, 2006.

37. Rendón, Versión Libre, July 12, 2007.

38. Bushnell 1993; Appelbaum 2016, 16.

39. How much support is impossible to quantify but consider: Álvaro Uribe, often described as the most popular politician in Colombian history, made the exact same appeals using the exact same discourses. Even the courts noted the eerie resemblance between Uribe's published political platform for his presidential campaign and the book about "constructing the regions" by Ernesto Báez that I mentioned at the beginning of this chapter.

40. Robin 2010, 375.

41. Robin 2010, 372.

5. THE MASQUERADES OF GRASSROOTS DEVELOPMENT

1. Freddy Rendón, Versión Libre, Fiscalía General de la Nación, Justicia y Paz, Medellín, July 10, 2007.

2. Quoted in CNMH 2010, 364.

3. Rendón, Versión Libre, June 6, 2007.

4. These integral links between crime, illegality, violence, and state formation have been well established by scholars (Blok 1974; Bayart, Ellis, and Hibou 1999; Volkov 2002; Hibou 2004; Nordstrom 2004; Roitman 2005; E. D. Arias and Goldstein 2010).

5. It is often forgotten that *Discipline and Punish* is in many ways a story about the relationship between primitive accumulation and the emergence of disciplinary power (Foucault 1995, 80–91, 221, 270–300). Foucault's concept of "regimes of truth" bears a striking resemblance to Gramsci's conceptualization and analysis of "common sense" (Foucault 1972; S. Hall 1992).

6. The trailblazing accounts of scholars like Ferguson (1985), Escobar (1995), and Sachs (1992) have been enriched by later critiques such as Hart's (2001, 2009), which have also highlighted the tight and formative ties between what she calls capital D Development as a project of Third World interventions and changes in the ongoing (lowercase d) development of capitalism.

7. I prefer "grassroots development" to related terms such as "sustainable" or "alternative" development. "Sustainable" has gained a primarily environmental connotation, while "alternative development," in Colombia, refers to crop-substitution programs aimed at weaning farmers off the cultivating of drug-related crops. "Grassroots" also usefully retains the presumed rationality of its approach in contrast to what's being problematized, i.e., top-down development. It is not lost on me that the spatial metaphors of development (top, down, bottom, up) closely relate to critiques by Ferguson and Gupta of fetishized understandings of the state through discourses of "vertical encompassment" (Ferguson and Gupta 2002; Ferguson 2006).

8. World Bank 1989, 37.

9. U.S. Undersecretary of State Chester Bowles, quoted in Latham 2000, 105.

10. José María Isaza, "La reforma agraria y el Plan Kennedy," *El Colombiano*, February 1, 1962.

11. "Banana Program Helping Colombia," *New York Times*, May 3, 1964.

12. Quoted in Latham 2000, 69.

13. Hart 2009, 123; Ruttan 1984.

14. Escobar (1995, 131) discusses the onset of integrated rural development in Colombia, while Restrepo (2010) and Aparicio (2012) provide complementary and more Urabá-focused accounts.

15. Quoted in Aparicio 2009, 100.

16. Michael Goldman provides a fascinating account of how these ideas worked their way through the entrails of the World Bank, where "Green Neoliberalism" eventually reared its head. He describes this "greening" as "the Bank's latest and most profound discursive framework" (Goldman 2005, 5). While highlighting additional discursive articulations, my understanding of grassroots development lines up perfectly with Goldman's findings. Others have incisively deconstructed discourses related to the local, empowerment, and ownership, showing how they tend to gloss over all kinds of power relations and injustices (Mohan and Stokke 2000; Mosse and Lewis 2005).

17. Healy 2001; Hayden 2003; Asher 2009.

18. Bodley 1975; Hayden 2003.

19. Several scholars have tracked the gendered—specifically, feminized—turn in development ideology and practice (Boserup 1970; Moser 1993; Hart 1997).

20. Hart 2009.

21. The way in which these four elements have been problematized is well covered in the critical development studies literature (Escobar 1995; Mohan and Stokke 2000; Sheehan 1998; Hart 2001; Appadurai 2001; Hayden 2003; Goldman 2005; Elyachar 2005; Asher 2009; Ballvé 2013).

22. R. Wade 1997, 611–12; Goldman 2005.

23. Winograd 1994, 62.

24. Ng'weno 2007; Oslender 2008; Asher and Ojeda 2009; Asher 2009; Ballvé 2012; Cárdenas 2012; Ojeda 2012.

25. The scholars in this camp (Escobar 1995, 2008; Aparicio 2009, 2012) stand in contrast to those who have directly critiqued their views or who provide alternative analyses (P. Wade 1999; Restrepo 2004; Agudelo 2005; Ng'weno 2007; Oslender 2008; Asher 2009).

26. Arguably, the first case of paramilitaries use and abuse of grassroots development was in the middle region of the Magdalena River, the cradle of the contemporary paramilitary movement. It was there that Acdegam, the local ranchers' association and sponsor of a local paramilitary group, engaged in many kinds of social projects (Ronderos 2014, 46–66).

27. The project straddled the basins of both the Curvaradó and Jiguamiandó Rivers, but since the vast majority of it was in the former I have simplified things by referring just to Curvaradó.

28. Author interview with displaced campesino in Zona Humanitaria Caño Claro, Curvaradó, Chocó, May 23, 2008.

29. In November 2000 the government titled 46,084 hectares to the Curvaradó communities and 54,973 hectares to the neighboring Afro-Colombian communities of the Jiguamiandó River. Afro-Colombians' struggles for territory have been the subject of several excellent books (P. Wade 1995; Ng'weno 2007; Escobar 2008; Asher 2009; Restrepo 2013; Oslender 2016).

30. "Habla Vicente Castaño," *Semana*, June 5, 2005.

31. Author interview with Jens Mesa, the president of Fedepalma, in Bogotá, June 18, 2008.

32. From 170,000 to 400,000 hectares, according to data culled from the annual statistical reports of the National Federation of Palm Growers (Fedepalma).

33. Section 7.3 of CNMH 2016.

34. "Natural accession" is a legal term referring to the enlargement of a property due to biophysical changes in the land, such as when a river changes course or dries up.

35. It is possible to trace numbers from one registry document to another all the way back to the original property of unparceled land, but iterative parceling out makes it unlikely that this ever happens.

36. "Contrato de Comodato," Asoprobeba, two pages, undated, obtained by author.

37. "El fantasma de Sor Teresa Gómez en territorio chocoano," *Verdad Abierta*, November 5, 2013.

38. The number is from "Caracterización Jurídica y saneamiento de los territorios colectivos de Curvaradó y Jiguamiandó," Instituto Colombiano de Desarrollo Rural (Incoder), July 12, 2012.

39. In Colombia they also go by the name of productive alliances or simply productive projects, but for consistency I use "strategic alliances."

40. Letters dated April 20, 2001, and September 27, 2002, from the Banco Agrario de Colombia to the President of Urapalma's Board of Directors.

41. Quoted in Watts 1994.

42. Presidencia de la República, "Plan Colombia: Plan for Peace, Prosperity, and the Strengthening of the State," (Bogotá: Presidencia, 1999).

43. "Proyecto afrocolombiano de siembra y desarrollo de palma Africana de aceite: Extractora Bajirá S.A. & Consejo Comunitario La Larga—Tumaradó," draft application to USAID, obtained by author, July 13, 2003. I wrote a journalistic article that exposed that Plan Colombia financed (via USAID) other paramilitary-linked strategic alliances (Ballvé 2009).

44. Teo Ballvé, "The Darkside of Plan Colombia," *The Nation*, June 15, 2009.

45. Ferguson 1985.

46. ". . . *y recuperar el sentido de presencia del Estado en las regiones*" (DNP 2003, 75).

47. Tribunal Superior del Distrito Judicial de Bogotá, Sala de Justicia y Paz, Magistrada Ponente Alexandra Valencia Molina, decisión Bloque Central Bolívar, August 11, 2017, 5, 133–37.

48. DNP 2003, 68.

49. DNP 2003, 55.

50. Acción Social 2007.

51. Author interview with Freddy Rendón (alias El Alemán), paramilitary chief, in Itagüí, Antioquia, September 17, 2012.

52. Author interview with displaced campesinos (anonymous) in Turbo, Antioquia, October 30, 2013.

53. The senator who brokered the meeting was the now-convicted *parapolítico* Antonio Valencia Duque: Corte Suprema de Justicia, Sala de Casación Penal, Proceso No. 30126, Acta No. 419, December 14, 2010.

54. Author interview with Cocinero (pseudonym), demobilized paramilitary and former PDS, in Necoclí, Antioquia, September 23, 2013, and December 6, 2013. Apparently there were two pilot projects: the one in Tulapas and another on the other end of the Caribbean coast.

55. ". . . *estuvo más pendiente de nosotros.*" Author interview with displaced campesina (anonymous) in Necoclí, Antioquia, December 7, 2013.

56. Fattal (2018, 101) makes this connection between stagecraft and statecraft.

57. Speech by President Álvaro Uribe in Necoclí, Antioquia, March 19, 2004.

58. Author interview with displaced campesina (anonymous) in Necoclí, Antioquia, September 25, 2013.

59. Statistics from UNODC, "Encuentro PCI 2009: Siete años construyendo legalidad," August 22, 2009; the quote is from Acción Social (2010a, 16).

60. Acción Social 2010a, 18, 31.

61. Razavi and Hassim 2006, 26; also, Hart 1997; Molyneux 2006.

62. USAID 2004, 6.

63. USAID 2009, 99.

64. Acción Social 2007, 107.

65. Acción Social 2007, 25.

66. Acción Social 2007, 26.

67. Acción Social 2008, 25.

68. Juanita León, "El paso del Alemán," *Semana*, September 18, 2005.

69. Communiqué from the Bloque Elmer Cárdenas to Luis Carlos Restrepo, the president's high commissioner for peace, March 24, 2004.

70. Author interview with Antonio García, lawyer and the BEC's civilian adviser, in Medellín, Antioquia, September 20, 2013. El Alemán has confirmed the origins of the idea, which is also detailed in an official report (Acción Social 2010b).

71. "Colombia es líder mundial en erradicación de cultivos ilícitos, destacó la ONU," Secretaría de Prensa, Presidencia de la República, August 22, 2009.

72. Rendón, Versión Libre, June 6, 2007.

73. Audiencia Cancelación de Títulos Fraudulentos, Postulado Fredy Rendón Herrera, Tribunal Superior de Medellín, Sala Justicia y Paz, September 16, 2011.

74. I culled the information on the companies from publicly available corporate documents on file at the Urabá Chamber of Commerce.

75. Despite my having interviewed USAID officials in Bogotá for past projects, they refused my request for an interview on this subject, insisting I send my questions about the projects by email. After sending my list of questions, USAID replied, declining to respond. The grants appear in "Second Quarter Report FY 2007: MIDAS Program," April 30, 2007.

76. Carlos Alberto Bohórquez, "Tulapas: Horizonte de esperanza," Asocomún, press release, January 10, 2006.

77. "Compra irregular de tierras en el Fondo Ganadero de Córdoba," *Verdad Abierta*, January 7, 2014.

78. Rendón, Versión Libre, June 11, 2007.

79. Rendón, Versión Libre, June 6, 2007.

80. Author interview with Freddy Rendón (alias El Alemán), September 17, 2012.

81. I'm borrowing the phrase from Ferguson (2006, 91), who uses it to make the same point vis-à-vis "civil society."

82. Watts (2014) offers a wide-ranging critical overview of the reemergence of resilience in the worlds of policy and academia.

83. World Bank 2011, 18, 25.

6. THE POSTCONFLICT INTERREGNUM

1. "Paz, justicia y libertad: Autodefensas Gaitanistas de Colombia," one-page flier dated, January 2012.

2. "Desolación en Córdoba," *El Espectador*, January 5, 2012.

3. Benjamin 1996, 246.

4. "Palabras del Presidente Juan Manuel Santos en la marcha 'Encuentro de apoyo a la ley de víctimas y de restitución de tierras,'" Presidencia de la República, Necoclí, Antioquia, February 11, 2012.

5. The "antinomies of community," a phrase I borrow from Watts (2004), are especially fraught in the context of postconflict reconciliation (Theidon 2013; Thomson 2013). For a wider critique of the postconflict apparatus as a mode of neoliberal rule, see Monk and Mundy 2014.

6. Gramsci 1971, 276.

7. Peluso and Vandergeest 1995; Scott 1998; Craib 2004; Moore 2005; Li 2007; Sikor and Lund 2009.

8. Although the Urabeños called themselves the Gaitanista Self-Defense Forces of Colombia (or AGC, its Spanish initials), they are more widely known as Los Urabeños. The authorities have started referring to the group as the Clan del Golfo to avoid stigmatizing the region of Urabá.

9. Emphasis added. The announcement of their existence through a flier on October 15, 2008, was also their first declaration of an armed general strike (the first of many).

10. Author interview with César Acosta, director of the Unidad de Tierras, in Apartadó, Antioquia, August 1, 2013.

11. "Segundos ocupantes, la otra cara de la restitución," *Verdad Abierta*, February 3, 2015.

12. *Reclamantes* and *ocupantes* (occupants) were the most common and neutral terms with which these groups identified themselves and each other. However, the rhyming Spanish words in the text might have been confusing for English readers, so I refer to the *ocupantes* as squatters.

13. Author interview with Elsy Galván, displaced peasant and land rights activist, in Turbo, Antioquia, September 3, 2012.

14. Author interview with Víctor Martínez, campesino leader, in Turbo, Antioquia, July 31, 2013.

15. Author interview with Víctor Martínez, October 30, 2013.

16. Author interview with displaced campesino (anonymous) in Apartadó, Antioquia, September 3, 2012.

17. Author interview with displaced campesina (anonymous) in Apartadó, Antioquia, March 23, 2013.

18. Author interview with Víctor Martínez, July 31, 2013.

19. Author interview with junta president (anonymous) in Turbo, Antioquia, March 18, 2013.

20. Author interview with displaced campesina (anonymous) in Apartadó, Antioquia, November 9, 2013.

21. Author interview with Víctor Martínez, September 3, 2012.

22. "Alianza de buen gobierno: Informe de implementación 2013–2014," Unidad Administrativa de Consolidación Territorial, August 2015.

23. UNDP 2013, 56.

24. ". . . *como Pedro por su casa*." Author interview with demobilized paramilitary (anonymous) in Turbo, Antioquia, May 22, 2013.

25. Author interview with demobilized paramilitary (anonymous) in Turbo, Antioquia, May 22, 2013.

26. Letter, one page, dateline "Apartadó, July 11, 2013," obtained by author.

27. ". . . *a una de su gente que anda por ahí*." Author interview with displaced campesino (anonymous) in Turbo, Antioquia, March 19, 2013.

28. ". . . *sin hacer much bulla*." Author interview with displaced campesino (anonymous) in Turbo, Antioquia, May 25, 2013.

29. Author interview with Unidad de Tierras official (anonymous) in Apartadó, Antioquia, August 2, 2013.

30. Author interview with César Acosta, August 1, 2013.

31. Author interview with OAS official in Apartadó, Antioquia, August 1, 2013.

32. Author interview with displaced campesina (anonymous), March 19, 2013.

33. "Las AGC haciendo presencia," YouTube video, 6:17. Posted by Autodefensas Gaitanistas de Colombia, May 25, 2017. The Urabeños' media campaigns are clear cases of what Alex Fattal calls "brand warfare" (2018).

34. Emphasis added. Autodefensas Gaitanistas de Colombia, "En pie de lucha por una Colombia más justa e incluyente," September 16, 2016.

35. For the Urabeños' role in the strike, see "Paro de plataneros estaba infiltrado por 'Los Urabeños,'" *El Espectador*, August 8, 2014. For their social work, see "Trabajo social de las Autodefensas Gaitanistas de Colombia," YouTube video, 2:02. Posted by Autodefensas Gaitanistas de Colombia, September 30, 2016: https://www.youtube.com/watch?v=7rzG0OOfuGs.

36. Watts 2004.

7. URABÁ: A SEA OF OPPORTUNITIES?

1. Law 935 of 2004, which began as Proyecto de Ley 233 de 2004 Cámara, *Gaceta del Congreso*, 90/04, March 25, 2004.

2. The bill was cosponsored by three congressmen and senators accused (or now convicted) of paramilitary ties: Luis Alfredo Ramos, Oscar Suárez Mira, and Manuel Ramiro Velásquez. The PEUD's explicit inclusion of "El Darién," which refers to the lands on the western fringe of the gulf, was a way of signaling its concern with not just Antioquia's portion of the region but also Chocó's. By dividing the two areas, the name symbolically avoids the erasure of Chocó by the expansionist tendencies of Antioquia.

3. "... *de una vez por todas*." Author interview with Luis Fredy Mejía, regional manager of the Strategic Plan, in Apartadó, Antioquia, May 29, 2013.

4. Ibid.

5. "The Most Dangerous City," *Time*, March 21, 1988. Ede Ijjasz-Vasquez, "How is Medellin a Model of Urban Transformation and Social Resilience?" The World Bank's "Sustainable Cities" Blog, June 2, 2017. John Borell and Stewart Stanley, "How Medellin Went from Murder Capital to Hipster Holiday Destination," *The Telegraph*, January 4, 2018.

6. Hylton 2007.

7. Concejo de Medellín, Sesión Plenaria Ordinaria, Acta 370, November 15, 2017.

8. Marx 2018, 3.

9. For a full account of social urbanism in Medellín, see Guerra 2014; Maclean 2015.

10. UN Habitat, arguably the world's leading urban policy institution, called Medellín an "international example of urban transformation" in its promotional materials when the city hosted UN Habitat's World Urban Forum in 2014. The Organization of American States (OAS), too, has trumpeted the "Medellín Model" (OAS 2011).

11. "Informe final de gestión: Plan de desarrollo, 2008–2011," Alcaldía de Medellín, December 15, 2011, 33.

12. "Balance Grupo EPM 2014," Press Release, Empresas Públicas de Medellín (EPM), March 18, 2015.

13. Sergio Fajardo, "Medellín, La Más Educada." *CEE Participación Educativa*, November 6, 2007.

14. At 34 per 100,000 in 2007, Medellín's murder rate was less than the 2016 rates of St. Louis (60), Baltimore (51), Detroit (45), New Orleans (44), and Cleveland (35).

15. Medellín won the 2012 Innovative City of the Year, an award given by Citibank, the *Wall Street Journal*, and the Urban Land Institute; in 2016 it won the Lee Kuan Yew World City Prize.

16. Emphasis added. Giraldo 2010, 52.

17. Author interview with Federico Restrepo, director of Plan Urabá, in Medellín, Antioquia, July 23, 2013.

18. Manuel de Solà-Morales, the urban planning guru associated with the Barcelona Model, coined the term "urban acupuncture."

19. "Parque Educativo abre la puerta de las oportunidades en Vigía del Fuerte," Gobernación de Antioquia, press release, May 7, 2014.

20. DNP et al. 2006, 16–17.

21. Letter dated May 7, 1927, accompanying report "Siemens–Bauunion: Informe Comisión Urabá, Carretera del Mar." AHA, in Carretera del Mar Folder, "Informe 1927," 1.

22. Gobernación de Antioquia, "*Urabá: Antioquia Caribe, Un Mar de Oportunidades, Estrategia Regional Integral,*" slideshow presentation, 90 pp., 2012, 54.

23. Ibid., 56.

24. Interview with Governor Luis Pérez, "Antioquia también es Costa," *Visión Total Caribe,* July 7, 2016; "Urabá, tras la búsqueda de una nueva ciudad," Gobernación de Antioquia, press release, January 25, 2017.

25. "2200 hombres le siguen el rastro a 'Otoniel,'" *El Colombiano,* March 10, 2015.

26. Alfredo Molano, "El caso Arboletes," *El Espectador,* October 14, 2012.

27. "'Otoniel,' auge y crisis del capo más buscado del país," *El Colombiano,* March 30, 2015.

28. Serje 2012, 111–12.

29. The Fund for Peace, a Washington-based think tank, produces a yearly Fragile States Index. Before its more politically correct rebranding, it was called the Failed State Index. Its accompanying world map paints perennial "failures" (Afghanistan, DRC, Somalia, Sudan, etc.) in alarmist reddish hues. Mazarr (2014) provides a good overview of the "failed state" as global threat paradigm.

30. Benjamin 1968, 257; cf. Agamben 2005, 87.

31. Kipfer 2009.

32. The blurry and in many ways unanswerable question of intent is why I find Berman and Lonsdale's (1992) distinction between state building and state formation (terms I use interchangeably) as unworkable—even as a heuristic (see introduction).

33. Scott 1998; Li 2007; Brenner and Elden 2009; Lefebvre 2009.

34. For these arguments and related debates, see Homer-Dixon 1999; Kaldor 1999; Berdal and Malone 2000; Collier and Hoeffler 2000; Peluso and Watts 2001; Collier et al. 2003; Berdal 2005.

35. Blomley 2010, 2016; Lund 2018; Peluso and Lund 2011; D. Hall, Hirsch, and Li 2011.

36. Fukuyama 2004, 19, 17.

37. Weber 2004, 33.

38. This was written into the framing document signed in 2003 by both the national government and the paramilitary leadership in Santa Fe de Ralito, Cordobá, that resulted in the paras' demobilization.

39. Greg Grandin, "Gabriel García Márquez—a Rebel Against Form, an Artist Against the Forces of Oblivion," *The Nation,* April 21, 2014.

40. García Márquez 1970, 316.

41. Gabriel García Márquez, "The Solitude of Latin America," Acceptance Speech for the Nobel Prize in Literature, December 8, 1982.

References

Abrams, Philip. 1988. "Notes on the Difficulty of Studying the State (1977)." *Journal of Historical Sociology* 1 (1): 58–89.

Acción Social. 2007. *Sembramos y ahora recogemos: Somos Familias Guardabosques.* Bogotá: Acción Social and UNDOC.

——. 2008. *Informe ejecutivo: Encuentro nacional del Programa Presidencial Contra Cultivos Ilícitos. Erradicación, prevención y sustitución de cultivos.* Bogotá: Acción Social and UNDOC.

——. 2010a. *Des-cifrando las Familias Guardabosques: Municipios Fases I-II.* Bogotá: Acción Social and UNDOC.

——. 2010b. *Informe ejecutivo: Encuentro Nacional del Programa Presidencial Contra Cultivos Ilícitos. Siete años construyendo legalidad.* Bogotá: Acción Social and UNDOC.

Agamben, Giorgio. 2005. *State of Exception.* Chicago: University of Chicago Press.

Agnew, John. 1994. "The Territorial Trap: The Geographical Assumptions of International Relations Theory." *Review of International Political Economy* 1 (1): 53–80.

——. 2010. "Still Trapped in Territory?" *Geopolitics* 15 (4): 779–84.

Agudelo, Carlos E. 2005. *Retos del multiculturalismo en Colombia.* Medellín: La Carreta Editores.

Alonso, Ana María. 1995. *Thread of Blood: Colonialism, Revolution, and Gender on Mexico's Northern Frontier.* Tucson: University of Arizona Press.

Anderson, Benedict. 1991. *Imagined Communities: Reflections on the Origin and Spread of Nationalism.* London: Verso.

Anderson, Malcom. 1996. *Frontiers: Territory and State Formation in the Modern World.* London: Routledge.

Antonsich, Marco. 2011. "Rethinking Territory." *Progress in Human Geography* 35 (3): 422–25.

Aparicio, Juan Ricardo. 2009. "La 'mejor esquina de Suramérica': Aproximaciones etnográficas a la protección de la vida en Urabá." *Antípoda* 8: 87–115.

——. 2012. *Rumores, residuos y estado en 'la mejor esquina de América': Una cartografía de lo humanitario en Colombia.* Bogotá: Universidad de Los Andes.

Appadurai, Arjun. 2001. "Deep Democracy: Urban Governmentality and the Horizon of Politics." *Environment and Urbanization* 13 (2): 23–43.

Appelbaum, Nancy P. 2003. *Muddied Waters: Race, Region, and Local History in Colombia, 1846–1948.* Durham: Duke University Press.

——. 2016. *Mapping the Country of Regions: The Chorographic Commission of Nineteenth-Century Colombia.* Chapel Hill: University of North Carolina Press.

Aranguren, Mauricio. 2002. *Mi confesión: Carlos Castaño revela sus secretos.* La Oveja Negra.

Aretxaga, Begoña. 2003. "Maddening States." *Annual Review of Anthropology* 32 (1): 393–410.

Arias, Enrique Desmond, and Daniel M. Goldstein. 2010. *Violent Democracies in Latin America.* Durham: Duke University Press.

Arias, Julio. 2007. *Nación y diferencia en el Siglo XIX colombiano: Orden nacional, racialismo y taxonomías poblacionales*. Bogotá: Universidad de Los Andes.

——. 2016. "La antropología del estado desde Akhil Gupta: A propósito de *Red Tape*. Burocracia, violencia estructural y pobreza en India." *Universitas Humanística* 82: 463–73.

Arjona, Ana. 2016. *Rebelocracy: Social Order in the Colombian Civil War*. Cambridge: Cambridge University Press.

Arjona, Ana, Nelson Kasfir, and Zachariah Mampilly. 2015. *Rebel Governance in Civil War*. Cambridge: Cambridge University Press.

Asher, Kiran. 2009. *Black and Green: Afro-Colombians, Development, and Nature in the Pacific Lowlands*. Durham: Duke University Press.

Asher, Kiran, and Diana Ojeda. 2009. "Producing Nature and Making the State: Ordenamiento Territorial in the Pacific Lowlands of Colombia." *Geoforum* 40 (3): 292–302.

Ávila, Ariel. 2010. "Injerencia política de los grupos armados ilegales." In *Y refundaron la patria. . . . De cómo mafiosos y políticos reconfiguraron el estado colombiano*, ed. Claudia López, 79–214. Bogotá: Debate.

Ballvé, Teo. 2009. "The Darkside of Plan Colombia." *The Nation*, June 15, 2009. http://www.thenation.com/article/dark-side-plan-colombia.

——. 2011. "La Telaraña de Los 'paras' en Urabá." *Verdad Abierta*, June 14, 2011. http://www.verdadabierta.com/index.php?option=com_content&id=3330.

——. 2012. "Everyday State Formation: Territory, Decentralization, and the Narco Land-Grab in Colombia." *Environment and Planning D: Society and Space* 30 (4): 603–22.

——. 2013. "Grassroots Masquerades: Development, Paramilitaries, and Land Laundering in Colombia." *Geoforum* 50: 62–75.

——. 2019. "Investigative Ethnography: A Spatial Approach to Economies of Violence." *Geographical Review* (early view, online): 1–13. DOI: 10.1111/gere.12347.

Banner, Stuart. 2005. *How the Indians Lost Their Land: Law and Power on the Frontier*. Cambridge: Harvard University Press.

Baretta, Silvio Duncan, and John Markoff. 2006. "Civilization and Barbarism: Cattle Frontiers in Latin America." In *States of Violence*, ed. Fernando Coronil and Julie Skurski, 33–74. Ann Arbor: University of Michigan Press.

Bayart, Jean-François, Stephen Ellis, and Béatrice Hibou. 1999. *The Criminalization of the State in Africa*. Bloomington: Indiana University Press.

Benjamin, Walter. 1968. *Illuminations: Essays and Reflections*. New York: Schocken.

——. 1996. *Selected Writings: 1913–1926*. Cambridge: Harvard University Press.

Berdal, Mats. 2005. "Beyond Greed and Grievance—and Not Too Soon." *Review of International Studies* 31 (4): 687–98.

Berdal, Mats, and David Malone, eds. 2000. *Greed and Grievance: Economic Agendas in Civil Wars*. Boulder: Lynne Rienner.

Bergquist, Charles W. 1978. *Coffee and Conflict in Colombia, 1886–1910*. Durham: Duke University Press.

Berman, Bruce, and John Lonsdale. 1992. *Unhappy Valley: Conflict in Kenya and Africa. Book One: State and Class*. Athens: Ohio University Press.

Blok, Anton. 1974. *The Mafia of a Sicilian Village, 1860–1960: A Study of Violent Peasant Entrepreneurs*. Cambridge: Waveland Press.

Blomley, Nicholas. 2003. "Law, Property, and the Geography of Violence: The Frontier, the Survey, and the Grid." *Annals of the Association of American Geographers* 93 (1): 121–41.

——. 2010. "Property, Liberty, and the Category." *Geoforum* 41 (3): 353–55.

——. 2016. "The Territory of Property." *Progress in Human Geography* 40 (5): 593–609.

Bodley, John H. 1975. *Victims of Progress*. Menlo Park, CA: Cummings Publishing.

Boserup, Ester. 1970. *Woman's Role in Economic Development*. New York: St. Martin's Press.

Botero, Fernando. 1990. *Urabá: Colonización, violencia y crisis del Estado*. Medellín: Editorial Universidad de Antioquia.

Brenner, Neil, and Stuart Elden. 2009a. "Henri Lefebvre on State, Space and Territory." *International Political Sociology* 3 (4): 353–77.

———. 2009b. "Introduction: State, Space, World: Lefebvre and the Survival of Capitalism." In *State, Space, World: Selected Essays*, ed. Neil Brenner and Stuart Elden, 1–48. Minneapolis: University of Minnesota Press.

Brown, Kate. 2004. *A Biography of No Place: From Ethnic Borderland to Soviet Heartland*. Cambridge: Harvard University Press.

Bushnell, David. 1993. *The Making of Modern Colombia: A Nation in Spite of Itself*. Berkeley: University of California Press.

Calvo, Fabiola. 1987. *Colombia: EPL, una historia armada*. Madrid: Ediciones Vosa.

Cárdenas, Roosbelinda. 2012. "Green Multiculturalism: Articulations of Ethnic and Environmental Politics in a Colombian 'Black Community.'" *Journal of Peasant Studies* 39 (2): 309–33.

Castro, Jaime. 1998. *Descentralizar para pacificar*. Bogotá: Editorial Ariel.

Chomsky, Aviva. 2008. *Linked Labor Histories: New England, Colombia, and the Making of a Global Working Class*. Durham: Duke University Press.

CNMH. 2010. *La tierra en disputa: Memorias del despojo y resistencias campesinas en la costa Caribe, 1960–2010*. Bogotá: Centro Nacional de Memoria Histórica.

———. 2016. *Tierras y conflictos rurales: Historias, políticas agrarias y protagonistas*. Bogotá: Centro Nacional de Memoria Histórica.

Collier, Paul, V. L. Elliott, Havard Hegre, Anke Hoeffler, Marta Reynal-Querol, and Nicholas Sambanis. 2003. *Breaking the Conflict Trap: Civil War and Development Policy*. Washington, DC: World Bank.

Collier, Paul, and Anke Hoeffler. 2000. *Greed and Grievance in Civil War*. Washington, DC: World Bank.

Coronil, Fernando, and Julie Skurski, eds. 2006. *States of Violence*. Ann Arbor: University of Michigan Press.

Corrigan, Philip, and Derek Sayer. 1985. *The Great Arch: English State Formation as a Cultural Revolution*. Oxford: Basil Blackwell.

Craib, Raymond B. 2004. *Cartographic Mexico: A History of State Fixations and Fugitive Landscapes*. Durham: Duke University Press.

Das, Veena, and Deborah Poole, eds. 2004. *Anthropology in the Margins of the State*. Santa Fe: School of American Research Press.

Delaney, David. 2005. *Territory: A Short Introduction*. Oxford: Wiley-Blackwell.

DNP, Departamento Nacional de Planeación. 2003. *Hacia un Estado Comunitario: Plan Nacional de Desarrollo, 2002–2006*. Bogotá: Departamento Nacional de Planeación (DNP).

DNP, Departamento Nacional de Planeación; Departamento Administrativo de Planeación de Antioquia; and Junta de Efemérides. 2006. *Plan Estratégico para la región de Urabá–Darién: Primera fase, insumos para el proceso en la región*. Medellín: DNP and Gobernación de Antioquia.

Dudley, Steven. 2004. *Walking Ghosts: Murder and Guerrilla Politics in Colombia*. New York: Routledge.

Dugas, John C. 2014. "Old Wine in New Wineskins: Incorporating the 'Ungoverned Spaces' Concept into Plan Colombia." In *US National Security Concerns in Latin America and the Caribbean*, ed. Gary Prevost, Harry Vanden, Carlos Oliva Campos, and Luis Fernando Ayerbe, 143–78. New York: Palgrave Macmillan.

Duncan, Gustavo. 2006. *Los señores de la guerra: De paramilitares, mafiosos y autodefensas en Colombia*. Bogotá: Planeta.

Eilenberg, Michael. 2012. *At the Edges of States: Dynamics of State Formation in the Indonesian Borderlands*. Leiden: KITLV Press.

Ekers, Michael, Gillian P. Hart, Stefan Kipfer, and Alex Loftus, eds. 2012. *Gramsci: Space, Nature, Politics*. Malden, MA: Wiley-Blackwell.

Elden, Stuart. 2004. *Understanding Henri Lefebvre: Theory and the Possible*. London: Continuum.

——. 2010. "Land, Terrain, Territory." *Progress in Human Geography* 34 (6): 799–817.

——. 2013. *The Birth of Territory*. Chicago: University of Chicago Press.

Elyachar, Julia. 2005. *Markets of Dispossession: NGOs, Economic Development, and the State in Cairo*. Durham: Duke University Press.

Escobar, Arturo. 1995. *Encountering Development: The Making and Unmaking of the Third World*. Princeton: Princeton University Press.

——. 2008. *Territories of Difference: Place, Movements, Life, Redes*. Durham: Duke University Press.

Escobedo, Luis Rodolfo. 2009. *Dinámica de la violencia en el Departamento de Córdoba, 1967–2008*. Bogotá: Observatorio del Programa Presidencial de Derechos Humanos y DIH.

Fattal, Alexander. 2018. *Guerrilla Marketing: Counterinsurgency and Capitalism in Colombia*. Chicago: University of Chicago Press.

Faulkner, William. 2011. *Requiem for a Nun*. New York: Knopf.

Felbab-Brown, Vanda. 2005. "The Coca Connection: Conflict and Drugs in Colombia and Peru." *Journal of Conflict Studies* 25 (2): 104–28.

Ferguson, James. 1985. *The Anti-Politics Machine*. Minneapolis: University of Minnesota Press.

——. 2006. *Global Shadows: Africa in the Neoliberal World Order*. Durham: Duke University Press.

Ferguson, James, and Akhil Gupta. 2002. "Spatializing States: Toward an Ethnography of Neoliberal Governmentality." *American Ethnologist* 29 (4): 981–1002.

Foucault, Michel. 1972. *The Archaeology of Knowledge and the Discourse on Language*. New York: Pantheon Books.

——. 1995. *Discipline and Punish: The Birth of the Prison*. New York: Vintage Books.

Frank, Andre Gunder. 1967. *Capitalism and Underdevelopment in Latin America: Historical Studies of Chile and Brazil*. New York: Monthly Review Press.

Fukuyama, Francis. 2004. "The Imperative of State-Building." *Journal of Democracy* 15 (2): 17–31.

Gadda, Carlo Emilio. 1957. *That Awful Mess on the Via Merulana*. Translated by William Weaver. 2007 Edition. New York: NYRB Classics.

García, Clara Inés. 1996. *Urabá: Región, actores y conflicto, 1960–1990*. Bogotá: Cerec.

García Márquez, Gabriel. 1970. *One Hundred Years of Solitude*. Translated by Gregory Rabassa. London: Penguin Books.

——. 1972. *Leaf Storm and Other Stories*. Translated by Gregory Rabassa. Perennial Classics, 2005 edition. New York: Harper and Row.

Gill, Lesley. 2016. *A Century of Violence in a Red City: Popular Struggle, Counterinsurgency, and Human Rights in Colombia*. Durham: Duke University Press.

Giraldo, Huber. 2010. "Parques Biblioteca de Medellín, Colombia." *Ciudad Viva* 4: 53–55.

Goldman, Michael. 2005. *Imperial Nature: The World Bank and Struggles for Justice in the Age of Globalization*. New Haven: Yale University Press.

González Casanova, Pablo. 1965. "Internal Colonialism and National Development." *Studies in Comparative International Development* 1 (4): 27–37.

González, Fernán E. 2014. *Poder y violencia en Colombia*. Bogotá: Centro de Investigación y Educación Popular (CINEP).

González, Fernán E., Ingrid J. Bolívar, and Teófilo Vásquez. 2003. *Violencia política en Colombia: De la nación fragmentada a la construcción del Estado*. Bogotá: Centro de Investigación y Educación Popular (CINEP).

Goodhand, Jonathan. 2005. "Frontiers and Wars: The Opium Economy in Afghanistan." *Journal of Agrarian Change* 5 (2): 191–216.

Goonewardena, Kanishka, Stefan Kipfer, Richard Milgrom, and Christian Schmid, eds. 2008. *Space, Difference, Everyday Life: Reading Henri Lefebvre*. New York: Routledge.

Goswami, Manu. 2004. *Producing India: From Colonial Economy to National Space*. Chicago: University of Chicago Press.

Gottmann, Jean. 1973. *The Significance of Territory*. Charlottesville: University of Virginia.

Grajales, Jacobo. 2017. *Gobernar en medio de la violencia: Estado y paramilitarismo en Colombia*. Bogotá: Universidad del Rosario.

Gramsci, Antonio. 1971. *Selections from the Prison Notebooks of Antonio Gramsci*. Translated by Quintin Hoare and Geoffrey Nowell Smith. New York: International Publishers.

——. 2011. *Prison Notebooks*. Translated by Joseph Buttigieg. Vols. 1–3. New York: Columbia University Press.

Grandin, Greg. 2010. "Living in Revolutionary Time: Coming to Terms with Latin America's Long Cold War." In *A Century of Revolution: Insurgent and Counterinsurgent Violence during Latin America's Long Cold War*, ed. Greg Grandin and Gilbert M. Joseph, 1–42. Durham: Duke University Press.

Grandin, Greg, and Gilbert M. Joseph, eds. 2010. *A Century of Revolution: Insurgent and Counterinsurgent Violence during Latin America's Long Cold War*. Durham: Duke University Press.

Guerra, Mónica Inés. 2014. "Regulating Neglect: Territory, Planning, and Social Transformation in Medellín, Colombia." PhD diss., University of California Berkeley.

Gupta, Akhil. 2012. *Red Tape: Bureaucracy, Structural Violence, and Poverty in India*. Durham: Duke University Press.

Gutiérrez, Francisco. 2010. "¿Estados fallidos o conceptos fallidos? La clasificación de las fallas estatales y sus problemas." *Revista de Estudios Sociales* 37: 87–104.

Gúzman, Germán, Orlando Fals Borda, and Eduardo Umaña. 1980. *La Violencia en Colombia*. 2 vols. Bogotá: Carlos Valencia Editores.

Hall, Derek, Philip Hirsch, and Tania Li. 2011. *Powers of Exclusion: Land Dilemmas in Southeast Asia*. Honolulu: University of Hawaii Press.

Hall, Stuart. 1977. "Culture, Media and the 'Ideological Effect.'" In *Mass Communication and Society*, ed. James Curran, Michael Gurevitch, and Janet Woollacott, 315–48. London: Open University Press.

——. 1992. "The West and the Rest: Discourse and Power." In *Formations of Modernity*, ed. Stuart Hall and Bram Gieben, 275–320. Cambridge: Polity.

Hansen, Thomas Blom, and Finn Stepputat, eds. 2001. *States of Imagination: Ethnographic Explorations of the Postcolonial State*. Politics, History, and Culture. Durham: Duke University Press.

Hart, Gillian P. 1997. "From 'Rotten Wives' to 'Good Mothers': Household Models and the Limits of Economism." *IDS Bulletin* 28 (3): 14–25.

——. 2001. "Development Critiques in the 1990s: Culs de Sac and Promising Paths." *Progress in Human Geography* 25 (4): 649–58.

——. 2009. "D/Developments after the Meltdown." *Antipode* 41 (1): 117–41.

——. 2014. *Rethinking the South African Crisis: Nationalism, Populism, Hegemony.* Athens: University of Georgia Press.

Harvey, David. 2001. "Globalization and the 'Spatial Fix.'" *Geographische Revue* 3 (2): 23–30.

——. 2006. *Spaces of Global Capitalism: Towards a Theory of Uneven Geographical Development.* London: Verso.

Harvey, Penelope. 2005. "The Materiality of State Effects: An Ethnography of a Road in the Peruvian Andes." In *State Formation: Anthropological Perspectives*, ed. Christian Krohn-Hansen and Knut G. Nustad, 123–41. London: Pluto Books.

Hayden, Cori. 2003. *When Nature Goes Public: The Making and Unmaking of Bioprospecting in Mexico.* Princeton: Princeton University Press.

Healy, Kevin. 2001. *Llamas, Weavings, and Organic Chocolate: Multicultural Grassroots Development in the Andes and Amazon of Bolivia.* South Bend: University of Notre Dame Press.

Hecht, Susanna B., and Alexander Cockburn. 1989. *The Fate of the Forest: Developers, Destroyers and Defenders of the Amazon.* London: Verso.

Hibou, Béatrice, ed. 2004. *Privatizing the State.* Translated by Jonathan Derrick. New York: Columbia University Press.

Hobbes, Thomas. 1987. *Leviathan.* Edited by C. B. Macpherson. New York: Penguin.

Homer-Dixon, Thomas. 1999. *Environment, Scarcity, and Violence.* Princeton University Press.

Hough, Phillip A. 2011. "Guerrilla Insurgency as Organized Crime: Explaining the So-Called 'Political Involution' of the Revolutionary Armed Forces of Colombia." *Politics and Society* 39 (3): 379–414.

Hristov, Jasmin. 2009. *Blood and Capital: The Paramilitarization of Colombia.* Athens: Ohio University Press.

HRW, Human Rights Watch. 2001. "The 'Sixth Division' Military–Paramilitary Ties and U.S. Policy in Colombia." New York: Human Rights Watch.

Hylton, Forrest. 2006. *Evil Hour in Colombia.* London: Verso.

——. 2007. "Medellín's Makeover." *New Left Review*, no. 44: 71–89.

Jessop, Bob. 1990. *State Theory: Putting the Capitalist State in Its Place.* Cambridge: Polity Press.

——. 2015. *The State: Past, Present, Future.* Cambridge: Polity.

Joseph, Gilbert M., and Daniel Nugent, eds. 1994. *Everyday Forms of State Formation: Revolution and the Negotiation of Rule in Modern Mexico.* Durham: Duke University Press.

Kaldor, Mary. 1999. *New and Old Wars: Organized Violence in a Global Era.* Stanford: Stanford University Press.

——. 2013. "In Defence of New Wars." *Stability: International Journal of Security and Development* 2 (1): 1–16.

Kalyvas, Stathis. 2006. *The Logic of Violence in Civil War.* Cambridge: Cambridge University Press.

Kilcullen, David. 2010. *Counterinsurgency.* London: Oxford University Press.

Kipfer, Stefan. 2009, "The times and spaces of hegemony: Antonio Gramsci's spatial historicism." Paper presented at Gramscian Geographies Conference, Royal Holloway University, January 8–9; available from author at kipfer@yorku.ca.

Koopman, Sara. 2015. "'¡Mona!': Whiteness, Tropicality, and the International in Colombia." Manuscript.

Latham, Michael E. 2000. *Modernization as Ideology: American Social Science and 'Nation Building' in the Kennedy Era*. Chapel Hill: University of North Carolina Press.

Lefebvre, Henri. 1991. *The Production of Space*. Translated by Donald Nicholson-Smith. Oxford: Wiley-Blackwell.

———. 2009. *State, Space, World: Selected Essays*. Edited by Stuart Elden and Neil Brenner. Minneapolis: University of Minnesota Press.

LeGrand, Catherine. 1986. *Frontier Expansion and Peasant Protest in Colombia, 1850–1936*. Albuquerque: University of New Mexico Press.

Lemke, Thomas. 2007. "An Indigestible Meal? Foucault, Governmentality, and State Theory." *Distinktion: Journal of Social Theory* 8 (2): 43–64.

León, Juanita. 2006. *País de plomo: Crónicas de guerra*. Bogotá: Aguilar.

Li, Tania. 2007. *The Will to Improve: Governmentality, Development, and the Practice of Politics*. Durham: Duke University Press.

———. 2014. *Land's End: Capitalist Relations on an Indigenous Frontier*. Durham: Duke University Press.

López, Claudia. 2007. *La ruta de la expansión Paramilitar y cambios en el mapa político de Antioquia, 1997–2007*. Bogotá: Corporación Nuevo Arco Iris.

———, ed. 2010. *Y refundaron la patria. . . . De cómo mafiosos y políticos reconfiguraron el Estado colombiano*. Bogotá: Debate.

Lund, Christian. 2018. "Nine-Tenths of the Law: Enduring Dispossession in Indonesia." Manuscript.

Maclean, Kate. 2015. *Social Urbanism and the Politics of Violence: The Medellín Miracle*. New York: Palgrave.

Mampilly, Zachariah. 2011. *Rebel Rulers: Insurgent Governance and Civilian Life During War*. Ithaca: Cornell University Press.

Markoff, John. 2006. "Afterword, 2002." In *States of Violence*, ed. Fernando Coronil and Julie Skurski, 75–82. Ann Arbor: University of Michigan Press.

Marquette, Heather, and Danielle Beswick. 2011. "State Building, Security and Development: State Building as a New Development Paradigm?" *Third World Quarterly* 32 (10): 1703–14.

Marx, Karl. 1990. *Capital: A Critique of Political Economy*. Vol. 1. New York: Penguin Classics.

———. 2018. *The Eighteenth Brumaire of Louis Bonaparte*. Singapore: Origami Books.

Mazarr, Michael. 2014. "The Rise and Fall of the Failed State Paradigm." *Foreign Affairs* 93 (1): 113–21.

Mitchell, Timothy. 1991. "The Limits of the State: Beyond Statist Approaches and Their Critics." *American Political Science Review* 85 (1): 77–96.

Mohan, Giles, and Kristian Stokke. 2000. "Participatory Development and Empowerment: The Dangers of Localism." *Third World Quarterly* 21 (2): 247–68.

Molyneux, Maxine. 2006. "Mothers at the Service of the New Poverty Agenda: Progresa/Oportunidades, Mexico's Conditional Transfer Programme." *Social Policy and Administration* 40 (4): 425–49.

Monk, Daniel, and Jacob Mundy, eds. 2014. *The Post-Conflict Environment: Investigation and Critique*. Ann Arbor: University of Michigan Press.

Moore, Donald. 2005. *Suffering for Territory: Race, Place, and Power in Zimbabwe*. Durham: Duke University Press.

Moore, Donald, Jake Kosek, and Anand Pandian, eds. 2003. *Race, Nature, and the Politics of Difference*. Durham: Duke University Press.

Moore, Jason W. 2015. *Capitalism in the Web of Life: Ecology and the Accumulation of Capital*. New York: Verso.

Moser, Caroline. 1993. *Gender Planning and Development: Theory, Practice, and Training*. New York: Routledge.

Mosse, David, and David J Lewis, eds. 2005. *The Aid Effect: Giving and Governing in International Development*. London: Pluto.

Mundy, Jacob. 2011. "Deconstructing Civil Wars: Beyond the New Wars Debate." *Security Dialogue* 42 (3): 279–95.

Múnera, Alfonso. 2005. *Fronteras imaginadas: La construcción de las razas y de la geografía en el Siglo XIX colombiano*. Bogotá: Planeta.

Ng'weno, Bettina. 2007. *Turf Wars: Territory and Citizenship in the Contemporary State*. Stanford: Stanford University Press.

Nielsen, Morten. 2007. "Filling in the Blanks: The Potency of Fragmented Imageries of the State." *Review of African Political Economy* 34 (114): 695–708.

Nordstrom, Carolyn. 2004. *Shadows of War: Violence, Power, and International Profiteering in the Twenty-First Century*. Berkeley: University of California Press.

Nuñez, Joseph R. 2001. *Fighting the Hobbesian Trinity in Colombia: A New Strategy for Peace*. Carlisle, PA: Strategic Studies Institute.

OAS, Organization of American States. 2011. *Culture, Common Denominator for Development: 18 Successful Practices*. Washington, DC: OAS.

Ocampo, José Antonio. 1994. *Entre las reformas y el conflicto: Economía y política en Colombia*. Bogotá: Grupo Editorial Norma.

Ojeda, Diana. 2012. "Green Pretexts: Ecotourism, Neoliberal Conservation and Land Grabbing in Tayrona National Natural Park, Colombia." *Journal of Peasant Studies* 39 (2): 357–75.

Oquist, Paul H. 1978. *Violencia, conflicto y política en Colombia*. Bogotá: Instituto de Estudios Colombianos.

Ortíz, Carlos Miguel. 1999. *Urabá: Tras las huellas de los inmigrantes, 1955–1990*. Bogotá: ICFES.

——. 2007. *Urabá: Pulsiones de vida y desafíos de muerte*. Medellín: La Carreta Editores y IEPRI.

Oslender, Ulrich. 2008. "Another History of Violence: The Production of 'Geographies of Terror' in Colombia's Pacific Coast Region." *Latin American Perspectives* 35 (5): 77–102.

——. 2016. *The Geographies of Social Movements: Afro-Colombian Mobilization and the Aquatic Space*. Durham: Duke University Press.

Parsons, James J. 1967. *Antioquia's Corridor to the Sea: An Historical Geography of the Settlement of Urabá*. Berkeley: University of California Press.

Pecaut, Daniel. 2001. *Guerra contra la sociedad*. Bogotá: Planeta.

Peluso, Nancy Lee, and Christian Lund. 2011. "New Frontiers of Land Control: Introduction." *Journal of Peasant Studies* 38 (4): 667–81.

Peluso, Nancy Lee, and Peter Vandergeest. 1995. "Territorialization and State Power in Thailand." *Theory and Society* 24 (3): 385–426.

——. 2011. "Political Ecologies of War and Forests: Counterinsurgencies and the Making of National Natures." *Annals of the Association of American Geographers* 101 (3): 587–608.

Peluso, Nancy Lee, and Michael Watts, eds. 2001. *Violent Environments*. Ithaca: Cornell University Press.

Pratt, Mary Louise. 2008. *Imperial Eyes: Travel Writing and Transculturation*, 2nd ed. London: Routledge.

Radcliffe, Sarah A. 2001. "Imagining the State as a Space: Territoriality and the Formation of the State." In *States of Imagination: Ethnographic Explorations of the Postcolonial State*, ed. Thomas Blom Hansen and Finn Stepputat, 123–45. Politics, History, and Culture. Durham: Duke University Press.

Ramírez, María Clemencia. 2011. *Between the Guerrillas and the State: The Cocalero Movement, Citizenship, and Identity in the Colombian Amazon.* Durham: Duke University Press.

Ramírez, William. 1997. *Urabá, los inciertos confines de una crisis.* Bogotá: Planeta.

Rangel, Alfredo. 2000. "Parasites and Predators: Guerrillas and the Insurrection Economy of Colombia." *Journal of International Affairs* 53 (2): 576–601.

Rasmussen, Mattias Borg, and Christian Lund. 2018. "Reconfiguring Frontier Spaces: The Territorialization of Resource Control." *World Development* 101 (January): 388–99.

Rausch, Jane M. 1984. *A Tropical Plains Frontier: The Llanos of Colombia, 1531–1831.* Albuquerque: University of New Mexico Press.

——. 1993. *The Llanos Frontier in Colombian History, 1830–1930.* Albuquerque: University of New Mexico Press.

Razavi, Shahra, and Shireen Hassim. 2006. *Gender and Social Policy in a Global Context: Uncovering the Gendered Dimensions of "the Social."* London: Palgrave Macmillan.

Redclift, Michael. 2006. *Frontiers: Histories of Civil Society and Nature.* Cambridge: MIT Press.

Restrepo, Eduardo. 2004. "Ethnicization of Blackness in Colombia: Toward a De-Racializing Theoretical and Political Imagination." *Cultural Studies* 18 (5): 698–753.

——. 2010. "Genealogía e impactos (no-intencionados) de las intervenciones de desarrollo en el Chocó: El Proyecto Desarrollo Integral Agrícola Rural (DIAR)." Quibdó, Colombia: Universidad Tecnológica del Chocó, Diego Luis Córdoba.

——. 2013. *Etnización de la negridad: La invención de las "Comunidades Negras."* Popayán, Colombia: Universidad del Cauca.

Reyes, Alejandro. 1997. "Compra de tierras por narcotraficantes." In *Drogas ilícitas en Colombia*, ed. Francisco Thoumi, 279–346. Bogotá: Ministerio de Justicia y del Derecho, Dirección Nacional de Estupefacientes (DNE) and United Nations Development Programme.

——. 2009. *Guerreros y campesinos: El despojo de la tierra en Colombia.* Bogotá: Grupo Editorial Norma.

Richani, Nazih. 2002. *Systems of Violence: The Political Economy of War and Peace in Colombia.* Albany: SUNY Press.

Ries, Nancy. 2002. "'Honest Bandits' and 'Warped People': Russian Narratives about Money, Corruption, and Moral Decay." In *Ethnography in Unstable Places: Everyday Lives in Contexts of Dramatic Political Change*, ed. Carol Greenhouse, Elizabeth Mertz, and Kay Warren, 276–315. Durham: Duke University Press.

Robin, Corey. 2010. "You Say You Want a Counterrevolution: Well, You Know, We All Want to Change the World." In *A Century of Revolution: Insurgent and Counterinsurgent Violence during Latin America's Long Cold War*, ed. Greg Grandin and Gilbert M. Joseph, 373–80. Durham: Duke University Press.

Roitman, Janet. 2005. *Fiscal Disobedience: An Anthropology of Economic Regulation in Central Africa.* Princeton: Princeton University Press.

Roldán, Mary. 2002. *Blood and Fire: La Violencia in Antioquia, Colombia, 1946–1953.* Durham: Duke University Press.

Romero, Mauricio. 2000. "Changing Identities and Contested Settings: Regional Elites and the Paramilitaries in Colombia." *International Journal of Politics, Culture, and Society* 14 (1): 51–69.

———. 2003. *Paramilitares y autodefensas, 1982–2003*. Bogotá: IEPRI, Universidad Nacional de Colombia.

———. 2005. "The Banana Workers of Urabá: From 'Subjects' to 'Citizens'?" In *Democratizing Democracy: Beyond the Liberal Democratic Canon*, ed. Boaventura De Sousa Santos, Maria Jose Arthur, Leonardo Avritzer, Sakhela Buhlungu, and Patrick Heller, 256–76. London: Verso.

———, ed. 2011. *La economía de los paramilitares: Redes de corrupción, negocios y política*. Bogotá: Debate.

Ronderos, María Teresa. 2014. *Guerras recicladas: Una historia periodística del paramilitarismo en Colombia*. Bogotá: Aguilar.

Roseberry, William. 1994. "Hegemony and the Language of Contention." In *Everyday Forms of State Formation: Revolution and the Negotiation of Rule in Modern Mexico*, ed. Gilbert M. Joseph and Daniel Nugent, 355–65. Durham: Duke University Press.

Rubio, Mauricio. 1999. *Crimen e impunidad: Precisiones sobre la violencia*. Bogotá: Tercer Mundo Editores.

Ruttan, Vernon W. 1984. "Integrated Rural Development Programmes: A Historical Perspective." *World Development* 12 (4): 393–401.

Sachs, Wolfgang, ed. 1992. *The Development Dictionary: A Guide to Knowledge as Power*. London: Zed Books.

Sauer, Carl O. 1966. *The Early Spanish Main*. Berkeley: University of California Press.

Schmitt, Carl. 1985. *Political Theology: Four Chapters on the Concept of Sovereignty*. Translated by George Schwab. Chicago: University of Chicago Press.

———. 2003. *The Nomos of the Earth in the International Law of the Jus Publicum Europaeum*. Translated by G. L. Ulmen. New York: Telos Press.

Schwarz, Benjamin C. 1991. *American Counterinsurgency Doctrine and El Salvador*. Washington, DC: Rand, National Defense Research Institute.

Scott, James C. 1998. *Seeing Like a State: How Certain Schemes to Improve the Human Condition Have Failed*. New Haven: Yale University Press.

Serje, Margarita. 2005. *El revés de la nación: Territorios salvajes, fronteras y tierras de nadie*. Bogotá: Universidad de Los Andes.

———. 2012. "El mito de la ausencia del Estado: La incorporación económica de las 'zonas de frontera' en Colombia." *Cahiers des Amériques latines* 71: 95–117.

Sharma, Aradhana, and Akhil Gupta, eds. 2006. *The Anthropology of the State: A Reader*. Oxford: Blackwell.

Sheehan, James M. 1998. "The Greening of the World Bank: A Lesson in Bureaucratic Survival." Cato Foreign Policy Briefing No. 56. Washington, DC: Cato Institute.

Sikor, Thomas, and Christian Lund. 2009. *The Politics of Possession: Property, Authority, and Access to Natural Resources*. Oxford: Wiley-Blackwell.

Smith, Neil. 2008. *Uneven Development: Nature, Capital, and the Production of Space*. Athens: University of Georgia Press.

Soto, Martha Elvira, ed. 2007. *El poder para ¿qué?* Bogotá: Intermedio.

Stanek, Łukasz. 2008. "Space as Concrete Abstraction: Hegel, Marx and Modern Urbanism in Henri Lefebvre." In *Space, Difference, Everyday Life: Reading Henri Lefebvre*, ed. Kanishka Goonewardena, Stefan Kipfer, Richard Milgrom, and Christian Schmid, 62–79. New York: Routledge.

Stavenhagen, Rodolfo. 1965. "Classes, Colonialism, and Acculturation." *Studies in Comparative International Development* 1 (6): 53–77.

Steiner, Claudia. 2000. *Imaginación y poder: El encuentro del interior con la costa en Urabá, 1900–1960*. Medellín: Editorial Universidad de Antioquia.

Storey, David. 2001. *Territory: The Claiming of Space*. Newark: Prentice Hall.

Suárez, Andrés Fernando. 2007. *Identidades políticas y exterminio recíproco: Masacres y guerra en Urabá, 1991–2001*. Medellín: La Carreta Editores and IEPRI.

Tate, Winifred. 2015. *Drugs, Thugs, and Diplomats: U.S. Policymaking in Colombia*. Stanford: Stanford University Press.

——. 2018. "Paramilitary Politics and Corruption Talk in Colombia." *Culture, Theory and Critique* 59 (4): 419–41.

Taussig, Michael. 1984. "Culture of Terror—Space of Death: Roger Casement's Putumayo Report and the Explanation of Torture." *Comparative Studies in Society and History* 26 (03): 467–97.

——. 1987. *Shamanism, Colonialism, and the Wild Man: A Study in Terror and Healing*. Chicago: University of Chicago Press.

——. 1992. *The Nervous System*. New York: Routledge.

——. 2003. *Law in a Lawless Land: Diary of a Limpieza in Colombia*. New York: New Press.

Theidon, Kimberly. 2009a. "Pasts Imperfect: Reintegrating Former Combatants in Colombia." *Anthropology News* 50 (5): 11–15.

——. 2009b. "Reconstructing Masculinities: The Disarmament, Demobilization, and Reintegration of Former Combatants in Colombia." *Human Rights Quarterly* 31 (1): 1–34.

——. 2013. *Intimate Enemies: Violence and Reconciliation in Peru*. Philadelphia: University of Pennsylvania Press.

Thomas, Peter D. 2009. *The Gramscian Moment: Philosophy, Hegemony and Marxism*. Boston: Brill.

Thompson, E. P. 1975. *Whigs and Hunters: The Origin of the Black Act*. New York: Pantheon Books.

Thomson, Susan. 2013. *Whispering Truth to Power: Everyday Resistance to Reconciliation in Postgenocide Rwanda*. Madison: University of Wisconsin Press.

Tsing, Anna L. 2005. *Friction: An Ethnography of Global Connection*. Princeton: Princeton University Press.

UNDP, United Nations Development Program. 2013. *Perfil productivo municipio Turbo: Insumo para el diseño de las estrategias y alternativas para la generación de empleo a las víctimas de la violencia*. Bogotá: UNDP.

Uribe, María Teresa. 1992. *Urabá: ¿Región o territorio? Un análisis en el contexto de la política, la historia y la etnicidad*. Medellín: INER-Corpourabá.

——. 2001. *Nación, ciudadano y soberano*. Medellín: Corporación Región.

Uribe, Simón. 2017. *Frontier Road: Power, History, and the Everyday State in the Colombian Amazon*. Hoboken, NJ: Wiley.

Urrutia, Miguel. 1994. "Colombia." In *The Political Economy of Policy Reform*, ed. John Williamson, 285–315. Washington, DC: Peterson Institute for International Economics.

USAID, U.S. Agency for International Development. 2004. *Colombia Forestry Development Program: Quarterly Progress Report, First Quarter 2004*. Bogotá: Chemonics Intl. for USAID.

——. 2009. *Más inversión para el desarrollo alternativo: Work Plan 2009–2010*. Bogotá: ARD Inc. for USAID Colombia.

Villarraga, Álvaro, and Nelson Plazas. 1994. *Para reconstruir los sueños: Una historia del EPL*. Bogotá: Fondo Editorial para la Paz.

Volkov, Vadim. 2002. *Violent Entrepreneurs: The Use of Force in the Making of Russian Capitalism*. Ithaca: Cornell University Press.

Wade, Peter. 1995. *Blackness and Race Mixture: The Dynamics of Racial Identity in Colombia*. Baltimore: Johns Hopkins University Press.

——. 1999. "The Guardians of Power: Biodiversity and Multiculturality in Colombia." In *The Anthropology of Power: Empowerment and Disempowerment in Changing Structures*, ed. Angela P. Cheater, 73–87. New York: Routledge.

Wade, Robert. 1997. "Greening the Bank: The Struggle over the Environment, 1979–1995." In *The World Bank: Its First Half Century*, ed. Devesh Kapur, 611–734. Washington, DC: Brookings Institution Press.

Watts, Michael. 1992. "Space for Everything (A Commentary)." *Cultural Anthropology* 7 (1): 115–29.

——. 1994. "Life under Contract: Contract Farming, Agrarian Restructuring, and Flexible Accumulation." In *Living Under Contract: Contract Farming and Agrarian Transformation in Sub-Saharan Africa*, ed. Peter D. Little and Michael Watts, 21–77. Madison: University of Wisconsin Press.

——. 2004. "Antinomies of Community: Some Thoughts on Geography, Resources and Empire." *Transactions of the Institute of British Geographers* 29 (2): 195–216.

——. 2014. "Resilience as a Way of Life: Biopolitical Security, Catastrophism, and the Food—Climate Change Question." In *Biosecurity and Vulnerability*, ed. Nancy N. Chen and Lesley A. Sharp, 145–72. Santa Fe: School for Advanced Research Press.

——. 2017. "Frontiers: Authority, Precarity, and Insurgency at the Edge of the State." *World Development* 101: 477–88.

Weber, David J., and Jane M. Rausch, eds. 1994. *Where Cultures Meet: Frontiers in Latin American History*. Wilmington, DE: Rowman and Littlefield.

Weber, Max. 2004. "Politics as Vocation." In *The Vocation Lectures*, ed. David Owen and Tracy B. Strong, 32–94. Translated by Rodney Livingstone. Indianapolis: Hackett.

Williams, Raymond. 1973. *The Country and the City*. Oxford: Oxford University Press.

——. 1977. *Marxism and Literature*. Oxford: Oxford University Press.

Winograd, Manuel. 1994. *Environmental Indicators for Latin America and the Caribbean: Toward Land-Use Sustainability*. Washington, DC: Inter-American Institute for Cooperation on Agriculture.

World Bank. 1989. *Sub-Saharan Africa: From Crisis to Sustainable Growth*. Washington, DC: World Bank.

——. 2011. "The World Development Report 2011: Conflict, Security, and Development." Washington, DC: World Bank.

Žižek, Slavoj. 2004. *Organs without Bodies: Deleuze and Consequences*. New York: Routledge.

Index

Page numbers in *italics* refer to figures.

CPSIA information can be obtained
at www.ICGtesting.com
Printed in the USA
BVHW082128310120
571144BV00001B/34